MORE ADVA...
A GUEST IN THE

"… an entertaining and richly ... both seasoned and budding allies. —*Kirkus Reviews*

"It's often said that much of the power of white supremacy lies in the invisibility of whiteness, thus making whiteness visible is key to dismantling white supremacy. *A Guest in the House of Hip Hop* places a sharp new spotlight on whiteness, showing us previously unseen facets of racism and classism. This is a bold and necessary work."
—**Rion Amilcar Scott**, author of *Insurrections*, Winner of the 2017 PEN/Robert W. Bingham Prize for Debut Fiction

"Mickey Hess's brilliantly insightful book challenges us to think deeply about what is required of us, both individually and collectively, as we face the challenges of our racial history with greater courage and empathy. *A Guest in the House of Hip Hop* is an important, timely book, as well as a terrifically entertaining read."
—**Paul Edwards,** author of *How to Rap 1 and 2* and *The Concise Guide to Hip-Hop Music*

"So many people go out of their way to try and prove that they are 'down,' but with Mickey you know immediately that he loves, respects, and studies this culture with every fiber of his being. I rock with him for being a brilliant and caring teacher, but even more so for just being a good man who is clearly invested in the art form that he is teaching. Very rare, but oh so needed."
—**Reef the Lost Cauze**, hip hop artist

"In this fascinating and timely book, Mickey Hess combines personal honesty with a razor-sharp critical perspective, addressing the urgent need for racial learning and unlearning

ADVANCE PRAISE FOR

and exploring how hip hop knowledge can influence our understanding of US culture and improve the ways we co-exist."
—**Murray Forman**, co-editor of *That's The Joint: The Hip-Hop Studies Reader*

"The story of our country, how it came to be, how it came to thrive, is as complex as it is fascinating. To understand this story, it is essential that the issue of race is opened and explored with the brutal honesty that is necessary to induce dialogue, build bridges, and find real answers. I find *A Guest In The House of Hip Hop* to be a courageous and sincere effort and I salute Dr. Hess for his dedication to the art form that I have devoted my own life to expanding and preserving."
—**David "Traum Diggs" Shanks**, hip hop artist

A GUEST
in the HOUSE
of HIP HOP

How Rap Music Taught a Kid from

Kentucky What a White Ally Should Be

✕✕✕✕✕✕✕✕✕✕✕

Mickey Hess

tg
PUBLISHING

New York, NY

Printed in the United States of America.
10 9 8 7 6 5 4 3 2 1

Ig Publishing
Box 2547
New York, NY 10163

www.igpub.com

ISBN: 978-1-632460-77-6 (paperback)

To Danielle Hess, for her bravery in the face of injustice, and for always pushing me to be a better person.

And to Wanda Hess, for teaching me what was right.

Contents

FOREWORD

I have a good friend named John. Like me, he grew up in the heyday of hip-hop when biting wasn't allowed, anything good was either "FRESH" or "FLY," and every kid in the neighborhood was an aspiring DJ, rapper, break dancer, or graffiti artist. Some of us did, or attempted to do, all of the above. John gravitated toward DJing when he was young and to this day has a turntable setup in his basement, where he retreats after a long day to decompress over two copies of a classic breakbeat. He dated his share of "around the way girls," with their big door-knocker earrings and brightly colored 54/11 Reebok Aerobic sneakers, and was fully immersed in the culture like most of us were back then. He even dabbled in the drug game as a young man and found himself behind bars for a short stint. His Cocaine Cowboy days are behind him now.

With his fiftieth birthday on the horizon, I'm sure he looks back and wonders what happened to that bright-eyed kid that spun records for local parties for little to no money. Life is very different now. He's a husband with children. He and his attractive, dark brown-skinned wife, who he's known since high school, have been married for over a decade. His participation in hip-hop culture, which went from turntablist and party DJ to independent label owner and tour DJ, has now given way to working a "regular" job while he remains a fan of the music from a distance. But he still loves hip-hop. His love for his favorite rapper, Rakim, is only rivaled by his enthusiasm for his favorite rock band, The Grateful Dead. He considers himself a true "Dead Head" and he sometimes flies to other states to meet like-minded buddies for concerts and festivals.

Hip-hop has always been, with limitations, a culture celebrated in the spirit of inclusion. A twenty-something-year-old German kid from Berlin can feel the same urge to bob his head and make "the ugly face" when he hears the undeniable boom bap of a DJ Premier beat blasting through refrigerator-sized speakers as a black kid who was born and raised in the Mecca, New York City. When Rakim uttered the phrase, "It ain't where ya from, it's where ya at," that rule of inclusion was cemented into the unwritten Constitution of Hip-Hop. All are welcome; just come correct. From what John tells me, Rock & Roll doesn't share that same spirit.

I'm guessing, based on the above description of my friend John, you were picturing a certain person in your mind, right up to the part about him being a Dead Head. You may have even gone back to read the previous paragraphs to see if you missed something. If you were picturing my friend as the only tie-dye-shirt-wearing black guy at the Grateful Dead Concert with a bunch of his white buddies, you'd be wrong. His buddies *are* white, but so is John. And yes, his wife is black. I have always considered John one of the white guys who "gets it." Not because of that old "Once you go black . . ." cliché, or because he's a Rakim fan who owns DJ equipment, but because despite the color of his skin he understands what *the struggle* is all about.

From the point John's wife gave birth to their son, that comprehension of the struggle became much more profound for him. He is no longer able to be a spectator to the black experience in America. He is on the field and in the game. As his child gets through his teenage years, John feels the target growing on his son's back. Each time a new report of an unarmed black person being shot by police goes viral, John's concerns for his own son grow. The conversations he hears among his rock friends when these stories hit the news has made him see some of those friends in a different light. He's had to become the only voice in those circles who sees the plight of Black and Brown Americans. It's frustrating . . . infuriating even. He's had quite a few arguments with good friends over these issues, especially the NFL player protests. Eventually he made the decision to drop out of his 2017 Fantasy Football Leagues and Pools because of these issues. When looking at his friends, he can't help but think, "What if this were my son? Would these guys be saying the same things? Would these buddies of mine look for ways to justify *his* murder by police?"

John admits he has had to stop associating with a few of the guys in his group, but others have been more open to seeing things from someplace other than their own perspective. Because of John, some of them have developed a different opinion of these issues, even entertaining feelings of empathy. This conversion of views came about through careful dialogue. Having those difficult conversations with his friends was important to John, if for no other reason than, in his mind, defending his children. You don't need to be married to a black woman/man or have half-black children to "get it," but sometimes it takes someone in your circle to lead you to the conversation. Getting a person to look at an issue introspectively helps them see things as they really are. The challenge is getting them to come down from the stands and get in the game.

This book looks to offer strategies and a framework for how those conversations can be initiated. The idea of being a "white ally" boldly challenges mainstream Americans to take a look into a broken mirror and see the shattered pieces for what they are. I believe that by picking up this book you are making the decision to try to see things differently. I'm hopeful that these writings will have you falling into one of two categories: recruiter or recruit. Our author, you will see, is clearly a recruiter. I believe his goal is to actively recruit more white allies into our society because he knows that having more people that are able to relate to and appreciate the plight of people of color, the better our world can become. Is that you? Will you take on the role of recruiter, bringing more friends and associates into a different way of thinking and being? Or will you become a recruit, one who after absorbing all his book has to offer, is now more sensitive to the very different path that people who "don't look like you" walk every day? Either are noble and honorable classifications and if you become either, society should applaud your bravery. My friend John started out as a spectator watching the world from the proverbial bleachers, but soon found himself right in the middle of the game.

MASTA ACE

Introduction

WHAT SHOULD A WHITE ALLY DO?

Don't start with this book. Or at least don't stop with it. Read Ijeoma Oluo, Claudia Rankine, Reni Eddo-Lodge, Kimberlé Williams Crenshaw, Patrisse Khan-Cullors and asha bandele, Michelle Alexander, Carol Anderson, Morgan Jerkins, Brittney Cooper, M.K. Asante, Ibram X. Kendi, Jeffrey O.G. Ogbar, Harry Allen, Ta-Nehisi Coates, Michael Eric Dyson, and other black writers at the heart of a renewed and much-needed conversation about race and racism in the United States. You certainly don't want the only book you read about race to have been written by a white author like me. Nobody's exactly clamoring to read what a middle-aged white guy has to say about hip-hop, but at the same time I see white authors too comfortable leaving the work of discussing race and racism to authors of color, which both overburdens their writing and reinforces the concept of race as a topic white people aren't asked to think much about. My perspective certainly shouldn't replace that of a black writer, but it may provide a point of entry to show the power of black voices on the developing mind of a white kid whose environment encouraged him not to listen. Too often white writers focus on showing they know the right things to say when it comes to race without addressing how they learned in the first place and how they worked to overcome the mistakes they made along the way. That's the story I'll try to tell here.

This is a book about how a white man born into racial isolation in small-town America grew up to study and teach the black culture of hip-hop. Born just outside of Science Hill, Kentucky, I grew up listening to the militant rap of Public Enemy while living in a place where the state song still included the word "darkies." If it weren't for hip-hop music and my mother's belief in higher education, I could have slipped into a lifetime of closed-mindedness and casual racism. Growing up in rural Kentucky in the Eighties and Nineties, I had no black teachers, few black classmates, and no black members of my church congregation. This racial isolation fostered a smug certainty about our way of life and a fear that it was threatened by the mere suggestion that there *were* other ways.

I saw a knee-jerk reaction to the 1990s iterations of multiculturalism and political correctness. When I left home for college in Louisville—the big city to me—my neighbors, coaches, and teachers warned me not to let my professors brainwash me. This was the mentality with which I embarked upon higher education. What were my neighbors clinging to? What were they afraid I might learn? Education is not indoctrination. It's no mystery why learning about black history tends to make white people less liable to buy into racist thinking and more likely to question the reasons whites invented and embraced those racist notions. It's no coincidence that the more history I learned, the less I could buy that there was a conspiracy against whites—as my neighbors had suggested—and the more I've come to understand the longstanding national conspiracy to keep black people out of white schools, pools, and neighborhoods, as well as the advantages that conspiracy continues to give a white man in 2018.

Listening to hip-hop made me have to think about what it means to be white, while the environment in my hometown encouraged me to avoid or even mock such self-examination. I listened to so much hip-hop, and read so many books about it, that when I went on to graduate school it was a natural choice of topic for my doctoral dissertation. Yet the more I studied hip-hop the more I came to look like part of the problem. I was another white professor teaching a black subject, landing a job that could have gone to a black scholar. My dissertation and the book it spawned got me a job teaching Hip-Hop and American Culture at one of the hundreds of US universities that offer plenty of hip-hop courses but employ embarrassingly low numbers of black professors. Schemes like this one make Americans mistrust white people who participate deeply in black culture, yet backing away from black culture entirely is too easy a solution. As a white professor with a long-standing commitment to teaching hip-hop music and culture, I maintain that white people have a responsibility to educate themselves by listening to black voices and then teach other whites to face the ways they benefit from racial injustices, even as I inevitably continue to benefit from them myself. As a white hip-hop scholar I can never allow myself to get too comfortable or too familiar, because writing about white people's fraught relationship with hip-hop might be my most important contribution.

I have not written a self-help book, but since my subtitle mentions what a white ally should be, I should address from the outset what a white ally should *do*. It's a sad fact that many white Americans put more stock in a white voice than a black one, so a conversation between whites offers me an opportunity to speak to America's history of race relations and introduce the ideas of black thinkers. Such conversations, in my experience, provide frequent opportunities to broach the subject, because white people, when alone, tend to speak their minds on race in a way they're afraid to do in front of people of color. The thinking goes that they won't be rebuked because they're among likeminded friends, and unfortunately, staying silent (as I've done too many times in my life) confirms my approval, or at least my acceptance, of hateful or ignorant thinking. In such conversations, I don't intend to substitute my voice for black voices, but to use the familiarity of my whiteness as a way to introduce the ideas of black thinkers to whites who've had too easy a time avoiding them.

Of course, racism is a more systemic problem than the ingrained prejudices of an individual white person. It's no accident that white Americans aren't asked to study black history much beyond a cursory nod to Dr. Martin Luther King Jr's "I Have A Dream" speech once every February. Nor is it an accident that around one in four black men will end up in an American prison,[1] or that one in four black Kentuckians has been permanently stripped of the right to vote.[2] The United States was founded on racial disparity and designed systems to maintain this disparity via our institutions—our courts, police departments, and prisons, our neighborhoods, schools, and voting booths. In a very real sense, America won't achieve true change until we change these institutions and systems, but don't forget that our attitudes are a key part of these systems. The more whites buy into racist thinking, the more invested they are in preserving the systems that advantage whites. We've changed systems before—from fair housing to school integration to health care—but then seen the new laws barely enforced and chipped away at and reversed. For legislative change to last, we need to change the way people think.

As a professor, I can have the most influence within the institution of higher education, teaching classes that introduce the history of racial disparity to college students who typically haven't learned much of it in twelve years of public education. Ideally, those students will become more racially-enlightened citizens who carry their educations forward to do some good in the institutions where they ultimately work. I've heard from graduates working as high school teachers and writers and editors. Some, like Robert Lefkowitz, have gone on to rap. J'na Jefferson writes for *Vibe*. John Gratton has done production work for dozens of hip-hop albums, including Chuck Strangers's *Consumers Park* and Joey Badass's *All-Amerikkan Badass*. Breanne Needles landed an internship booking shows for the Wu-Tang Clan and went on to work in publishing. Marcus Castro started a clothing line called 2 Familiar, which references an old joke from our hip-hop class. My former students are working as everything from TV cameramen to stand-up comics to cops. We need educated citizens in all those roles. Racism is so ingrained in American culture that it touches every aspect of our lives, so what should a white person do?

Listen to black voices. Study black history. "Education is the apology," wrote *Boston Globe* columnist Derrick Z. Jackson in 1997. "White folks need to study slavery to see that they are in the same trap as the 1800s" when "elite white industrialists raked in the profits [while] shafted white workers were left with the consolation that they were still better than black folks."[3] Seek out black voices and you'll find one introduces the next. I started with hip-hop, but I didn't stop there. I first heard the names Huey P. Newton and H. Rap Brown in a Public Enemy song. I first heard of Steve Biko and *Soul on Ice* from A Tribe Called Quest. I heard the Oakland, California rapper Paris mention Frantz Fanon before I saw my college professors assign his writing. I turned up my headphones and headed for the library. But education that isn't shared only benefits one learner, so make every effort to share your education with others.

Don't expect black people to take it upon themselves to educate you. Don't look to black people to reassure you your statements are inoffensive. Don't assume that you haven't said anything offensive just because a black person has not called you out.

Don't assume your black friends or colleagues want to talk about your studies or your journey toward racial enlightenment, but do reach out to ask how they're doing when a white nationalist march makes headlines, because, as my friend and colleague Sheena Howard once said, "This shit is traumatic." Don't say you can't believe this is happening in this day and age, because your black friends very likely can.

Speak for yourself. Don't present yourself as an expert on black thinking, but introduce your white friends and colleagues to the words of black thinkers. "Too long have others spoke for us,"[4] wrote John B. Russworm and Samuel E. Cornish in the first issue of *Freedom's Journal* in 1827. Nearly 200 years later, the book publishing industry remains nearly entirely white, and black professors make up only around 6% of the full-time university faculty nationwide. Russworm and Cornish saw the danger of such a lack of self-representation: "though there are many in society who exercise toward us benevolent feelings; still (with sorrow we confess it) there are others who make it their business to enlarge upon the least trifle, which tends to discredit any person of color; and pronounce anathema and denounce our whole body for the conduct of this guilty one . . .

Our vices and our degradation are ever arrayed against us, but our virtues are passed unnoticed."[5]

That problem hasn't changed enough since 1827. Even with hip-hop's cultural dominance, the control over what aspects of black lives get presented in the music can be traced back too often to white record executives.

Don't get too familiar. Don't believe that your track record of study or sensitivity allows you to make statements that might be considered racist if they came out of the mouth of a stranger. Don't make having read books by black authors the new "some of my best friends are black."

Don't let having aligned yourself with black causes convince you that you're better than other whites. Don't congratulate yourself for being conscious, woke, or informed, or having worked uniquely hard to achieve racial enlightenment. If you've had educational opportunities denied to other whites, find ways to share what you've learned while remembering to acknowledge your own advantages, even down to the all-important factor of having been born to parents who encouraged, rather than discouraged, your learning. Don't develop a white savior complex but this go-round the uncivilized natives are other whites. J. D. Vance in *Hillbilly Elegy* criticized poor whites in Kentucky for buying "giant TVs and iPads" rather than saving money, working hard, and pulling themselves out of poverty.[6] White Americans have made that same argument for years about black Americans. It was wrong in that cross-racial context and it's wrong when it's whites speaking about whites.

Admit your own complicity and work to correct it, but don't make a show of wallowing in white guilt. Don't apologize on behalf of generations of racist whites by way of distinguishing yourself from the past or the white masses. Don't cling to white pride by defending yourself (i.e., listing your antiracist credentials) or defending the white race (i.e., crying *Not ALL Whites*).

Don't get defensive. When an eighteen-year-old student asks me why he should have to come to college and be made to feel bad for being white, there's some power in my being able to admit I used to feel that same way—that I grew up encouraged to reject any talk of the advantages of white skin as an attack against white people. My goal is not to make him feel bad about being white so much as it is to make him *think* about what it means to be white in context of the history of this country. Since he's concerned about feelings, I'll have him read W.E.B. Du Bois' *The Souls of Black Folk*, which asks, "How does it feel to be a problem?" or Moustafa Bayoumi, who borrowed Du Bois's question for its title of his 2009 book *How Does it Feel to be a Problem? Being Young and Arab in America.* I'll have him read the words of Mamie Till-Mobley, whose fourteen-year-old son Emmett Till was brutally murdered after he was accused of having whistled in the direction of a white woman. If this student is still stuck on the idea that the real injustice here is the assault on *his* feelings, he needs to keep reading.

Don't expect to be congratulated. I stood at a New Jersey protest and vigil in the wake of the white nationalist march on Charlottesville, Virginia. One of the protest organizers—a white woman—kept encouraging cars at the intersection to honk their horns in solidarity with our cause. When a black motorist chose not to participate, the organizer, smiling, shouted, "Come on and join in! We're doing this for *you!*" Don't expect people of color to join in, or even acknowledge, whatever efforts you're making. Anticipate that people of all colors might be puzzled and even put off by your efforts.

How could someone so committed to organizing protests say something so ignorant? My guess is that she got so swept up in protesting that she was temporarily blinded by self-righteousness. She got so swept up in her conviction that she was being a good person that for a moment she forgot how to be one. It wouldn't be the first time I've seen it happen. I saw countless protestors step over a disabled veteran asleep by his cardboard sign as we marched to Philadelphia's City Hall for a health care repeal die-in. Perfectly healthy citizens planned to play dead to put on a show for our senators, while this man was actually dying on the street.

Confront hate, but correct ignorance. Boycott corporations. Demand resignations from the CEOs and celebrities. But approach private conversations less with the intent of winning an argument than winning a listener. The racism expressed in everyday interactions has a particular insidiousness that can make black Americans worry that they're being too para-noid or too over-sensitive or too stereotypically angry or that they can't help viewing the present moment in the context of so many centuries of bad history. Claudia Rankine's *Citizen* shows the poet finds it easier and more fulfilling to confront outright hate (a white man referring to a group of black teen-agers as "niggers," in front of Rankine, a black woman),[7] than an insidious comment from a white professor interviewing her for a job ("his dean is making him hire a person of color when there are so many great writers out there"[8]) or a friend complaining that her son lost his legacy-secured spot in the incoming class at a prestigious university ("because of affir-mative action or minority something—she is not sure what they are calling it these days and weren't they supposed to get rid of it?"[9]). It may be easier and more fulfilling to con-front outright racist aggression, but the most aggressive rac-ists are also the ones least likely to be persuaded to consider your point of view. Facing covert racism, Rankine finds herself caught between biting her tongue versus reinforcing the ste-reotype of being too sensitive, too aggressive, too quick to play the race card. It would take a tremendous amount of poise and restraint for her to take it upon herself to educate her aggres-sors, to see each daily slight or microaggression as an opportu-nity to serve as a patient instructor. I won't recommend black Americans remain patient in the face of ignorance. After all, it's been more than fifty years since Dr. Martin Luther King Jr. wrote that he could no longer wait. Why should this work of patiently educating white Americans fall squarely in the laps of black Americans?

White allies can do their best work when they find opportunities to take on the work of patient education. The vast majority of white Americans have the luxury of never having to think much about race, but they sure like to talk about it. We may be unsure if offhand racist comments are rooted more in lack of education than outright hate, or if the intimacy of a one-on-one conversation between whites simply allows for a passive-aggressive masking of hateful attitudes with the excuse of having innocently misspoken. But we cannot make the mistake of using someone's positive qualities (she's a protest organizer, he volunteers every Thanksgiving at a homeless shelter) as a way to convince ourselves that such a good person couldn't possibly mean the racist things he says. Instead, see his potential: he could be an even better person if he studied more history and listened to more black voices and learned how misguided his thinking is. I don't mean to spare white feelings so much as keep a white friend or colleague from closing her ears to the message, but my strategic patience must not be mistaken for coddling ignorance or acknowledging ignorance as a position as valid as any other.

As a white ally, I can do my best work by heeding the calls for patience and politeness that it would be ridiculous to ask back folks to heed. Without letting racists off the hook or even taking it easy on them, white allies can strategically take on the burden of the restraint that America has for far too long encouraged from black activists. From Martin Luther King Jr's "This 'Wait' has almost always meant 'Never'"[10] to the notion that Black Lives Matter should be more polite, critics have tended to see a particular rudeness in the calls for white Americans to stop killing black Americans. An ostensible commitment to politeness underlies the calls for us to listen to each other, but I don't buy into the idea that we should give racists a platform so that they can explain where they're coming from. Racist thinking is rooted in ignorance, and what good is understanding where someone is coming from if it's a place of ignorance? "Whites, if must frankly be said," wrote Dr. Martin Luther King Jr, "are not putting in a similar mass effort to reeducate themselves out of their racial ignorance. It is an aspect of their sense of superiority that the white people of America believe they have so little to learn."[11] Too often that white sense of superiority feels assaulted by the suggestion that talking about the lives of black Americans does not require that we give white voices equal time.

That sense of superiority often leads whites to want to dictate not only who gets to talk but how the conversation should sound. Many whites support black causes so long as the activism doesn't make white people uncomfortable. After Black Lives Matter activists in Seattle snatched the mic at a Bernie Sanders fundraiser in 2015, Ijeoma Oluo wrote, "The reaction to these protesters shed light on the hidden Seattle that most black people know well—the Seattle that prefers politeness to true progress, the Seattle that is more offended by raised voices than by systemic oppression, the Seattle that prioritizes the comfort of middle-class white liberals over justice for people of color."[12] Just months later, the issue of politeness was raised again when Bill Clinton shouted at and admonished BLM protestors in Philadelphia. (The protestors didn't like the 1994 crime bill that President Clinton signed into law, worsening the mass incarceration of black Americans, and they didn't like Hillary Clinton's having referred to youth offenders as "superpredators" in 1996.) Lincoln Blades found Clinton's exasperation refreshing. "Often," he wrote in *Rolling Stone*, "liberals are so well-versed on the polite conventions of respectable and appropriate speech that they can become talking-point robots rather than individuals who have their own set of beliefs . . . There's nothing scarier for a minority than not really knowing what the person across from them actually thinks about their intrinsic worth and their fight against oppression."[13]

Both writers above point to a particular self-satisfaction on the part of whites who consider themselves forward-thinking or liberal-minded. This self-satisfaction is also wielded against other whites via the schism in class and social standing that makes it easy for educated white liberals to become comfortable in their superiority to the unwashed masses of whites whom they blame for everything from segregation to the election of Donald Trump. If my ambition is to spread knowledge, I cannot approach education by looking down on those I intend to teach. It's not enough for the most educated of whites to look down on the ones more dedicated to common sense and religion and anti-intellectualism. Attacking the white folks who sit around spewing offhand racism just makes them dig in their heels and take comfort in the old misguided notions of reverse racism and the liberal elite out to get them.

As a professor, I'm undeniably a part of this perceived elite. I won't deny that I'm fortunate to have a sphere of influence as meaningful as the college classroom, where I, in professor mode, can exhibit a patience I don't feel in the fight-or-flight reaction that kicks in in my everyday confrontations with my neighbors and cousins. When that student asked why he should have to come to college and be made to feel bad about being white, I didn't feel myself freeze up and write him off as a lost cause the way I probably would have done with someone so sure of himself in a one-on-one conversation outside my classroom. After all, this student and I were trapped together, like it or not, for the duration of the semester, so I might as well make every effort I can to shake him out of his certainty that reading books by black American authors about black American issues is an affront to his security as a white American. As I said, I could see myself in that student. I could see me, an eighteen-year-old freshman, much quieter and less confrontational but still feeling that I was being somehow punished for my backwoods ignorance when my professors required me to attend a poetry reading by black feminists rather than wait in line at the record store to buy Snoop Dogg's debut album *Doggystyle*. I can't deny that my small-town Kentucky neighbors got into my head when they warned me my professors would brainwash me. I could see myself at eighteen when I looked at my student, but I could also see those screaming white faces from Charlottesville, those marching white nationalists with their tiki torches. Too much patience on my part risks losing him to the hate groups, but too much impatience risks pushing him right into their ranks. My best strategy is to admit I once straddled the same fence he's straddling, and tell him the story of how I ended up on the right side.

A GUEST IN THE HOUSE OF HIP HOP

One

DON'T PUSH IT TOO FAR

I taught a class called Hip-Hop and American Culture, toting my infant daughter in a fabric sling they've since outlawed as a suffocation hazard; I fed her from a bottle while I led a discussion on cultural appropriation in popular music. Forty years after the first hip-hop parties in South Bronx rec centers, mine was one of the hundreds of hip-hop courses taught at US universities, from Turntable Technique at the Berklee College of Music to Queering Hip-Hop at Duke. Professors taught courses in the Rhetoric of Hip-Hop, Anthropology of Hip-Hop, and the Politics of the Hip-Hop Generation. The University of Arizona had instituted the nation's first minor in hip-hop culture. Twenty years after professors wrote their first books on hip-hop—Houston Baker's *Black Studies, Rap, and the Academy,* Tricia Rose's *Black Noise: Rap Music and Black Culture*—Hip-Hop Studies was thriving.

I joined the English Department at Rider University in New Jersey as America prepared to elect its first black president, Barack Obama. Somebody wrote "nigger" on the wall of one of our dormitories. Sixty miles north, at Columbia University, somebody hung a noose on the door of a black professor. Two white reporters from our student paper came to my office toting a Halloween costume—a "Rap Star" complete with fake gold chain and fedora—hoping I'd wear it for the photo

3

they'd run with their story on my class. I did not put on the costume. A white professor dressed up like Run DMC symbolized everything I feared could go wrong with a university teaching hip-hop; the fact that these two eighteen-year-olds didn't see it convinced me I might do some good.

I scrounged around campus for money to pay guest speakers, determined to let no student of mine exit a rap class without having sat in a room with a rapper. I pieced together a 300-dollar speaking fee for a man who'd toured the world performing with the Wu-Tang Clan; he asked if we could pay him in cash so he wouldn't risk messing up his public assistance. I brought in a childhood hero of mine, an old-school MC who sent me a last-minute request for an extra hundred dollars to pay his driver but then showed up alone, behind the wheel of a beat-up old borrowed car.

It paid better to teach a rap class than to rap, and how did we vet the professors? None of us had a PhD in Hip-Hop, after all; our degrees ranged from English to Architecture. We could have known nothing about rap music beyond how to use it to pack classrooms by pandering to our students' interests, and rappers suspected as much. The legendary hip-hop producer Prince Paul smiled and shook my hand when I picked him up from the New Jersey Transit station, but I watched his eyes light up in my car on the way to campus when I asked him about an obscure De La Soul b-side he'd produced. "Wow," he said. "So you're really an old hip-hop head, huh?" Paul wasn't the first guest speaker to express surprise that I knew the subject I'd been hired to teach. It puzzled me, at first; nobody would question if a physics professor were, you know, really into physics. Then I remembered that white people are so prone to steal—that's how we ended up with a rapping Pillsbury Doughboy—that it wouldn't surprise a rapper at all to see a rap class taught by a white professor who didn't know the first thing about rap. Never mind Miley Cyrus twerking on MTV; this scheme goes so far back that white people took the *Charleston* from black people. White people stole the banjo—an African instrument—so conclusively that if today, in America, you said, "I know a guy who plays banjo," no one would picture a black person.

I didn't exactly exude hip-hop. Bouncers, as I approached a rap club, once asked me if I was lost. I once invited one of the most important women in hip-hop to campus and when I met her in the parking lot she *aww*ed like she'd met an eight-year-old boy who taught a class on rap music. Was I so harmless as to inspire an *aww*, even though I was a white guy teaching a class on a music genre where many of the corporate moguls signing the checks remained white as ever and the black artists were still going to jail for the stories they sold in songs? In a country built on such a pattern of theft, I was full of myself to believe that one man teaching one class could do much good *or* harm. Standing behind the lectern, I looked like comedian Irwin Corey's bumbling old white professor pausing to define rap music at the beginning of Run DMC's "Rock Box." I looked like Spalding Gray's militant white professor goading Redman and Method Man to boycott his Black History class in their comedy *How High*. I looked like Fordham professor Mark Naison in his subtly self-deprecating turn as a white contestant on Dave Chappelle's trivia game-show spoof "I Know Black People." A white man teaching Black Studies: was it funny or tragic?

•

No matter how many guest speakers I brought in, my course was still designed and taught by a man rappers might mistrust. In 1993, in my first year of college, I sang along with De La Soul—"White boy Roy can-not feel it/but he's first to try and steal it/dilute it/pollute it/kill it . . ." In 2016, I nodded along with Vince Staples—"All these white folks chanting when I ask them where my niggas at"—while Kanye West asked white people to please stop writing about hip-hop.[1] Rappers welcome money from white fans, but they've always expected whites would someday take hip-hop away from them. Faced with Vanilla Ice in 1990, music journalist Havelock Nelson wrote, "Rock-and-roll was black back in the days when it began . . . I don't know if rap in the year 2050 will be seen as white. But it damn sure could be." I didn't believe it could happen, but now, halfway to 2050—with Iggy Azalea, and Tom Hanks' rapper son, and the scores of Scandinavian rappers—I'm start-ing to worry he may have been onto something.

The catch-22 for white rap fans is that deeper participation tends to look more suspect. It's more okay to be a white guy who recognizes Jay-Z from pictures in *People* magazine than it is to be a white guy who wants to parse Jay's lyrics and publish a book. Yet backing away from black cul-ture seems too easy a solution. After all, white people have been ignoring black culture for years. It's a problem that Elvis Presley got famous singing songs black artists had already recorded, but it's a bigger problem that so many Americans never heard those songs until Elvis sang them. An older white professor once clapped me on the back and, with a condescen-sion that said *I'm so racially enlightened I avoid black art entirely,* cracked a joke about a white guy teaching a rap course. He made jokes but I bet he couldn't name ten rappers. Could he name ten black novelists? At one extreme, nobody wants an African-American Studies department staffed entirely with white professors. At the other, nobody wants a white pro-fessor to leave James Baldwin off her American Lit syllabus because she thinks white scholars shouldn't teach black art.

White people shouldn't hide their silence behind the lofty ideal of avoiding cultural appropriation, but they also shouldn't speak on black issues with a casual overfamiliarity. Ice Cube called his white fans eavesdroppers, but added that "even though they're eavesdropping on our records they need to hear it."[2] Lord Jamar called white rappers houseguests. Macklemore used a song to promote tolerance—"If I was gay, I would think hip-hop hates me"—and Jamar took offense: "Okay, white rappers . . . you are guests in the house of hip-hop. Just because you have a hit record doesn't give you the right, as I feel, to voice your opinion."[3] I found myself wanting to agree with Lord Jamar, a rap legend I once saw share a bill with Nice & Smooth on the deck of the battleship USS New Jersey. But I can't agree entirely when I get paid to voice my opinion. I wouldn't be much of a professor if I never said anything critical of my subject. I can't agree entirely when he's essentially complaining, *We let a white guy into the party and he said we should let in gay people too.* "Don't push it too far," said Jamar. "Those of y'all who really studied the culture, that truly love hip-hop and all that, keep it real with yourself, you know this is a black man's thing." (Notice he said black *man.*) The paradox for the white hip-hop scholar is that to know hip-hop culture means to know it doesn't always welcome criticism from white professors.

For me to accept this paradox is not to buy into the tired old nonsensical claims of "reverse racism." First, the very fact that white people have to call it *reverse* racism reaffirms the direction the violence has flowed. There is no reverse bullying, reverse terrorism, or reverse rape. Second, it is *not* "reverse racism" when a white professor makes his living teaching a course on a black cultural form where some of the black musicians say they'd prefer whites step aside. Lord Jamar doesn't exclude white people—the ones who've done their homework, at least—from participating in hip-hop; he just doesn't want to see a white guest walk into hip-hop's house and start changing the wallpaper. I imagine he'd approve of my taking a class in hip-hop, but tell me I sure as hell shouldn't *teach* one. Michael Eric Dyson—one of the black scholars whose books I assign as required reading—sees a much bigger problem than one person leading one classroom. "I'm not saying," he writes, "that non-black folk can't understand and interpret black culture. But there *is* something to be said for the dynamics of power, where nonblacks have been afforded the privilege to interpret and—given the racial politics of the nation—to legitimate or decertify black vernacular and classical culture in ways that have been denied to black folk." In other words, it's not only about how well the professor knows hip-hop; it's about who approved the curriculum and gave that professor his job. My personal experience illustrates Dyson's point: I wrote a doctoral dissertation on hip-hop that was approved by a committee of four white men and one black woman; I've published four books on hip-hop but never been assigned a black editor. My work has, of course, gone through the anonymous peer-review which is the foundation of academic publishing, so I can hope—but not assume—some of the unnamed readers who voted to publish my writing were black scholars who specialize in the study of hip-hop. But it's no stretch of the imagination to believe that a white man could become a credentialed and published expert in a black cultural form without ever having a black person check his work.

American universities offer hundreds of hip-hop courses even as they employ embarrassingly low numbers of black professors—only around six percent of university faculty nationwide. I hope we are facing a sea change and that six percent will soon double and triple—there is certainly some momentum to the call for more black professors—but hiring more black faculty members won't, on its own, correct an imbalance of power that is about more than percentages. Critic Alex Nichols, writing about the musical *Hamilton*, rejected the notion that filling more roles with black people solves racial disparity: "Contemporary progressivism has come to mean papering over material inequality with representational diversity. The president will continue to expand the national security state at the same rate as his predecessor, but at least he will be black. Predatory lending will drain the wealth from African American communities, but the board of Goldman Sachs will have several black members. Inequality will be rampant and worsening, but the 1% will at least 'look like America.' The actual racial injustices of our time will continue unabated, but the power structure will be diversified so that nobody feels quite so bad about it."[4] Electing a black president didn't end racism; rather, the prospect of his election brought out the hangman nooses to a Selma, Louisiana schoolyard and the campuses of Maryland and Columbia, and his two terms inspired racists to run for office. If history teaches us anything, it's that a boom in black professors will probably prompt a similar backlash. Race in America is more complicated than black vs. white, although every time we think we've moved beyond that binary something drags us back into the past.

Of course universities need to hire more black professors, and I can't disagree with the assertion that black scholars should lead the discussion about black culture and vet the white scholars who research and teach that culture. White scholars studying hip-hop should first and foremost listen to black rappers and scholars, but to stop at listening alone is a cop-out. I worry that plenty of white professors would be happy to hire new black professors and direct minority students to them and leave matters of race to be taught in their classrooms so that the white professors don't have to risk saying the wrong thing. Race permeates every subject; the university shouldn't delegate to newly hired black professors the responsibilities of confronting race in the classroom.

But even though white professors can't shirk the responsibilities of discussing race, we could read hundreds of books by black scholars and it still won't completely wear down the edges of our blinders. Vetted by peer review or vouched for by rappers, a white scholar remains an outsider. I'm never all that satisfied with the self-justifications of the other white scholars, and I'm by no means looking to inspire a new legion of white people to become hip-hop professors. Yet I stand firm in my conviction that I'm a white person doing it well—even if the best way I know to do it is to keep questioning that conviction. I am undeniably part of the forces taking hip-hop further away from its roots, into college classrooms and onto library shelves. I know my hip-hop, but I don't know how it feels to be black in America, so it would be grossly irresponsible for me not to ask my students to think about the problems and contradictions inherent in what their professor does for a living. But I haven't quit teaching yet, so I don't want to sound like I'm going through the motions of making excuses. Saying I know my history— even if it might look like I'm only repeating it—might come off as a self-serving and insincere gesture. My self-examination has to allow for the real possibility of my being wrong; otherwise it's only a show I put on for my critics. But I can't say I've studied hip-hop for this long just to reach the conclusion that I shouldn't be doing it.

I've been teaching hip-hop in colleges for fifteen years, after all. Having recently turned forty-two years old—almost as old as hip-hop itself—I've become keenly aware that my students were born after Tupac was already dead. I am a forty-two-year-old white man who makes his living studying music created by black youth, and my course feels more and more like a history lesson. I can hustle to keep up with the new rappers, but I'll still never quite get it. I'll never hear the new songs the way a twenty-year-old hears them. It's a harsh realization, but worse is its corollary: if I can get too old to write about hip-hop, was I always too white?

Two

WHY WHITE KIDS SHOULD
LISTEN TO HIP-HOP

The true power of hip-hop on my individual imagination is that it made me have to think about being white. Born into racial isolation in rural Kentucky, I grew up never having to think about whiteness as anything other than a default position. This luxury is granted to a great deal of white Americans whose ancestors fought to keep black Americans out of their schools, pools, and neighborhoods. I grew up at a distance, culturally and geographically, from the communities where hip-hop was created. My friend, the rapper Traum Diggs, spent his childhood on Brooklyn playgrounds where Kangol Kid from UTFO would come through and toss a football back and forth with the kids; I lip-synched to UTFO at a talent show at my south-central Kentucky elementary school, where I didn't have a single black classmate.

I grew up among Appalachian poverty, miles and miles from that ever-important "metaphysical root" of hip-hop, the ghetto.[1] I first heard rap music in the woods, on a Cub Scout hike at Kentucky's Wolf Creek Dam. We stopped to eat lunch—baloney-and-cheese sandwiches and beef stew out of pop-top cans. We ate in the quiet of nature until Scoutmaster Larry tuned in his little portable radio to the country station playing, for what seemed like the thousandth time, "I'm just a common man, drive a common van, my dog ain't got a pedigree . . ."[2]

Larry scanned to the next channel: a Van Halen song faded out; a voice emerged from an echo chamber, shouting, "Run . . . Run . . . DMC!" I'd never heard anything like it. I heard guitars but it wasn't rock; they weren't singing, exactly. Two men shouted the ends of each other's sentences as they bragged about their success:

> You're the type of guy that girl ignored
> I'm drivin Caddy, you're fixin a Ford

I was the son of an auto-body repairman, but I didn't quite catch the paradigm shift: we'd changed the channel from a white man boasting about his modest vehicle to a black man celebrating his Cadillac.

My dad played bluegrass guitar. He and his friends preferred country musicians who dressed like they were headed home from a day of hard labor, so they resented these rappers with their fedoras and gold chains. "I reckon they think they're big stuff, don't they?" they'd ask, shaking their heads at the TV screen. "I reckon they think they're something." I didn't understand it then, but their resentment smacked of the age-old American stereotypes of the uppity Negro, the Zip Coon, the minstrel-show caricature of the black man who so earnestly aspired to symbols of white success that white people found it funny to watch him fail.

The stereotype solidified in the context of working-class pride, in the racist jokes told by customers and hangers-on in my dad's shop. "What does Pontiac stand for? Poor Old Nigger Thinks It's A Cadillac." The resentment of black aspirations compounded among the low-income white Southerners whose ancestors had built their wealth on the backs of slaves and then lost it in the wake of the Civil War. When their great-great-grandparents lost their slaves, they lost the free labor at the foundation of their economy; now, generations into the future, any new gain for black people still came to feel like a new loss for whites. The more *they* got, went the thinking, the less left for *us*. So my dad's friends shook their heads at the rappers on television and climbed back into their dented and rusted pickup trucks, convincing themselves they didn't need to dream about gold chains and Cadillacs; they had everything a man could ever want, right there in small-town Kentucky.

•

I remember looking forward to leaving.

I grew up on the border between Eubank and Science Hill, Kentucky, with an unwavering certainty that I lived in a place that people on TV did not want to come from. I used to stand in the woods and pretend I was standing in Central Park, out for a quick run before I headed back to my Upper West Side high-rise. In real life I lived between the woods and a pig farm. If my family wanted a pizza delivered, we had to drive one town over and meet the driver at the edge of his territory— the Junior's Food Mart parking lot. I spent a lot of time reading library books and listening to bootleg rap cassettes bought at the truck stop. I spent a lot of time in the woods. A lot of time bouncing a tennis ball against the side of the house and wishing I were somewhere different.

My childhood home, where my mother still lives, had once been a one-room schoolhouse. Old couples, former students at the schoolhouse, would stop by to marvel at how far they'd gotten from where they began. My father ran an auto-body repair shop from the shack he and his friends built out back; he made the outsides of cars look pretty but could not keep our own car running. At the end of our gravel driveway, the white-and-black metal sign for Mike's Body Shop; two nights after Daddy bought and installed the sign, some asshole drove past and threw a rock out his car window. The impact left a cracked asterisk, which over the years turned into a softball-sized starburst of rust.

I swept cigarette butts into a pile on the body-shop floor and watched my father prep cars for paint jobs, protecting headlights and windshields with newspaper and masking tape, with its sweet chemical smell. I used to chew on masking tape rolls, ruin them with my teeth imprints. One of my first words was *Bondo*, a putty used to fill in dents in the bodies of automobiles. Bondo comes in two little tubes: mix the white chemicals with the red chemicals and it dries Pepto-Bismol pink. Sand it smooth and breathe in the cloud of pale pink dust. Daddy always had a coat of Bondo dust in his hair, which made it look grayer than it already was. And on his clothes, which made them look more worn out and faded than they already were.

I found comfort in the paint fumes and the heat from the wood stove even as the cars my dad painted promised escape: semi-truck cabs with silhouettes of big-breasted women airbrushed onto the back windows, a van with a New York license plate and a thick Brooklyn phone book shoved between the console and the passenger seat. I looked up landmarks mentioned in rap songs—Biz Markie's Albee Square Mall, MC Lyte's Empire Rollerdrome. I knew they were real places, of course, but holding that phone book in my hands somehow made them more tangible. I called Albee Square Mall and when somebody answered I hung up, my heart racing like I was calling to ask out a girl.

What began as escapism opened my ears to perspectives some of my classmates rejected. I can't say that at nine years old I set out to listen to rap music to hear stories of how it felt to be black in America, but those messages did come to resonate with me. Black History Month at my elementary school taught me that Martin Luther King had a dream, but Public Enemy taught me that two decades after his murder they still didn't celebrate his birthday in Arizona. School showed me the grandfatherly George Washington Carver, but X-Clan name-dropped the militant Nat Turner and Huey Newton. I heard Q-Tip say *Soul on Ice* and I sought out Eldridge Cleaver's prison memoir by that name at the public library. I watched Prince Paul introduce a De La Soul video about the power of being an individual by saying, "If you take three glasses of water and put food coloring in them, you have many different colors, but it's still the same old water," and I wanted to believe he was not just pointing out the lack of logic to racism, but welcoming a white kid in Kentucky into the hip-hop fold. When I felt ashamed to whisper "free lunch" to the cafeteria workers at school, I thought about the rappers who wrote such compelling songs about growing up in housing projects. It was childish escapism, not much different from watching cowboy movies or mafia flicks, but it developed into a lifelong allegiance to one of hip-hop's distinct iterations of the American Dream—the idea of making it out of a place by telling its story so vividly.

The place you're from follows you when you're dealing with a music genre where the artists still shout out the housing projects they left behind decades ago, and stars from Ali Shaheed Muhammad to J. Cole put their actual childhood street addresses in their music. Their journeys toward fame and fortune had me planning a similar route of my own as I traveled down gravel roads on the school bus, crammed between the window and a man-sized fifth-grader named Jonas, who lived on the pig farm one stop before my house. When we dropped off Jonas, kids would yell, "Soo-ey! Slop them pigs, Jonas!" Our bus driver, Zenith—who was missing fingers from a table-saw accident—would point his index stump at them and tell them to shut up. How did Science Hill get its name? When it came to evolution or climate change, people there were defiantly anti-science. "The community," the Internet tells me, "was named by geologist William J. Bobbitt, who visited to gather and analyze the local rocks."[3] Makes sense. There was nothing much more exciting to do.

I don't mean to say it was Mayberry. Our county sheriff: shot in the head by an Oxycontin addict hired for the hit by the other man running for sheriff. My mother's across-the-street neighbor: shot in the face over cocaine. My wife's brother, who swears his Bible tells him blacks are "a cursed people": shot in the stomach by rival meth dealers. Yet we scared ourselves away from big-city crime. *They'll steal the Nikes right off your feet out there. They'll pull you right out of your car.* I listened to rappers sound the alarm about police violence before I ever saw four white cops beat Rodney King on the streets of LA, but my classmates were more moved by the riots that took place after the cops were acquitted. My classmates, with their truck-driver dads, watched four black men pull Reginald Denny from the cab of his semi truck and beat him nearly to death in the street. *By God, that could have been me,* they thought, but they couldn't see themselves in King. They justified the cops beating King because of the fact that he was drunk, high, and driving erratically, then they headed home to drink beer, smoke weed, and crash their cars into farmers' fences. My neighbors watched South Central Los Angeles burn and congratulated themselves on living in South Central Kentucky and passing on to their kids a mentality that didn't encourage them to expand their horizons so much as ask why would anyone *want* to.

Here's the conundrum: I made it out of a place so insular and sure of itself because I was sure I was better than the people who thought that way. I thought I was *too good* to go to the community college a few miles from the house I grew up in. I wanted to leave Kentucky in my rearview mirror and go to college in New York or Boston, but my mother, who'd told me since preschool that I was going to college, begged me to stay close to home.

When I decided to leave home to attend college two hours away in "the big city" of Louisville, my older cousin, the long-haul trucker, shared a piece of worldly advice: "Just make sure you don't get caught out in Niggertown."

"Are you sure you want to live up there in Louisville," asked a friend's older sister. I asked what she meant and she huffed and then said, in a tone like she was speaking the name of a disease I might catch, "*Niggers.*"

Black people had congregated in cities like Louisville, of course, because they'd been run out of rural Kentucky by white people. Once black Kentuckians could no longer be used for free labor on farms, white Kentuckians began to lynch them for offenses as minor as "bad character," "insulted white woman," "criticized mob," and the ever-popular "unknown."[4] These lynchings were a campaign of terrorism meant to run the rest of the black people out of town. The rural white Kentuckians had scared themselves to death of the black Kentuckians, so they'd chased them away from the farmland and into the city. But in the process of scaring black people into leaving town, they'd scared themselves into staying put.

I grew up less than two miles away from the farms where my parents grew up, but I broke the cycle by convincing myself I was destined for bigger and better things. I made it out by teaching hip-hop culture and creative writing to young people who will come out of college stuck with nearly one hundred thousand dollars in student loans. I teach the legacy of bootstraps and rags-to-riches, the story of America as a place where we start out one thing and end up another. They are in college to do just that, but so much tells them it is no longer possible. I was told the same thing twenty years earlier: well-meaning uncles told me I would never make money writing books or teaching college, not in this economy; one of my English professors told me I would never have a job like his.

Yet today I am an English professor teaching a class on American success stories, from Ben Franklin to 2 Chainz in sixteen weeks. I don't teach only the stories, but the ways we use the stories against each other. If you succeed, some say *Look what America made possible for you*, but if you fail it's your own fault. Others of us are taught the inverse: to see success as one person's triumph over a system designed to keep us down, and our individual setbacks as America working the way it was designed to work. Thus, the rap music of my youth showed me the toe-tagged Uncle Sam on the cover of Ice Cube's *Death Certificate* and Uncle Sam as the (white) devil in Paris's "The Devil Made me Do It" video.

It was a short walk from Johnny Paycheck's "Take this job and shove it" to Ice Cube's "Take this job and stick it, bigot." Before I ever heard rap, I saw country music artists sell songs about working hard but not ending up with much. I mulled over this message as I swept cigarette butts from the floor of my dad's body shop, his radio too high to reach and tuned to the country station. Daddy was determined to be his own boss, so he'd quit school in eighth grade to learn to paint cars. Mom believed college was the key to success: the longer you spent listening and learning, the better you'd do. I watched her re-enroll in college and finish her bachelor's degree, our car's floorboards littered with her textbooks and papers. Daddy restored antique cars from the rusted shells he found in the woods, but Mom drove a dirt-brown, dented Corolla. She studied in that car, windows iced over in winter—with three kids in the house, it was the only place she could find any peace. I came to see college as a welcome inevitability; I was going, Mom said, even if she had to scrub floors to pay my tuition. But when it came down to it, I paid with student loans, same as she'd done before me.

•

When the conversation turns to race, white people tend to start talking about money, as if growing up with less wealth makes a person less white. As if growing up with less of an inheritance than the richest white Americans is a sign of solidarity with the black Americans whose ancestors were owned as property. Wealth accrues across generations, so I resent my friends who inherited a family business or whose parents were well-off enough to give them the down payment on their first house; imagine the difference between having a great-grandmother who owned a farm she could pass down to her children and having a great-great-grandmother who was herself passed down to the master's kids when he died. As of 2018, the US Census Bureau lists the median net worth of white families at $132,000, while Latino families have less than one-tenth of that wealth ($12,000), and the median for black families is a mere $9,000. Slaves owned nothing for their kids to inherit, so after slavery ended, the next generation had to start from square one. Local police departments came up with new schemes to put the freed slaves back into chains, but even the ones who remained free were kept out of the best jobs and schools and terrorized into fleeing the South and then staying in their own neighborhoods in the North lest they give white people the impression that black people might expect them to share.

There is no logic to racism, but there certainly is a design. No matter how hard the freed slaves and their children worked, they still didn't end up with much to leave to the next generation, so their descendants ended up going to the same failing and underfunded schools their parents had attended, and working the same kinds of jobs. America shrugged off the idea of reparations and instead, gradually, grudgingly, told schools they had to start letting in students of all colors; the country encouraged employers, in situations where all qualifications were equal, to hire the minority candidate first. When white Americans came to realize they were doing worse than their parents (the antithesis of the American Dream), they didn't blame the billionaires whose share of the wealth was increasing to a percentage never before seen in history; they blamed desegregation and Affirmative Action. White politicians ran for office on a platform of reclaiming a gone and lost greatness from an earlier era. What white Americans may have missed most was their claim to the bootstraps stories this country was founded upon. There was the lingering resentment that white people were at a distinct disadvantage when it came to American Dream stories: no matter how poor a white man was, he would never be black.

In a country obsessed with the dream of the individual clawing his way to the top, white Americans began to resent that the humblest beginnings went to black Americans. Being born with white skin gave them an undeniable head start they sought to reject. Jerry Heller, the white, Jewish manager of Niggaz With Attitudes, prefaced his memoir with the bold statement, "I wanted to call this book *Nigga 4 Life*, but the fucking corporate gangstas who've taken over the bookselling dodge in this country wouldn't support it if I did."[5] N.W.A. were early icons in the fight for the right for rappers to say whatever the fuck they wanted, and decades later—after the group split up and accused Heller of stealing their money and Ice Cube shouted, "Fuck Jerry Heller and the white superpowers"[6]—Heller railed against the timidity of corporate publishing. *No one*, he argued, should be able to stop a white man from calling himself black:

> "I was a nigga on the streets of Cleveland when I was growing up, only they pronounced it 'kike' back then. I was a nigga in the late fifties at Ohio University in Athens, Ohio, when my first college roommate asked me if Jews were allowed to vote. After that I was a nigga on the campus of the University of Southern California, when WASP bullyboys spray-painted anti-Semitic graffiti on the walls of ZBT—the Jewish frat house where I roomed."[7]

Jews certainly heard their share of slurs. Thirty years after Heller saw that anti-Semitic graffiti, such hateful notions persisted. In 1989, Heller was making money managing Niggaz With Attitudes when Public Enemy's Professor Griff proclaimed, "The Jews are wicked. And we can prove this."[8] But Heller suggested that being Jewish entitled him to claim a slur that had been designed to hurt black people, so that having been called a "kike" entitled him to call himself a "nigga," even though he was a white record executive working in an industry built on the exploitation of black musicians, and even though his own black musicians accused him of keeping more than his share of their money.

America made being born powerless, hated, and poor such a compelling start to our stories that everyone wanted in, regardless of skin color. America was born out of rebellion, so my white Kentucky classmates felt like rebels listening to Public Enemy's great call to action "Fight the Power" just one year after we felt like rebels listening to Hank Williams Jr's revisionist daydream "If the South Woulda Won."

As much as Hank had preached self-reliance and living off the land in his earlier anthem "A Country Boy Can Survive," he still pined for the good old days when slaves would have cooked him his pancakes. Two decades later, in 2011, the South still hadn't risen again. Hank didn't like our black president one bit and he wasn't shy about sharing his views. ESPN parted ways with Hank after he compared President Obama to Hitler; America had become so oppositional, said Hank, that the Republican speaker of the house playing golf with the Democrat president was like Israel's prime minister playing golf with Hitler. "Working-class people are hurting," said Hank, who was worth $45 million, "and it doesn't seem like anybody cares. When both sides are high-fiving it on the ninth hole when everybody else is without a job—it makes a whole lot of us angry. Something has to change."[9] We were a country born of rebellion. We just couldn't agree on which powers to fight.

White politicians gave a perfunctory nod to the stories of black Americans; this, they believed, made them look compassionate and worthy of voting for. But theirs was a self-congratulatory form of white enlightenment; it didn't fool the black voters, and it frustrated those white voters who remained convinced that the better black people did in this country the worse the white people would do. Watching the perfunctory nods of compassion, my Kentucky neighbors came to see a conspiracy in which one class of white people (wealthy, educated in college rather than church) turned on the other white people for speaking in racist terms. They came to see a white liberal urban coastal elite bent on controlling the very language working-class white people can use. *We* made it, they might have heard the white elites saying, so something must be wrong with the people we left behind. *We* left home and got smarter and richer, so we can look back and shake our heads at the people still stuck in Kentucky, even as we pride ourselves on our ostensible dedication to the plight of the black people *they* look down on. People in my part of Kentucky saw the whites who had everything using perceived prejudices as a reason to look down on the whites who had nothing. They were certain the problems of this country were rooted in skin color, and they were tired of being told they were the wrong kind of white.

The white elites who gave so much lip service to racial justice were the ones who had benefitted the most from our country's racism. They got the best pools, schools, and neighborhoods—and did little to nothing to invite in more black people—while poor whites in rural Kentucky resorted to baseless grudges and racist jokes. I wouldn't say all, or even most, rural whites or Southern whites or even small-town Science Hill, Kentucky whites thought this way, but it was a mentality I saw and one that undoubtedly influenced my own. I certainly don't speak for the state I left a decade ago, or the small town I left two decades ago, but I can't escape the fact that growing up there shaped my outlook as a young man. In telling my Kentucky stories, I don't mean to advertise my humble origins so much as show how the place I came from shaped the way I approach hip-hop and the way I think about my own role in relation to it. Some whites growing up in the Eighties and Nineties were taught that overt racism would no longer benefit them; I was shown that it would. I didn't just hear racist jokes; I repeated them. I invented my own. In a place where these jokes served as social currency, I couldn't help seeing *In Living Color* and my bootleg Eddie Murphy cassettes as an extension of the same brand of humor. I counterbalanced my love for what some of my neighbors called "nigger music" with a healthy dose of laughing along with those neighbors at our ignorant notions of what it meant to black.

I wish I could forget that part of my past, but to do so seems dangerous. Americans are fascinated with stories of overcoming poverty, but the more important success story is overcoming the mentality of the place in which we were born. I was taught racist thinking from such a young age that I could have easily fallen into a lifetime of casual racism. I was born in a Kentucky town so insular and sure of itself, but thanks to the dual influences of hip-hop and higher education, I ended up in a job that gives me the luxury of time to think, read, and write about the ways I relate to black culture. I look back at the mentality of my Kentucky upbringing as something I've studied enough history to overcome; I make a living teaching this history to college students, even as this history very likely gave me my job—a job that a more just society would have given a black person.

Three

"IT'S ABOUT CLASS, NOT RACE" (NO, IT'S NOT)

Americans are tied to the idea that we've earned what we have. I belong here because I fought hard to get here, say the rappers and the politicians alike. It is our American mythos of overcoming the circumstances of our birth and escaping the place we came from, our American dream that a kid from Kentucky, no matter the hopelessness of his neighbors, can "one day leave those worthless hicks behind while still using their story to enhance my own credibility."[1] America tells me the stories I was most ashamed of growing up should become a point of pride now that I've made some money, that the value in these experiences is in looking back at them to congratulate myself on how far I've come. It benefits me to use these stories to brand myself a particular kind of white who still had things easy but not as easy as the white people who grew up rich. But having grown up on food stamps doesn't qualify me to write about hip-hop, even if it does affect the way I look at its stories of rising out of poverty to buy your mother a mansion.

The more I read and write, the more I question the role of my race in relation to my subject matter. I used to find some solace in the fact that I'd spent more on hip-hop than I'd made from it, but with the hip-hop class paying a piece of my salary that is likely no longer the case. Not to say I'm getting rich. I'm not making money like Lyor Cohen

27

or Jimmy Iovine, the white record executives who've made millions from hip-hop. Tuition has skyrocketed, but students' dollars haven't exactly ended up in their professors' pockets; by one estimation, tuition rose 72% more than the rate of inflation between 2001 and 2011, while faculty salaries at the end of that decade stayed right where they were when the decade began.[2] Still, the money was good enough to lure me away from Kentucky for a move to my job at Rider. My wife and I rented an apartment in nearby Philadelphia, in a neighborhood where the tattooed twenty-somethings lived their lives like Kentucky grandmothers: they make and sell beeswax candles and butterscotch pies; they weed rooftop gardens and run knitting workshops. Many of them had degrees from elite colleges, but weren't putting them to any vocational use other than to lean on theories they'd learned about late capitalism to rationalize their conviction that people should know how to make something other than money.

When faced with the birth of our first child, my wife and I turned to the Internet to ask where we should raise her. Our search began logically enough, with the *Philadelphia Inquirer*'s Murder Map and the National Sex Offender Registry, but—scared out of Philly—we found ourselves studying the standardized test scores and median household incomes of the South Jersey suburbs. How quickly the Internet presented me a pie chart of the racial makeup of each school. I'd like to picture a Mexican-American family seeking this information to assure their daughter she won't be the only Chicana in her class, but I know it's probably white people using it to make sure the whole school looks just like them.

I see myself as the kind of person who'll send my daughter to public school. Philly schools were bad, so I moved to the small town of Haddonfield, New Jersey, where the schools were good. Friends of mine see themselves as the kind of people who live in the city; they want their daughter to grow up around diversity, so they stayed in Philly and sent her to a pricey private school where she met her best friends, that diverse body of kids whose parents can afford to send them to a pricey private school. Another couple I know found a lower tuition rate at a Catholic school, so they send their kids there, even though they aren't Catholic and don't want their kids to be. What a lot of effort we expend to protect our children from the other children whose parents can't afford to choose where to send them to school.

Where we live is who we are, or at least who we look like to other people. I have set aside aspects of my identity in order to live in a small town where the schools score high on standardized tests I don't even believe in teaching to. When I told a friend I was moving to Haddonfield, he frowned and asked, "But aren't they all Republicans?" A whole town of Republicans: the prospect frightened me. What would they be like? What would they do to my daughter?

I've never voted Republican. I've barely voted at all, considering the countless opportunities I've ignored in state and local elections. But as an eleven-year-old boy in Kentucky I wore a T-shirt with Ronald Reagan drawn, boardwalk-caricature style, as an Old West gunslinger: sheriff's badge, sagging holster, spurred cowboy boot kicking the ass of a turban-headed Muammar Gaddafi. The shirt was an adult large, big as a nightgown on me, but I begged my mother to buy it. "Why?" she asked. I had never expressed an interest in politics. My knowledge of President Reagan came almost entirely from "Ronnie's Rap," a novelty record I played incessantly. One verse, in particular, made me laugh:

Met with Gorbachev in '85
To talk about how everyone could stay alive.

And though he seemed to be a guy with class
If he doesn't play ball, we'll nuke his . . . country.

I begged for the Reagan shirt. Mom bought it for me on the condition I would not wear it to school, but I wore it anyway, the very next day. The gym teacher gave me a wink and a furtive thumbs-up. "How come you're wearing that Ronald Reagan shirt?" my friend Scott Hurt asked. I didn't know. There were two shirts for sale and I chose one.

"Democrat or Republican," said my dad, "all of em's crooks." He shook his head at my Reagan shirt and told me the last vote he'd cast was for Richard Nixon, so he'd never vote again. We are all voting for crooks, yet we see ourselves as very different from a person who chooses the opposing crook. At what point did I come to hear *Republican* as a slur?

A Haddonfield neighbor who grew up in Georgia told my wife and me she was happy to see some more Southerners. I felt a tinge of pride at being so warmly called a Southerner, same as I'd felt insulted at the suggestion I would join the Republicans. Although I've never claimed either label. Although I once spent an hour trying to convince a near-stranger that Louisville was more Midwestern than Southern. He had written off the South so conclusively that it seemed easier for me to redraw the map than to change his mind. It's a rare New Jerseyan who doesn't see my leaving Kentucky as a move toward success. Mostly they congratulate me for having left the land of red-state Republicans. And now I've stumbled onto an exclave.

But if I can move to a garbage town, or a garbage state, what's to say I can't live in a garbage country? Our national elections are neck-and-neck races, each side certain the other is wrong, so most of us must believe America is 50% awful. Where do we draw the lines: Democrat vs. Republican? Rural vs. Urban? North vs. South? White vs. Not

White? Rich vs. Poor? I like my news blunted by comedy; my mother likes hers panicked as a horror film trailer. You may not have much, her news tells her, but people less deserving are coming to take it; if the government would stop helping them take what's yours, you might have been rich by now. My news makes fun of her for being so easily fooled. Mine tells me the rich—not the poor—are the villains, and I believe it.

I once saw a free concert—a rap group called Black Landlord— in Philly's Rittenhouse Square and cheered along with the rest of the crowd when the MC pointed up at the expensive high-rises surrounding the park and said, "Fuck all those rich people up in them towers." Weeks later, my department hired a new English professor and he moved right into one of those towers. He was no richer than I was. I was no less rich than he was. Yet I look at the people with houses bigger than mine and I harbor the illusion they do not deserve what they have. They were born rich, I tell myself. Or if they worked for it, they worked too hard, traded their lives for money, made a deal with the devil. Do I deserve what I have? Books about rap music bought me my house. Things could have gone very differently.

•

My Haddonfield neighbors convince themselves they've earned what they have and that they're teaching their kids that hard work—not inheritance—will earn them a large home in a nice neighborhood. They assume I got here not only by hard work, but a legacy of it. "My father got up in the morning and put on his suit and went to the office," a neighbor proclaimed. "I see people on food stamps and they're perfectly happy to sit at home all day and wait for their handout to come in the mail. What kind of lesson is that for their kids? I mean, what did you see *your* dad get up and do in the morning?"

I saw my dad trade twenty dollars in food stamps for ten dollars in cash so that he could buy cigarettes. I saw my dad pull his own wisdom teeth with a pair of pliers and a bottle of Old Granddad. We didn't have health insurance. My sister broke her arm when she jumped through our backyard sprinkler and landed on a beach ball; Daddy wanted to set it at home. I saw my mom, when she went to take a sip of her Pepsi, stop short and hold the bottle up to her eye like a pirate's spyglass to make sure no roaches had crawled inside. Roaches infested our cabinets so we kept cereal boxes inside an old Styrofoam cooler on the kitchen table and stored our dishes inside our broken dishwasher. Fake brick paneling in the kitchen. Fake wood grain in the living room. What were we trying to hide?

Coalminers and war veterans on one side, farmers and schoolteachers on the other. My mom's family made its living growing tobacco, the poison that killed my dad. The Japanese captured Papaw Hess during World War II and starved him until he was hungry enough to strangle and eat the chicken they tossed into his cell. He came home from the war different, I was told. Burned his son's toys in the heat stove, laughed at him for carrying a baby doll, like a *girl*, until Daddy, seven years old, finally took an axe and chopped off the doll's head. Daddy started smoking before he was ten years old, quit middle school to learn to rebuild cars. He spent months restoring a 1955 Chevrolet and, while he was serving in Viet Nam, Papaw sold it and spent the money.

Having taken his share of orders in the Air Force, my father refused to work for any boss but himself. He was too stubborn to look for a better-paying job painting cars for one of the lots down the road in the bigger town of Somerset. He played country guitar at late-night parties and slept through AM appointments while Mom dealt with customers. If it was a potential new paintjob, she'd pray they called back. If it was a friend or neighbor seeking a quick repair, she'd invite him into the house to try, himself, to shake Daddy awake. One morning, a man Mom knew from church stopped by and claimed he'd already paid, so she gave him his keys and he drove off with all Daddy's hard work. When Daddy finally got out of bed and saw the car gone, he drove around town, raging, until he spotted the car parked in front of the Science Hill pool hall. He took a tire iron out of his trunk and smashed every part of that car that he'd fixed.

Daddy wasn't home much and when he was he was in the body shop working and avoiding his family. I stayed in the house where I could watch TV and avoid him and his friends and the cars they worked on. I took Mom's side because she talked about her side and he didn't talk much. When she tried to talk to him, he broke a chair over the kitchen table. She asked her brother to talk to him, *his* brother to talk to him, but he would not listen to anyone. We were his wife and kids and he lived with us, but he also lived with some woman in a trailer behind Oran's truck stop. When my dad was at home, I remember him most for his anger at me and my sisters for having woken him up watching our Saturday morning cartoons. He'd stomp through the kitchen to stir Folgers Crystals into a cup of microwaved water and sit silently at the table looking tired and introspective and put-out. He'd smoke a few cigarettes and then paint cars until it was time to play music again. Back home at 2:00 AM, still on a performer's high, he'd brew a pot of coffee and paint some cars and finally go to sleep. He'd lie in bed until late in the afternoon, screaming, "Shut them kids up! I can't take it." He'd peel out of our gravel driveway and mom would say, "Well, you ran him off again. I hope you're happy."

My mother felt as tied to our house as my dad felt imprisoned by it. She told me I was going to go places in life, but she was scared to let me leave the front yard. She shook her head at the prospect of traveling an hour's distance to take me to watch the Harlem Globetrotters at Lexington's Rupp Arena, named after an old racist who never wanted to let black people play basketball. "I don't know how to get there," Mom would explain. "And even if I could get to Lexington I wouldn't know how to drive once I got there." She was comfortable driving only to places she'd already driven, and only until dusk, when she said her night blindness became too severe to drive anywhere at all. We left my friends' autumn birthday parties before the cake, Mom wringing her hands and mouthing prayers that we'd make it home before nightfall. Back home, safely, she sat in her recliner underneath an electric blanket, her upper lip shiny with Vicks Vapo Rub, her eyes red and watery, toilet paper wadded in her fists and stuffed between the cushions, and anti-anxiety meds and a can of caffeine-free Pepsi on the floor beside her. "He's not coming back this time. I just know it."

My father didn't want to be an auto-body man with a wife and three kids. He was good enough at guitar to believe it should make him famous. He wanted to be on stage at the Grand Ole Opry. And when my sisters or I pled for a trampoline or cable TV, he'd say, "Well we don't always get what we want, do we? I wanted to be a famous guitar player."

It wasn't enough to be famous in small town Kentucky, to play Saturday nights at his friends' pig roasts and Sunday afternoons at the flea market. He wanted to be on television, so he hated the guitarists he saw on TV. I listened to him blame the stars for being more good-looking than talented, for having it too easy, for knowing somebody. He didn't say much, but I latched onto the bit he said: things were unfair.

•

I saw white resentment of black success when I stayed up late to watch *Saturday Night Live*. Daddy and his friend Kenny watched me watch Eddie Murphy put on makeup to pass as a white man—a satirical reversal of the social experiment from *Black Like Me*, a book I'd seen on my teacher's shelf. "Slowly I began to realize," said the white Eddie Murphy, "that when white people are alone they give things to each other for free."

Kenny shook his head. "Shoot, ain't nobody ever give me nothin. Have they you, Mike?"

"They sure ain't," said my dad. "They wouldn't give me air if I was in a jug."

Kenny's was a common resentment among the adults I knew: they resented that black people had cornered the market on pity; they resented that black people were free to assume white people had it easy by virtue of being white, even as black people had also—*somehow*, after centuries of being subjected to the offhand vitriol of whites—cornered the market on taking offense to jokes about race. In 1961, less than twenty-five years before I watched Eddie Murphy on *Saturday Night Live*, Dick Gregory—one of the first black comedians to regularly perform for white crowds—joked, "Segregation is not all bad. Have you ever heard of a collision where the people in the back of the bus got hurt?" In 1961, the joke was on segregation. In 1984, the joke was at long last on white people.

I laughed as the white Eddie Murphy sat, stiff and pale, as the last black man exited a bus and the remaining passengers—all white, or so they thought—began to sing and dance, free at last from the burden of his presence. I laughed at Eddie Murphy, in another SNL sketch, playing a grownup Buckwheat from the *Little Rascals*, mispronouncing the lyrics of popular songs. "Shoot," said Kenny. "He don't even know he's making fun of himself, does he?" Buckwheat kept mispronouncing lyrics. "Well, that's a nigger for you, ain't it? Hell, I can't stand 'em, can you, Mike?"

And Daddy said, "Aw, now I reckon some of 'em's okay. There's good ones and bad ones, same as us." He believed that—or I choose to tell myself he did—but I watched him set aside his convictions to make a joke. I watched him get big laughs in our kitchen on Martin Luther King Jr. Day—the first one our school district had deigned to observe; Kenny asked why I was off school and Daddy shrugged and grinned and said, "Some nigger's birthday." Listening to him, I learned that it was okay to make jokes as long as you didn't mean it. But as irresponsible as he was in leaving me with that lesson, I still find myself wanting to defend my dad, to say he dropped out of school in the eighth grade, didn't have the advantages of a higher education, grew up in racial isolation in rural Kentucky, or was just joking. White Americans have spent so many decades making these kinds of excuses for our ancestors, and devoted so little time to trying to distinguish the jokes from the threats, or to ask ourselves if there was ever any difference at all.

I heard the word "nigger" as frequently in my dad's body shop as I did on my N.W.A. cassettes. When presented with a repair estimate, a customer might respond, "Well, I ain't got the money to fix it right, so I reckon we'll just have to nigger-rig it." To barely fix a car was to "nigger-rig" it, but to make a car look too flashy was to "nigger it up," e.g., "My cousin put ground effects on his pickup, but it just looks too nigger for me." Black people couldn't win.

My teachers and church deacons clung to the stereotype of the young black male criminal, but they didn't like to see young black males getting rich rapping about being criminals. They told me rappers were not as poor as they claimed to be—if they were really from the street they wouldn't even get past security to sign a record deal. It was all exaggeration, they assured me. The white grownups around me made jokes about black people using food stamps and stealing hubcaps, but they didn't like to see them use crime or poverty as a means to succeed. "Just look at them waving their guns and their gold chains around," they might say. "Martin Luther King would be ashamed of them, the way they act." White people kept buying songs and movies that told those stories— the desperation of drug-dealing, the power of the gun—even as they used those same stories to keep black people right where they were.

White rock bands sued rappers for stealing little slices of sound, after all the moves rock bands had stolen from black guitarists. White rappers stole stories about growing up poor and desperate so that their biographies fit some stereotypical sense of what it meant to be black. White rapper Vanilla Ice outsold any rapper to come before him, his promotional materials presenting a "colorful teen-age background full of gangs, motorcycles and rough-and-tumble street life in lower-class Miami neighborhoods, culminating with his success in a genre dominated by young black males."[3] Black journalist Ken Parish Perkins pulled Vanilla Ice's high school yearbook from the Dallas suburb of Carrollton, Texas—1,300 miles from Miami—and called Ice's manager to question the contradiction. His upbringing "could have been well-off," said his manager, "but maybe he chose to go to the street and learn his trade. When he said he's from the ghetto, it may not be true that he grew up in the ghetto—but maybe he spent a lot of time there."[4] Makes sense. If there's one thing rap tells us the ghetto welcomes, it's well-off white kids dropping by for apprenticeships. "If you ain't never been to the ghetto," warned Treach of Naughty by Nature, "don't ever come to the ghetto. Cause you wouldn't understand the ghetto. So stay the fuck out of the ghetto."[5]

Ice's lies might have struck a nerve with Perkins, a black man who'd grown up in the kind of neighborhood Vanilla Ice only visited. One of the few black journalists at the *Chicago Tribune*, Perkins rejected the paper's plan to publicize his rise from the housing projects to the *Tribune* newsroom in order to promote its commitment to diversity. He refused to allow the paper to publish his photograph with his column; "[Readers] see a black man," he reasoned, "they think he'll be a certain way."[6] A black journalist hid his face and his life story from readers, even as he exposed a white rapper for faking his life story to appear something closer to black. A black journalist brought down a white rapper for having stolen his struggle story from his black peers, but when it came to presenting his own struggle, he preferred readers assume he was white.

A white rapper cribbed his struggle story from black rappers and outsold any rapper before him. When black rappers complained, he tried to turn the backlash into a struggle in itself. "People are out to bust Vanilla Ice," his publicist Elaine Schock told the *Philadelphia Inquirer*, "because he's successful and because he's white. I do think it's reverse racism."[7] Was it, though? Vanilla Ice was a guest in the house of hip-hop and he sneaked out with a piece of its foundation and stood on it to reach the top of the pop charts. Facing the backlash, Ice brought Public Enemy's Flavor Flav with him to his interview on *The Arsenio Hall Show*, but his strategy backfired when Hall asked Flav to wait offstage while he took Ice to task. "A lot of black rappers," he said, "are probably angry because some of the white people screaming [for you] didn't buy rap until you did it, until they saw a vanilla face on the cover of an album."[8]

"You saw Flavor Flav. Me and him, we're homies,"[9] Ice asserted, although only moments earlier he'd received the man's handshake so awkwardly it looked more like they'd met for the first time ever right there on stage. "Is that why you brought him out? Just to show you have a black supporter?" asked Arsenio.[10] I was fifteen years old when I watched this interview air live on *Arsenio Hall,* and it was the first time I felt like rap didn't belong to me; I'd discovered it, after all, on that hike through the woods to Wolf Creek Dam. Now, re-watching the clip when I'm forty-two and preparing to teach a lesson on white rappers, I have to ask myself this question—when I bring rappers as guest speakers, how pure are my motives? I'm dedicated to having students talk face-to-face with rappers, but I can't deny that I also mean to enhance my own credibility by making my course look legitimate enough that a rapper would drop by.

Vanilla Ice positioned himself as an anomaly among white people, telling Hall he was the unicorn among "the majority of white people" who "cannot dance."[11] Being white and thus rhythmically disadvantaged, Ice suggested, had made succeeding even harder for him, yet he overcame biology to develop an undeniable skill that sold records and concert tickets: "People who said I never could make it, that I'd never amount to S-H-I—you know the rest—said a white boy can't make it in rap music, kiss my white . . . you know the rest."[12] Once it came out that he'd exaggerated his link to the ghetto, fans were less willing to take his word on his skills as an artist. Perkins exposed Ice's lies, but Ice's fans were at fault for finding his fake story compelling. Why were listeners so eager to hear about a white man who'd ventured into a black neighborhood and outshined the black musicians?

Vanilla Ice was so thoroughly discredited that for the next ten years, any emerging white rapper was haunted by his inauthenticity. No rapper wanted to look like another Vanilla Ice. House of Pain wore shamrocks and Celtics jerseys in a sort of racial rebranding effort. We're not white, these symbols suggested; we're *Irish.* The group's frontman,

Everlast, had released a solo album just two years earlier and never said "Irish" once, yet his House of Pain album included "Top O' the Mornin' to Ya," "Danny Boy, Danny Boy," and "Shamrocks and Shenanigans." The Irish, who endured indentured servitude but never the chattel slavery that brought Africans to the Americas,[13] had endured social and economic exclusion in the US at the hands of other whites, but that exclusion was very much in the past by the time House of Pain's hit single "Jump Around" reached number 3 on the US charts, and number 6 in Ireland.

Not until 1999, nearly a decade after Vanilla Ice, did another white rapper reach (then exceed) his level of sales and fame. Eminem convinced listeners that not only did he really, truly grow up poor in Detroit, but Vanilla Ice had made things even harder for him by making white rappers look like liars. *8 Mile*'s most powerful scene shows Eminem's character B. Rabbit win a freestyle battle by revealing his black opponent, Papa Doc, is not who he appears to be. Rabbit disarms Doc by owning up to living in a trailer with his mom—"I'm a piece of fucking white trash, I say it proudly"—as he accuses Doc of posing as something he's not:

> I know something about you
> You went to Cranbrook, that's a private school.
> What's the matter, Dawg, you embarrassed?
> This guy's a gangster? His real name's Clarence.
> And Clarence lives at home with both parents.
> And Clarence's parents have a real good marriage.

The revelations rendered Doc mute, but I imagine that late that night, tucked into bed, he might have thought, *Yeah, but a cop would still shoot me first.*

If Doc could have thought faster on his feet in the battle, he might have put into rhyme the notion that when strangers see him they see a black man, rather than a man with a private-school diploma. *Why do you think the crowd was so willing to believe I was a gangster,* he could have asked Eminem's character, *and so unwilling to believe you've faced a struggle?*

White rappers try to shift the discussion from race to class, as if the wealthiest boardrooms and schools and neighborhoods had not been designed to keep black people out, while ghettoes and prisons were designed to keep black people in. When I tell stories about my childhood, I don't mean to suggest that class trumps race, or that food stamps even the playing field. My parents, unlike Clarence's, didn't have a real good marriage, but that doesn't make me less white. Eminem certainly admits being white made it easier for him to sell platinum; he attends to the advantages white skin gave him in selling records to white fans who might not have owned one song by a black rapper: "See the problem is/I speak to suburban kids/who otherwise would have never knew these words exist . . . they connected with me too because I looked like them." Yet Jimmy Iovine, the record exec who signed Eminem, claimed hip-hop had so torn down racial binaries in this country that *8 Mile* was "about class, not race."[14] "A white label head," responded Public Enemy's "media assassin" Harry Allen, "discusses a movie, ostensibly about a Black art form, in which the lead character is white, the screenwriter is white, the director is white, the producer is white, most of the productions talent, no doubt, white, and, of course, the film itself owned by a company run by, mostly owned by, and deriving the majority of its income from white people. Yet, something or other is 'about class, not race.'"[15]

Eminem's childhood poverty was so verifiable that he could put his childhood home, at 19946 Dresden Street in Detroit, on his album cover. Eminem's old neighborhood was so impoverished that in 2013, the Michigan Land Bank put the house up for auction, with bids starting at only one dollar, despite the house's fame. A reporter dropped by for a firsthand look at the place Eminem grew up: "A man who lives on Dresden," he wrote, "told me that the neighborhood has been terrorized by drug and gang activity for several years. He also mentioned, while walking a 200-plus pound pit bull on a choke chain, that I should be careful because dope dealers often prey on Eminem fans who stop by and visit the home."[16] A white rapper found success in a genre invented by black men; his old neighbors menaced his fans. The fans came on a pilgrimage, determined to see for themselves the unsafe neighborhood and the crumbling childhood home that had made the white rapper who he was. You'd think one of them might have put down a dollar to purchase the house, but before it could sell, it burned down. Eminem's employees recovered bricks from the rubble and sold them to fans via his website.

Just across town, Ben Carson—a black, Yale-educated surgeon—was running for president. In a 2015 campaign video, he posed in front of a dilapidated house much like the one Eminem put on his album cover. "Poverty and the mean streets of Detroit could have defined my life," he said. "I'm Dr. Ben Carson, and this is my story."[17] That was his story, maybe, but that wasn't his *house*. Reporters traveled to the house where Carson actually lived as a child and a teenager, and found that it "sits on a tree-lined block of well-kept, middle-class houses."[18] Carson's childhood neighbor, who still lives on the same block, said, "This has always been, I would say, a pretty decent neighborhood—people working, kids playing. We used to keep the doors unlocked. Doors would be open at night. You could just walk in."[19] A black man rose from a pretty decent neighborhood to run for President but settle for a cabinet position as secretary of Housing and Urban Development. He worried that if public housing were made too comfortable it wouldn't inspire its residents to claw their way out of there, so he took $31,000 of the taxpayer money that could have gone to improve public housing and spent it instead on a dining-room set for his own office.[20]

Wasn't this the American Dream? Ben Carson had beaten the odds to become a renowned pediatric surgeon, an inspiration to millions. He didn't need to pretend he'd grown up in a worse house than he actually did. He didn't need to claim to have overcome a "pathological temper"[21] that caused him to attack and stab his classmates in incidents CNN was unable to verify. Ice-T suggested Vanilla Ice didn't have to lie either: "One of his mistakes was he came into the rap business saying he was from the street. He didn't have to say that. All he had to do was say hey, I'm a white kid, I'm trying to rap, and I want to be accepted. You don't have to lie and say you're from someplace you're not, you know?"[22] We had become obsessed with whether or not our public figures were telling the truth—and rightly so—but our fact-checking distracted us from the bigger problems with our impulse to buy into such stories. Being born poor made for a good story, once you got rich. Growing up poor was worth so much that our rappers and politicians were willing to lie about it, yet all it did for most people was keep them poor for the rest of their lives.

Four

HIP-HOP COMES TO CAMPUS

MF Grimm arrived at campus in the back seat of a taxi cab, having taken a 300-dollar ride from New York City to my campus more than halfway across New Jersey. "Professor Hess!" he said. "It made my mom's day to hear that I'm speaking at a college. So, this is embarrassing, but I don't have any cash. Can you cover the cab fare? I promise I'll pay you back." Grimm had waived his meager speaking fee. The creative-writing club paid for his flight from Los Angeles, and the American Studies program put him up in a hotel, but I paid the ornery cab driver with cash from my own pocket. *What are you doing?* I asked myself. *This man is a stranger who lives on the other side of the country. You will never see this money again.* I was ashamed of myself for thinking that way, for worrying Grimm would steal my three hundred dollars even as I worried I'd stolen much more from him. I thought of his song "Taken," where he borrows Rakim's old line "Ladies and gentlemen, you're about to see / a pastime hobby about to be . . . taken to the maximum" but changes that last part to "taken away from us." I worried I'd taken hip-hop out of its proper context and that teaching hip-hop to college students was just yet another way to remove it from where it began.

Grimm captivated my students with a talk that ranged from his experiences riding on top of Mr. Snuffleupagus as a child actor on

Sesame Street to recording MF DOOM's album *Operation: Doomsday* next door to a meth lab. He autographed some books, then I volunteered to personally drive him to the very clean and affordable New Jersey Transit train that would take him back to New York. I waved goodbye, then I opened my new copy of Grimm's memoir, *Sentences*, to read the inscription: "To Dr. Hess—Thanks for keeping hip-hop alive." I couldn't pat myself on the back for it—even Vanilla Ice had his black supporters—but I found it encouraging that a rapper saw the value in a college course on rap. A week later, Grimm called to ask for my address so he could mail me my three hundred dollars.

Old-school rap legend Greg Nice burst into my classroom, red-eyed from a studio all-nighter. He beamed at the roomful of American Studies majors assigned his music as required listening. "What's going on, Rider?" he shouted. "And they said I'd never make it to college." His playful defiance echoed "Juicy," Biggie's song about dreaming of making it big, dedicated to the teachers who'd told him he'd never amount to nothing. Despite, or because of, such discouraging remarks, Biggie hit the street corner and sold drugs to make money to feed his child. Despite, or because of, such discouraging remarks, Biggie kept rapping and rapping until he got so good he could leave the street corner behind him and make millions selling songs about selling drugs, his songs likely poisoning more minds than his drugs ever did.

There were only so many roles available, Biggie argued on "Things Done Changed": the only routes out of the ghetto were basketball, crack, or rap—which for many of the best-selling rappers meant rapping about selling crack. Those were the kinds of songs that sold well, which was nothing new; things hadn't changed that much in terms of the roles black people got paid to play. Sixty years before Biggie played a crack dealer on his records, Hattie McDaniel played the devoted housemaid, Mammy, in *Gone With the Wind*, and similar housemaid figures in dozens of other films. *The slaves were freed seventy years ago*, said her critics, *so why are you still playing Mammies in movies?* "Why should I complain," McDaniel asked, "about making seven hundred dollars a week playing a maid? If I didn't, I'd be making seven dollars a week actually being one!"[1] But Biggie wasn't so sure the decision came that easy. Sean Combs had to beg him to stop selling crack down in North Carolina, where he'd already spent nine months in jail, and come home to New York and sign a record deal. "This better work out," Combs says Biggie told him. "I could have made a lot of money down there."[2]

Millionaire rappers bragged about their days in the drug trade the way millionaire politicians bragged about their grandparents' turns in the coalmines and factories. *We did this because we had to*, each of them said in their own way, *in the hope that our children would not have to resort to the same*. But the factories belonged to the past: so many of them had been shut down and outsourced to countries where people were even more desperate, and it's no surprise that manual labor didn't have quite the same romance for the people whose forebears were forced to build our country for free. Rap romanticized selling drugs as an education in entrepreneurialism, like business school without the student loans. Jay-Z claimed the drug trade helped him hone the skills he needed to navigate the music business, where corporate record labels trafficked in songs about making it out of the ghetto. But how harmful was the story, told by so many rappers, that selling drugs was less of a last resort than a stepping stone on the path to success? Crack, rap, or basketball, said Biggie. "You will not play in the NBA," said Barack Obama, on his way to a White House where no black president before him had slept. "You are probably not that good a rapper. Maybe you are the next Lil Wayne, but probably not, in which case you need to stay in school."[3] No way out, said the rapper, besides entertaining people with sports or music. But, said the president, you're not good enough at those things to succeed. What paths did that leave? Biggie said drugs and Obama said school. This clash of values cannot be ignored by those professors who bring hip-hop into the classroom. One of the first video clips I play in class is an interview in which Killer Mike, asked about hip-hop's focus on keeping it real, shrugs and says, "I sold dope *and* went to college. What's real?"[4]

Plenty of rappers went to college. Plenty of rappers grew up with middle-class incomes and middle-class values. But as much sense as it made to bring rappers to campus, professors couldn't invite *only* the rappers who had gone to college, or assume the rappers who'd earned degrees were somehow safer or more in line with the values we intended to teach. And even when I did invite the college-educated rappers, administrators still approached them very differently than they did other speakers. A Rider dean—who's since retired—stayed past midnight for the Traum Diggs and Rah Digga concert I organized. He showed up with our director of public safety and spent less time listening than lurking in the back of the room, asking how soon it'd be over. Public safety officers posted up backstage like they were afraid the rappers would steal something. Yet when I brought in a poet—a convicted shoplifter and MDMA enthusiast—no campus officials stopped by. Never mind that rappers I've brought in have degrees from better schools than the one I attended. Never mind that Rah Digga scored 1300s on her SATs and majored in electrical engineering, or that Traum Diggs matriculated at Temple University when he was just sixteen years old. When this dean saw black rappers were coming to campus, his mind didn't go to their grade point average, but to their potential as a threat.

This dean's assumptions were dangerous, same as it was dangerous for the white woman in scheduling to ask if the event couldn't wait for

Black History Month. Same as it would be dangerous for me, as a white professor, to assume a black student knows more about hip-hop than a white student, or that a black student necessarily embraces or even appreciates hip-hop. I think of Rider's own Semitic-themed rapper Robert "Lefty Da Jew" Lefkowitz, who said listening to Gangstarr helped him get through the death of his father. I think of sixty-two-year-old freshman Eugene Marsh, who'd been the first black student to enroll in his high school in South Carolina—and had the Ku Klux Klan burn a cross in his yard. Lefty lived and breathed hip-hop, while Eugene looked askance at it. Eugene took pride in hip-hop as an unprecedented worldwide cultural force rooted in the experiences of poor black Americans, yet he saw rappers reinforcing hateful stereotypes. For all hip-hop's progress in giving voice to poor black youth, its songs cemented racist notions their parents hoped to leave in the past. "I signed up for this class," Eugene told me, "because I wanted to understand the positive side of hip-hop. I knew it had to be there, but I couldn't see it. I still can't completely see it but I'm trying." He *was* trying; the semester ended and he got his grade and he still came back to hear every rapper who came to campus. My job was not to sell Eugene on hip-hop by convincing him of its positive contributions. My job was not to talk Lefty out of rapping. My job was to show both of them hip-hop's complexities and contradictions and get them to think more critically about them than they had before they signed up for the class.

•

The complexities and contradictions of my own relationship to hip-hop rose to the surface in 2008, when Mercer County Community College invited me to join a panel discussion on hip-hop's cultural impact. A black activist and community organizer was there to condemn hip-hop, and I was a white professor there to defend it. Nas had released an album called *Hip Hop is Dead*, and I'd published a book saying it wasn't dead, precisely because artists like Nas took such care in patrolling its borders. I argued that hip-hop had gone commercial even while criticizing going commercial, so that Nas could brag about seeing his face on SONY trucks even as he pined for the good old days when hip-hop still belonged to a few black and Latino neighborhoods. When faced with the threat of rap going pop, rappers wrote songs against pop rap. When faced with the threat of white rappers, rappers wrote songs about keeping rap black. Ewuare X. Osayande, my fellow panelist, disagreed with me: "Commercialized rap music is no more 'Black' than the *Amos and Andy* show from back in the day," said his book. "It is a mockery of Blackness. It is a pejorative parody of Blackness. Hip-hop has been disemboweled of any real socio-political value and stuffed with materialism, sexism and violence and now sits on the shelves of the corporate masters like the prized game that it is."[5] *Damn.* (Osayande, by the way, spends his free time counseling kids in Southwest Philly who've lost a family member to gun violence. So much for thinking I'm saving the world by teaching college students which Halloween costumes are racist.)

Psychologically speaking, I'm sure there was a measure of self-preservation to my book. The hip-hop purists were crying commercialization killed hip-hop, and if I accepted that New Orleans' Lil Wayne was an accessory to rap music's murder because he took its sound a different direction from its NYC pioneers, how could I justify taking it into the college classroom? I was writing a novel about nostalgia, so I saw nostalgia driving the call for hip-hop to return to its roots. If hip-hop never left the Bronx, I argued, it would have suffocated; its spread across the globe hadn't killed it but kept it alive. The rappers and listeners who'd grown up closer to hip-hop's birthplace disagreed with me. Hip-hop had once been theirs, they argued, before the record companies ruined it; hip-hop had once stood for something. During the panel at Mercer, an older black man in the audience argued hip-hop had lost its path: "In the Eighties, 'The Message' was a smash hit railing against the junkies and thieves in our communities," he said. "Today the rappers *are* the junkies and the thieves and the dope dealers. What is 'The Message' today?"

But Grandmaster Flash didn't even want to make that song, I wanted to interject. Flash wrote in his memoir that he'd wanted to make party music, not a song about his car getting repossessed. A studio musician wrote some lyrics and brought them to Sylvia Robison, the head of the record label, who pressured Grandmaster Flash and the Furious Five to let MC Melle Mel finish the song and record it. Grandmaster Flash didn't participate in any capacity; the label put his name on a Top Forty hit that he didn't have the first thing to do with. Rap's forgotten first mogul, Sylvia Robinson, brought Grandmaster Flash "The Message" because she thought it would make money;[6] four decades later, critics of rap's commercialization use it as an example of how much purer rap used to be.

But I bit my tongue. It was not a good look, a white man defending hip-hop to a black man who said it made black men look bad. (Wasn't much of a defense, anyway—he said rap today was terrible and I wanted to tell him it always had been.) I worried the underlying accusation would hang there in the room: *I know hip-hop*, I would suggest in correcting his facts, *a little better than you know it.* The idea of saying it felt wrong, and reminded me of the talk I gave at my alma mater, the University of Louisville, where a young black student during the Q&A

asked me, "Respectfully—and this is going to sound like more of an attack than I mean it to be—how do *you* know?"

How did I know? I had published three books about hip-hop, which the talk's organizers displayed on a folding table beside me onstage. But I suspected that the display came to speak more for self-promotion than expertise—not only did I believe I had the right to talk about hip-hop; I wanted the audience members to pay me money so they could read more at home. How do I know? I read *You Know my Steez: An Ethnographic and Sociolinguistic Study of Styleshifting in a Black American Speech Community.* I read "Paralinguistic Mechanisms of Production in Human 'Beatboxing': A Real-Time Magnetic Resonance Imaging Study." Of course I made a bad first impression—professors were sticking the word beatboxing inside quotation marks, sticking rappers inside MRI machines. The whole endeavor felt far too clinical.

Professors have long been criticized for writing from their ivory tower without engaging with the real world, and here I was teaching hip-hop music to college students while somebody spray-painted "No Nigger Mayor" on a South Carolina city hall.[7] Would I have done better patrolling for racist graffiti? In Kentucky, I once witnessed a faded red Oldsmobile resting on blocks in a neighbor's front yard; black spray-painted letters on the hood spelled NIGG. The house was not vacant—lights were on, other cars parked in the driveway. I like to picture the beating the homeowners gave the vandal when they caught him mid-word. But he probably just ran out of paint.

It was a powerful word he was spray-painting on that car. In 2015, the University of Kansas investigated a white professor, Andrea Quenette, after her graduate students—teachers in training—reported that she'd said the word in a class discussion of how they should approach addressing issues of race in their classrooms. What better way to strip its power, she may have been thinking, than to drag it into the open? But the word was not rare: the walls of the university had been whispering it for centuries, and on some campus every semester it bled through to the surface to appear on those walls in spray-paint. An open letter from the student in Quenette's COMS 930 class said that she told them, "As a white woman, I just never have seen the racism . . . It's not like I see 'Nigger' spray-painted on walls."[8] Quenette's students understood her to say that racism did not exist at the University of Kansas because she hadn't personally seen the word scrawled right in front of her eyes, but Quenette said she meant to compare Kansas to the University of Missouri, where students had recently seen the word rear its ugly head.[9] Quenette's version doesn't quite match her students' account of the words she spoke, but even if we accept her explanation, there's a sad irony to a Professor of Communications not understanding the impact of that word, heard through black ears, from the mouth of a white woman at the front of the room. Could Quenette have discussed the impact of the word without saying the word? Certainly. In fact, discussing her reasons, as a white professor, for refusing to say it might have prompted her students to really stop and consider what they will and won't say in their own classrooms.

Years ago, I used to say the word in my classroom when quoting texts by black authors, but I'll never say it again. I will quote the word in writing, but I will not say it out loud. In my early days as a professor, I was convinced that I would rob black authors of the impact of their words if I censored their lyrics, short stories, or poems. I used to operate under the principle that to censor the word gives it even more power to be used in a racist attack, or that to cushion it strips the power from texts—you can't do justice to an Amiri Baraka poem like "Black Art" when you're pausing to mutter ". . . N-word." I now realize, though, that it didn't matter that I was quoting a black author. What mattered was that the word left the lips of a white man, and that word is emblematic of a centuries-long campaign of terror on the part of whites against blacks. A student, in a discussion of the word, once asked me why white people can't say it but black people can. I told him we'd had our turn. Whites invented the word to dehumanize blacks. A white man certainly shouldn't feel like *his* freedom is impeded if he's afraid to say it today.

I worry that the lesson many white professors took away from the Quenette incident was not that there is a better way to discuss these issues, but that white professors would be smarter to avoid ever bringing them up at all. The most disturbing part is that Quenette walked away scared to bring race back up: "To be honest," she told *Inside Higher Ed*, "I am afraid of engaging in a discussion of race and diversity in the classroom . . . I believe it will be harder for me to respond to my students now because I am afraid of saying something wrong."[10] But should her fear of repercussions for offending her students trump the fear that word can provoke? That word was the rallying cry for a campaign of racist terror waged by whites against blacks. If we want to talk about the history of fear surrounding that word, we could talk about the fear of being disenfranchised and dehumanized, the fear of being lynched. In that context, it's absurd to focus on a white professor's fear of "saying something wrong." White professors have ignored race in their lectures for far too long, so I do worry about a culture that makes a professor afraid to try. But I worry more about a culture that does not encourage a professor to think before she speaks. Quenette suggested she might seek more training: "I hope that I can use resources on my campus . . . and support from other faculty to better equip myself for such a situation."[11] I'd like to think she doesn't mean she'll lean on her colleagues of color and leave the discussions of race in their hands. We need more black and Latino and Asian professors—no question—but we need the white professors to think more about race, not to avoid addressing race altogether.

·

We need white university presidents to stop dressing up like carica-tures of Mexican people for Halloween, the way the president of my alma mater, the University of Louisville, did along with his entire office staff in 2015. Only days before this incident at Louisville, Yale had sent an email encouraging its students to avoid precisely this kind of cos-tume, prompting one faculty member, Erika Christakis, to write her own email suggesting Yale should maybe reconsider creating a culture in which an institution of higher education tells adults how they ought to dress up for Halloween. Yale placed the onus on the costume-wearer, suggesting that students ask themselves, "Could someone take offense with your costume and why?"[12] Christakis placed the onus on those students who took offense, writing that her husband Nicholas, Head of Yale's Silliman College, recommends that when faced with a white stu-dent in blackface, yellowface, war paint, or feathered headdresses, Yale members might simply "look away, or tell them you are offended."[13] A student, perhaps heeding his advice, accosted Nicholas Christakis and shouted, "You should not sleep at night! You are disgusting!"[14]

The interchange between the Yale students and Nicholas Christakis centered on the clash between the goals of protecting students from emotional harm versus challenging them intellectually: as a residential college, was Silliman a "home," as one student insisted, or was it a place of learning, as Christakis maintained? Christakis, in fact, stood so firm in his conviction that he sought to reason with the students rather than apologize to them. "Many students," wrote Conor Friedersdorf in *The Atlantic*, "believed that [Christakis's] responsibility was to hear their demands for an apology and to issue it. They saw anything short of a declaration of wrongdoing as unacceptable. In their view, one respected students by validating their hurt feelings."[15] So, while University of Louisville President James Ramsey apologized for wearing his offensive costume and continued to serve as president, the Christakises did not apologize, but did heed the calls for their resignation as heads of Silliman College.

Meanwhile, in Staten Island, police officers lynched a black man on tape and went free. In the span of two months in 2013, a Florida jury acquitted a man who'd stalked and murdered a black child and Food Network fired celebrity chef Paula Deen after she admitted to, in her lifetime, having said the word "nigger." Deen was certainly not the most dangerous racist on the loose in 2013, but her defenders seemed to suggest she should face no consequences at all, and that *she*, in fact, was the victim here. The vampire novelist Anne Rice took to Twitter to write, "It's so easy to persecute an older, overweight, unwise, crude, ignorant woman who may very well be a good person at heart." (Imagine Paula Deen reading that tweet and thinking, *Um ... thanks?*) Rice argued that the reaction against Deen's racism was an example of prejudice against white Southerners. Then Rice, who'd published so many thousands of carefully-chosen words, tweeted this unfathomably poor choice of words: "Aren't we becoming something of a lynch mob culture?" Rice invoked lynching—the campaign of terrorism in which white mobs brutally murdered over 3,000 black Americans between 1882 and 1968—to defend Deen, whose deposition described at length her desire to hire an all-black wait staff for a wedding not because of her strong commitment to workplace diversity but because of her commitment to the authenticity of a "really Southern plantation wedding."[16] If we said nothing in the face of such backward thinking, we were guilty of condoning the culture that led George Zimmerman to kill Trayvon Martin because of the color of his skin, yet I could not escape the fear that our boycotts and calls for resignations served as a stand-in for the actual justice we'd been denied.

In my childhood I watched the War on Drugs not take down kingpins so much as sentence first-time offenders to lengthier terms than rapists. We've watched our war on drugs fail, and now I feared we were taking the same tack with our war on hate, attacking the dimebag dealers of racism while the armed and fanatical racists hide in plain sight. But we simply can't risk the possibility of their being one and the same. In 2010, two white students dumped cotton balls in front of the University of Missouri's Black Culture Center, a crime one of their lawyers dismissed as "kids doing dumb things."[17] But just seven years later, the NAACP issued an unprecedented statewide travel advisory for black people traveling to Missouri, and the cotton-ball incident looked far less isolated and far more serious than the misdemeanor littering charge the students to which the students pleaded guilty. In 2011, another white student spray-painted "nigger" on a statue on Mizzou's campus. In 2014, just over a hundred miles from campus, a white police officer shot and killed the unarmed black teenager Mike Brown, igniting weeks of protests in Ferguson. In 2015, a white student screamed "nigger" at black students and somebody smeared a poop swastika on a dormitory's bathroom wall. Mizzou president Tim Wolfe—a corporate businessman who'd never before held a job in an educational setting— seemed to, at best, drag his feet in reacting or, at worst, shrug and ask what he was expected to do. Graduate student Jonathan Butler went on a hunger strike; black members of the football team refused to play. So

Wolfe resigned, even as he declared, "This is not, I repeat, not the way change should come about."[18]

"Change comes from listening, learning, caring, and conversation,"[19] said the same president who just months after taking office announced he would close the prestigious University of Missouri Press, without having spoken to a single employee at the press. "We have to respect each other enough to stop yelling at each other and start listening, and quit intimidating each other," said the president who didn't like student protestors blocking his car after he'd done nothing to address the culture of racist threats on his campus. Wolfe couldn't justifiably say that the black and white members of the Mizzou community were intimidating "each other" when the aggressors were invariably white. A white man yelled "nigger" at the Legion of Black Collegians. White men in a pickup truck screamed slurs at Payton Head, president of the Missouri Students Association.[20] The intimidation all came from one direction, no matter what threat the intimidators may have perceived in their victims. "I really just want to know," wrote Head, "why my simple existence is such a threat to society. For those of you who wonder why I'm always talking about the importance of inclusion and respect, it's because I've experienced moments like this multiple times at THIS university, making me not feel included here."[21] Yet when black students pushed President Wolfe to take action, and ultimately to resign, he said we have to quit intimidating *each other*.

Wolfe's supporters believed he should have not allowed himself to be so intimidated by the students he was paid to serve; he should have stood his ground. After his resignation, a white nationalist posted on Yik Yak, invoking the name of the Florida law at the foundation of George Zimmerman's defense, "I'm going to stand my ground tomorrow, and shoot every black person I see."[22] Despite such intimidation, black student groups pressed forward nationwide. The momentum of the Mizzou protests spread to campaigns to rename buildings named after old racists at Georgetown, Princeton, and Vanderbilt. Students rallied for racial justice at Ithaca College, Occidental College, Johns Hopkins, The University of Alabama, Claremont-McKenna, and Purdue, to name a few. "Campus Protests Are Spreading Like Wildfire," cheered *Mother Jones* magazine; laugh along with us at "The Ten Most Ridiculous College Protests of 2015" jeered *Forbes*. America's disdain for political correctness—and the notion that we were coddling our youth into seeing themselves as victims—led us to find and focus on the ridiculous. Two days after Wolfe resigned, bloggers revealed that Jonathan Butler, the black grad student whose hunger strike gave so much power to the University of Missouri protests, was the son of a millionaire railroad tycoon. *Some struggle*, said his critics, rolling their eyes. They posted pictures of his father's mansion to discredit his activism, as if one black man's earning his fortune balanced the scales of injustice. They saw the heir to millions of dollars complaining he had things so *hard*; I saw the reach of our racism, the slim chances of escaping its grasp—we're even shouting slurs at the millionaires.

The thirst for mocking the notion of white privilege in no way negated Butler's hunger strike, but the focus on the "most ridiculous" protests shifted the discussion to sandwiches. In the span of two months, the biggest campus protest movement in forty-five years lost the spotlight to complaints about free yoga and bad cafeteria food. Students at a Canadian university shut down a free yoga class because Britain stole yoga from India. Diep Nguyen, a Vietnamese student at Oberlin College, criticized the inauthenticity of her cafeteria banh mi, a sandwich born from the colonialism that brought French bread to meet with Vietnamese daikon and pork. Nguyen came to an Ohio college and found the cafeteria serving Italian ciabatta filled with pulled pork and coleslaw from the American South. "How," she asked, "could they just throw out something completely different and label it as another country's traditional food?"[23] This was racism's version of broken-windows policing—the theory that small gestures like replacing smashed windows maintains an orderly environment that keeps vandals from turning to bigger crimes. It was this broken windows theory—devised in the 1980s and since debunked—which led to the stop-and-frisk policies that gave New York City police free rein to harass black and brown people for looking suspicious (which is to say for looking black and brown). Making a better banh mi, goes the logic, would make us all pay more attention to what we are stealing from each other; caring enough to keep that sandwich true to its roots would acknowledge the value of the culture that invented it. If we could educate people enough to value the history of something as seemingly small as a sandwich, that education could ideally make a cop think twice about who he was stopping and frisking.

True, Diep Nguyen could afford Oberlin's pricey tuition that the people paid low wages to cook that inauthentic banh mi could never afford, but the banh-mi backlash put a lot of heat on a college student, no matter how much money her parents might have—or no matter how much debt she was willing to take on for an Oberlin education. No less than the *Atlantic* printed a letter from a chef who said if she'd complained to him he "would have tried to knock [her] goddamn teeth out with a frying pan."[24] Jesus. Give the student some credit. When I was her age I wasn't writing cultural critique; I was making awful attempts at jokes. First coming to college, I asked a stranger (a white girl, pretty) if Orientation was where they turned us Asian so we'd be better at math. I *wish* I could say I'd spent my freshman year complaining about the cultural appropriation of sandwiches.

We've been conditioned to seek out what's silly when people sound the alarm over cultural appropriation, but Nguyen was not wrong to complain to her student paper about her sandwich, not even while college students were drawing poop swastikas. Not even while cops were shooting people and getting away with it. Her complaint rose out of the same spirit that drove the Missouri protests, so conflating them allowed pundits to mock a movement—to mock a generation—so that when the next complaint arose they could say *These spoiled kids complain about anything and everything.* But don't forget that white Americans supported a crackdown on minor offenses when broken-windows policing claimed that arresting vandals and graffiti artists kept them from turning to bigger crimes. They supported the NYPD's stop-and-frisk program that searched citizens for merely looking suspicious. To suggest that a Vietnamese student shouldn't complain about her fake banh mi is to argue that universities should not be subject to the same kind of harassment to which police regularly subject black and brown people.

In defending Nguyen's banh mi complaint, I don't want to risk making the same mistake and suggest that cultural appropriation is the same thing as racial terrorism. Seeing racist graffiti at the University of Missouri reminds a black student that they are in danger in Missouri and in danger on campus. Nguyen is fighting for cultural ownership, not fighting for the right not to be terrorized. But of course she should complain about the sandwich her college served her. College is exactly the place we should all learn how to listen to such a complaint rather than mock it. The online response to the Great Oberlin Banh-Mi Rebellion of 2015 turned nasty so quickly. A grown man threatened to knock out an eighteen-year-old woman's teeth with a frying pan because she didn't like the label on her sandwich. European food-labeling laws enforce a strict code that dictates that cheese can only be named Parmesan if it's cheese made in Parma. Champagne made outside of France's Champagne region can only be called Champagne-*style*. Labeling Oberlin's pulled pork "banh-mi style" might have prevented complaints but it wouldn't have made it a better sandwich. No more than distinguishing pop rap from real hip-hop quashes that border dispute. When criticized on Twitter for appropriating hip-hop, Iggy Azalea—an Australian woman who raps with a Tennessee accent—claimed she was making a whole different style of rap music that didn't have much to do with the original culture:

Talib Kweli: "Hiphop come from oppression & struggle that u don't experience."

Iggy Azalea: "Rap is global now and it has sub-styles . . . *pop-rap* is part of that."

Pop-rap is rap-style music, designed to reach the Top 40 charts more than speak to the street corners where rap began. Azalea— the first white woman to sustain any measure of sales and exposure in American hip-hop—had drawn the ire of rappers before she ever typed that tweet. Snoop Dogg called her ugly and mannish, and, pop-rapper or not, Iggy embraced his diss like a hip-hop pro. Snoop said she looked like the Wayans brothers in drag and whiteface makeup in their movie *White Girls*, so Iggy owned the insult and made it her Halloween costume—a white woman dressed as a black man dressed as a white woman. When Eminem, a white man twice Iggy's age, rapped about raping her, she responded, "I'm bored of the old men threatening young women as entertainment trend." White and Australian or not, she had a point. (See, above, "knock [her] goddamn teeth out with a frying pan.") But shifting the discussion from race to gender—a special move Iggy overrelied on—didn't solve either problem.

Rappers kept saying Iggy had said "nigger," but nobody'd actually caught her saying it. It was always fake quotes and misheard lyrics. Kweli was informed he'd called Iggy out for saying something she hadn't said; he responded with less of an apology than a shrug: "coulda sworn I seen that tweet but ok." Chuck D was informed he'd commented on a fake quote; he tweeted, "True or not the IGGY thing is a reality." Which is to say that the word hangs over Iggy's performance whether she says it or not. (She did once call herself "slave-master" on a song, after all, but don't forget that many hip-hop stars merely shrugged when Eminem held a whip on the cover of the February 2003 *Rolling Stone*.) She already said it, symbolically, with every verse she recorded, with every dollar she made from a rap record, and the idea of her saying it was so compelling that her critics heard it where it didn't exist.

Iggy Azaela heard her critics saying another word. Q-Tip sent her a series of measured and reasoned tweets suggesting she should better understand the context of her performance as a white rapper—the context of slavery, Jim Crow, redlining, and the murders of black men at the hands of police. To Azalea, his remarks sounded like *mansplaining* even though he was a black man explaining black culture to a white woman. She called it "patronizing" that Q-Tip (a forty-something black man) would suggest she (a twenty-something white woman) didn't already know this history. Rappers could certainly be patronizing; there was a word they used to talk down to women, whether Chuck D or Talib Kweli or Q-Tip said it to Iggy Azalea or not. If they heard her saying *nigger* whether she said it or not, I can certainly grant that she, in the same way, might have heard them saying *bitch*.

Never mind that Chuck D and Talib Kweli were poster boys for positivity and political engagement, while rappers like Rick Ross wrote a song about drugging and raping a woman and Dr. Dre brutally attacked music journalist Dee Barnes and joked about it on a song nearly a decade later. So much hip-hop is unabashedly anti-woman that I can understand Iggy Azalea's feeling attacked or at least put in her place by these men who never said "bitch" in their lyrics. Talib Kweli isn't beyond reproach but I will give him his credit: he was there on the front lines at Ferguson; I wasn't and Iggy Azalea wasn't. He won me over forever when I saw him rap at Bogart's in Cincinnati in July 2000, and as much as I gripe about the bestseller list being populated by celebrity chefs and disgraced politicians—anybody but *writers*—he certainly has a right to gripe at a white rapper for making money from a form that's more his than hers. But I can't help but feel sorry for Iggy Azalea for being criticized for things she didn't say, for being more an emblem of the problem than the problem itself.

If she already knew the history Q-Tip tried to teach her, she sure didn't talk about it much in her music. Her music was void of historical references, unless you count the line "Give me head, Abe Lincoln" in her song "Pu$$y." If she had done more to acknowledge the problem—if she wrote songs about history instead of her genitals—she could have potentially educated her listeners and convinced her black hip-hop elders that she'd done her homework. She wouldn't have changed history one bit by acknowledging the history of racial oppression and injustice, but she may have gained better footing. Two decades before Iggy Azalea, Eminem beat his critics to the punch by calling himself "the worst thing since Elvis Presley/to do black music so selfishly/and use it to make myself wealthy," then he went right on doing it, same as I went right on teaching my hip-hop class and writing my books.

A common move among white scholars speaking about race or racism is to give a sweeping acknowledgement of America's past and the advantages that past—and its influence on the present—continues to give the citizens with white skin. But that move tends to externalize racism, to put it in the hands of history rather than place it squarely in our own. It acknowledges that we all symbolically say the n-word, yet we still point the finger at the public figures who slip up and say it out loud. But racism is not rare—to scandalize it reaffirms our conviction that we have it under control, and in those few and far-between instances that our white rappers and celebrity chefs slip up, they are caught and punished. It reaffirms our conviction that we have conquered racism, or at least killed off the ways it manifested so openly in decades past. It reaffirms our sense of our own blamelessness: *Of course I'm not racist—remember how upset I was at Paula Deen?* We look the person who's been labeled racist and say she is not like me.

We police emails and tweets. We target and shame one person at a time, hoping the others catch on and change their ways and try harder to think before they speak. We fight ignorance and vitriol by demanding firings and resignations in the hopes that one man's downfall might dissuade others from speaking the way she spoke. We have the technology to shame celebrities for their comments; it's tempting to use it any chance we get.

Am I suggesting we should let everyday people rob us a little bit so that we don't become the boy who cried wolf when the real robbers come to town? No, I'm saying we shouldn't sound our slur alarm so loud that it drowns out the more insidious threats. Words can wield power—I get it. I'm an English professor; I work with words all day. Changing the words we use can change the whole way we think about something. We raised our children to choose their terms carefully, and now they confuse rudeness for an act of war. Do the public figures we chastise take a good look in the mirror and vow to change their ways, or will rudeness, attacked, harden into hate? Confrontations make us dig in our heels. Our minds race to rationalize what we've said, even when we didn't stop to think before saying it. Viewers at home, with their own biases, see not an individual attacking a group, but a group attacking an individual. *Look how they're all ganging up on him and all he did was speak his mind. It's not fair, by God. What if they come for me next?* Fired over one email, they say, shaking their heads. Fired over one *word*. But that one word was the last straw heaped onto a centuries-old pile of hate and injustice. If we let these transgressions slide, what hope do we have to catch the real killers and thieves?

Five

POLITICAL CORRECTNESS AND
WHITE IDENTITY

When talking about political correctness and which slurs we should censor, white people tend to draw a line between those whites who are too defiantly uneducated to know better and those whites who higher education has made so fragile they can't take a joke. I came of age in the Nineties, when political correctness had so taken hold in this country that people around my part of Kentucky prided themselves on speaking exactly the opposite. Politicians on TV showed off their polish by using clunkier terms to refer to people in the hopes of avoiding a scandal, but my neighbors saw right through the façade: "Ain't nobody gonna tell me what I can and can't say." We all want to see ourselves as the underdogs; it's the influence of our revolutionary heritage. White Southerners, who'd lost so much money and status in the process of having their slaves taken away from them, didn't like black people telling them what to call black people.

So they dug in their heels and kept calling Brazil nuts *nigger toes*, calling geodes *niggerhead rocks*—crack them open and they're empty inside. At school, we had the word *niggardly* on a vocabulary test— "He received a niggardly allowance." Brian Hargis shouted, "Does that mean they paid him in food stamps?" and even Mr. Bumgardner laughed.

Still snickering, I repeated the joke to my mom when I got home. She shrugged and reminded me, "*We're* on food stamps."

•

Kentucky's state song, Stephen Foster's blackface minstrel show standard "My Old Kentucky Home," included the word "darkies" until 1986, when Carl R. Hines—the only black member of Kentucky's House of Representatives—called for Kentucky to replace this word in its state song. I was eleven years old when we officially changed darkies to people. I was not yet born when in the 1960s Malcolm X rejected the term Negro and embraced the terms Black and African American. I was a child in the 1980s when Jesse Jackson codified African-American, in the minds of news anchors and politicians, as the term polite speakers were supposed to use, even though not all black people embraced the hyphen. KRS-ONE suggested it named a category that was something less than American: "White man never say Euro-American," he rapped, "so why should the black man say Afro-American?"[1] Terms changed; you could see the vestiges of America's old vocabulary in The National Association for the Advancement of Colored People and The United Negro College Fund. Kids took our turn-of-the-century clinical terms *moron* and *idiot* and used them to mock each other, so in the 1960s we invented the clinical term *retarded*, which by 2013 had come to sound so hateful we had to retire it too. No matter what new terms we came up with, people still found ways to make them sound hateful.

Some of us stuck with the old terms. In 1988, when I was thirteen years old, I witnessed the backlash against eighty-nine-year-old Happy Chandler—a former Kentucky governor and the man who'd been baseball commissioner when the major leagues first let Jackie Robinson play—who'd used the n-word to refer to African people. "Zimbabwe's all nigger now,"[2] he said, in urging the UK board of trustees to stop investing the university's money in Zimbabwe. UK's football team protested by refusing to practice. A few dozen students held a rally to demand Happy resign or at least apologize. "I did say it," he said in what was in no way an apology. "I wish I hadn't. I know enough about what's going on in the world to know there's a lot of people who, if you call them nigger now, they are going to object to it."[3] Happy held a press conference to remind his critics that he'd once allowed a black man play baseball with white men, after all, way back in 1947: "I don't reckon there's anybody in this lifetime has made any greater contribution to race relations and good feelings between black and white people than your humble servant, and I think the record will show that."[4] Happy Chandler did not resign. The UK football team went back to practice. Protestors went back to class.

Happy's a Kentucky institution, said my teachers and neighbors, and look how they're doing him—scandalizing an old man for speaking the way people spoke in his day. It was an excuse I'd heard before. When I was six years old, my granny sang, "Eeny meeny miney moe. Catch a nigger by the toe," and Mom told me not to think poorly of her, but to use tiger instead when I sang. "That's a word people used in your granny's time."

"What is it?" I asked. *Tiger* substituted so easily that I pictured a kind of animal—the way people used the word sure didn't sound like they were talking about human beings.

"It's like Arnold on *Diff'rent Strokes*. You wouldn't want to hurt Arnold's feelings, would you?"

Her explanation seemed to make perfect sense: people used to say this word but now we knew better. Yet younger people still said it so frequently. My second-grade classmate's father was decades younger than my granny or Happy Chandler when, having asked if we had crushes on girls in our class, told his son, "Don't you bring home no little nigger girl." My friend laughed. I laughed. His dad said it with a comic timing I tried to mimic when I relayed the event to my mom in the car on the way home. She tightened her grip on the steering wheel and said, "You bring home whoever you want. I thought his daddy knew better than that."

Some of us knew better and some of us didn't, I understood her to say. She and I knew better than the people we happened to live near. She kept me by her side, so she could keep an eye on me, when we went to visit Daddy's sister, my Aunt Marlene, who sent me into her little front yard to play with my Cousin Marty and his friend Alan with the little arm, his hand malformed and curled back on itself. They crashed radio-controlled police cars into G.I. Joes. Marty aimed a gun at a bird's nest. "It's just a BB gun," Marlene assured Mom. "It ain't even loaded." But she took it from Marty to appease my mother, who still insisted I stay inside the house with her and talk to Marlene about school. "Did you pass?" Marlene asked me, "Alan got held back. You want you a Moon Pie? You want you a RC Cola?"

As certain as I was that I was better than Alan (*what kind of a kid doesn't pass first grade?*), I didn't like the way he and Marty looked at me with pity (*what kind of kid doesn't like racecars and guns?*) When Mom went to the bathroom, Aunt Marlene pushed me back into the yard to play. I found Marty and Alan planting firecrackers in ant hills. "Your Daddy dip snuff?" asked Alan, spitting brown juice into the grass near my feet. He pulled a little puck-shaped container from his back pocket and offered it to Marty, who popped it open, took a pinch of the powdered tobacco and tucked it behind his bottom lip. "Want some?" he asked, extending the container to me. I went back inside.

•

On our own turf, during playdates at our house, the distinction between us and them crystallized. I hid toys, the good ones, at my mother's insistence when Daddy's friend Richard came over with his son Mike, a boy my age named after my father. Richard and Daddy had been buddies since high school and Richard tended to beam at Little Mike and me with a certain anticipation that didn't jibe with my stashing my best playthings before his son could set foot in my room. "Little Mike ain't going to break your toys," Daddy said, but Mom hid the Millennium Falcon under Daddy's old Air Force uniform in the top of our hall closet. Mom's goodwill had run out after the fate of the toys I took with me to school: Darth Vader stolen; Chewbacca's legs snapped off in the sandbox. Now even my own bedroom wasn't a safe haven.

Richard showed up with a six-pack of Michelob and set to reminiscing while Daddy masked the windshield of a customer's car to prep it for painting. Mike and I shrugged at each other. "Why don't you boys go on in the house," Richard suggested, "so the grownups can talk." My room void of toys, Mike suggested we vandalize the little plastic desk where I did my homework. We took magic markers and wrote the bad words we knew: *fart* and *butthole* and *peter*. "Don't you know any worse words?" asked Mike, so I added the worst word I knew—*nigger*.

Mike shrugged; the word was familiar enough to have lost its impact. "Write *pussy*," he told me. "That's really bad." And it was, from my mom's reaction. She rounded the corner, aghast, just as I finished writing the Y. She sent Little Mike out to the body shop to tell his dad what he'd done. I imagined Daddy bent over his work and Richard laughing and clapping Little Mike on the back. "You can't let the rougher kids put you up to things," said Mom. "I'd like to wring Richard's neck for teaching him that. I didn't learn that word until I met your daddy."

"What is it?"

"It's *this*," she said, clutching herself. "On a woman." Her gaze shifted to a more troubling word. "Which one of you wrote this one?" she asked, pointing to *nigger*. "Little Mike," I lied.

"Good," she said, studying my handwriting and giving me a look. "Because I know I taught you better than that."

She taught me I knew better—which I took for a kinder way to say I *was* better—but in the process I learned new words: *hick* and *redneck*. I learned to feel embarrassed for looking too much like the people I thought I was meant to look down on. I didn't want to look poor. I didn't want to speak with a Southern accent. I didn't want to dip snuff or wear anything with a John Deere logo. I saw a kid at school making engine noises and pretending to shift gears and spin out as his class rounded the corner to the cafeteria. *Look at him*, I thought. *So simple.* "Some of these kids," said Mom, "just can't wait to quit school and go back home to the farm. You're going to study hard and get good grades and go to college and they just want to play with their tractors." She told me I was destined for something better, so I took it there was something wrong with the people who couldn't imagine living anywhere different.

Mom's lesson backfired when she arrived at my second-grade Field Day, her face still numb from the dentist; she was missing a front tooth, like Donnie Belcher's mom. My teacher had told me to stop playing with Donnie after he and I got into trouble for writing all the kids' names but ours on the floor with crayons: *This isn't like you, Mickey. Did Donnie put you up to this?* I'd come to see Donnie as a very different sort of person than I was. His hair stayed a little longer and unwashed, and he came to school wearing ball caps that advertised farm equipment. I could make no sense of his priorities or his ideas about what kinds of work were worth doing. While my friends and I got excited on Field Day to take a break from our books and run outside for a sack race, Donnie—the same age as the rest of us but hardened by farm life—shook his head in exasperation that the teachers were wasting precious daylight on such frivolities: "I ain't got the time to be running around with no egg on no spoon. I got a heifer to tend to."

Races won and lost, Field Day ribbons and Lil Debbie snack cakes distributed, our teachers released us to our parents. I watched Donnie's mom pull off his cap to smooth down his hair. She smiled the gap-toothed smile that said *I am the wife of a farmer. I don't have the time, the money, or the vanity to concern myself with cosmetic dentistry.* I looked back to the line of Rocket readers and their moms who'd taken the time to apply make-up before coming to Field Day. I didn't see a missing tooth in the bunch. Mom walked me back to the car. "Your teeth aren't *done*, are they?" I asked. "The dentist can't fill in that big hole in the front?"

"No, it's too expensive for us," she whispered, hiding her smile.

In the back seat, clutching my Field Day ribbons, I said, "It makes you look like a hick."

What kind of monster had she created? If I unsettled Mom by making fun of her, I horrified her by making fun of my classmates. I made fun of poor Kevin Sneed's country accent so relentlessly that my own voice started to sound like his. I called Roger Phelps's father—Virgil the janitor—"Virgin," and fat Roger pinned me down and made me kiss the gym floor before he'd let me up. Roger was a bully, I told myself. He'd overreacted to a nonsensical insult, sat his fat ass on me over nothing. Virgil, after all, was a grown man with a son and clearly not a virgin like I was, like Roger and nearly all of us were. But to Roger, I'm sure it sounded like I was joining the chorus of voices he heard making fun of his father for being a janitor. This revelation, mind you, is one it took me *years* to arrive at. That afternoon I only thought, *Roger's a dickhead.* "I didn't really kiss it," I told him, hours later on the school bus. It was less of a taunt than my weak attempt to save face.

Roger shook his head, triumphant. He shifted a toothpick from one side of his mouth to the other. "You did too," he said, grinning. "I seen the slobber."

Growing up in Pulaski County, Kentucky, I had a Eubank address and a Science Hill phone number. I went to Eubank Elementary, but the county high school brought together the kids from the Eubank and Science Hill farmland with kids from the comparatively big town of Somerset, with its access to fishing and boating on Lake Cumberland. In the absence of racial diversity, we turned to ranking ourselves by social class. School never made me think about being white other than in terms of being ashamed to wear shorts that would expose my pale legs to the mockery of my tanned classmates. My skin stayed a paler white than the kids whose parents could afford beach vacations or swimming pools. Rich whites in the past used to keep their skin white as possible so they could set themselves apart from the poor people who turned darker toiling outside in the sun; now rich white people turn themselves orange to show that they had enough money to go to tanning salons. My tan didn't count, because I was two different shades. I had what was called a *farmer tan*, the term implying I did not come from the kind of white people who take off their shirts and relax on a beach—my kind only sunburned our faces and arms while we were *working.*

Rednecks were farmers who sunburned their necks in the fields while the wealthier people stayed inside. In my mind, the rednecks were classmates my age eroding their cheeks with chewing tobacco, caught with pot or Old Crow in their lockers, skipping school to strip tobacco on their family's farm. I didn't live on a farm, but there were farms on either side of our house, and my mother's side of the family had been farmers for generations. The anxiety of coming from small-town Kentucky—the anxiety that we *really might be* rednecks—drove my fascination with Jeff Foxworthy's *You Might Be a Redneck* routine:

Rednecks were poor and dirty: "You keep a can of Raid on the kitchen table."

Rednecks were violent and irrational: "You've ever shot anyone for looking at you."

Rednecks were unambitious: "Your father encourages you to quit school because Larry has an opening on the lube rack."

My farmboy classmates took what I considered an incomprehensible pride in the aspects of themselves Foxworthy pointed out, while I listened for clues for how to avoid looking like them. I worried I might be a redneck, so I cringed at my dad's practice of burning our garbage. Daddy refused to pay the town for trash collection so he dragged our trash outside and burned it behind the body shop, grumbling and cursing the whole time. He was convinced his wife and children were bankrupting him, so he'd dump out the garbage bags and dig through the jars and boxes and make sure they'd been emptied to his satisfaction. Once, he discovered a box of Captain Crunch with what he swore was a good half bowl left. He brought it inside to the kitchen table, picked out a cockroach, and poured himself a bowl. Seeing the terror and disgust on my face he shrugged and asked, "What if all we had to eat was spoiled milk and stale cereal?" He seemed to take such pride in eating it.

Mom started to burn the trash herself to avoid his surveillance of the things she had thrown away. The compromise suited them both, until one morning Daddy came running out of the bathroom, his hair wet from the shower, yelling, "What was in that trash you put out there? It looks like the whole damn back of the shop is on fire!" It was a hairspray can, the firefighters told us later. It exploded and ignited the back of the body shop. Daddy rushed outside to back customers' cars out of the shop before the flames reached them. Neighbors, seeing the smoke, drove to our house to see if they could help, but ended up only standing there with Daddy watching his body shop burn to the ground.

If I'd worried before about the impression we gave, I was downright mortified at the pile of scorched sheet metal and timber clearly seen from the road as cars drove past our house. Jo Ann Beard's novel *In Zanesville* opens with the narrator, a fourteen-year-old babysitter, saying, "We can't believe the house is on fire. It's so embarrassing first of all, and so dangerous second of all."[5] I knew just how she felt. I saw it as a basic requirement of being a competent and non-trashy human: you don't let the things you own burn. I didn't like that my family looked irresponsible. I didn't like that we looked pitiable. I didn't like that we looked like rednecks.

Daddy blamed Mom for being careless enough to toss that hairspray can into the fire. Mom blamed Daddy for being too stubborn to give up his dream of owning his own business and look for a better-paying job painting cars at one of the big Somerset, Kentucky car lots. Borrowing money to rebuild his body shop, Daddy looked at the state of the house we lived in and refused to fix or replace anything until Mom learned to take better care of the things she had; Mom looked at the house and said she refused to waste her time trying to make broken things work. It was a vicious cycle. The furnace went out so Mom opened the oven for heat and soon burned out the element. Now we had an oven *and* a furnace to fix. A leaking dishwasher ruined the kitchen floor. A leaking air conditioner caved in the hallway ceiling. When friends came over I told them we were remodeling. When Daddy disappeared for a week and our electricity got turned off, I told my friends he'd just forgotten to pay the bill.

I begged for a satellite dish so I could watch *Yo! MTV Raps*, and when Daddy swore he couldn't afford it, Mom drove me down Highway 27, past Oran's truck stop and its Wagon Wheel burger so big it was free if you could eat the whole thing, down the winding gravel road until it turned to dirt, past ramshackle houses with weedy front yards, down the hill to a trailer with makeshift wood steps. Daddy's unmistakable maroon Hudson Terraplane parked in the driveway next to what felt to me like his ultimate betrayal—a satellite dish the size of a swimming pool.

I understand now that Mom chose to hold her head high (or her nose in the air?) because she was embarrassed—as embarrassed to be seen paying for groceries with food stamps as she was by Daddy's running around town with his mistress. Daddy spent his nights in that trailer behind Oran's Truck Stop with a woman he preferred to his wife, so Mom had to feel like she was better than somebody, had to come up with ways she was better than Daddy (more educated, more refined, more religious). She traded food stamps for cash, under the table, at my uncle's convenience store, just to maintain the illusion we could pay for our groceries with hard-earned American dollars. "In the hierarchy of Southern poor," the novelist Tony Earley wrote about his childhood in North Carolina, "we were the good kind."[6] Was this the lesson my mother sought to teach me, or just the lesson I learned?

Six

RACIAL ESSENTIALISM

Having spent my childhood setting myself apart from my neighbors, I never believed the terms *hick, cracker,* or *redneck* applied to me. I laughed when Goodie Mob invoked the surname of *The Beverly Hillbillies'* patriarch to call Bill Clinton a Clampett. I cheered when Lil Wayne slammed George W. Bush *and* the "white cracker motherfucker that probably voted for him." I heard dead prez rhyme, "I went to school with some redneck crackers," and I thought *So did I.* My vision constrained by my own life experiences, it took me another listen to hear dead prez's assertion that public schools run by white people don't educate black kids so much as train minimum-wage workers to make money for white-owned businesses, or to hear Wise Intelligent ask, "Why do we try to believe/ that crackers ruling public schooling doesn't impede the seeds?"[1] I may have convinced myself I wasn't a Clampett, or a redneck, or a cracker, but I couldn't deny that I was a white teacher trained by a system that has failed black students.

There were a few ways to address teaching Hip-Hop and American Culture while white:

1. Apologize for it (smacks of *sorry not sorry* when you apologize but keep doing it anyway)

2. Try to blend in (be careful, as the effort may only make you stick out. One white author used his book's introduction to tell the story of how his parents took him to race rallies when he was a child. They sent him to school with black kids, he said, and he "was intensely attracted to some of the black girls."² Yeah? So were the white slave-masters.)

3. Be yourself and keep quiet and hope nobody brings it up (risks the elephant-in-the-room scenario, risks repeating the history of white folks snatching black sounds and styles without feeling the need to explain themselves)

4. Shrug and make a joke of yourself (if you're me, you might bring up Kentucky. You might play the J. Cole line "look around, my nigga, white people have snatched the sound,"³ then try to lighten the mood with a joke like, "They even got a white guy teaching it. A white guy from *Kentucky*. Wearing this sweater. And these glasses.")

There is power in self-deprecation, but making a joke about myself has its limitations. If *I'm* something to laugh at, what does that say for my ideas, or for my class on hip-hop and American culture? Where does the joke stop? Do I consider hip-hop a joke? Black art and culture a joke? The humor traffics in the same old racial essentialism: I'm *so white* I dress like a professor instead of a rapper.

"Almost every trope of blackness: single-parent household, born poor, working-class, saxophone-playing, McDonald's-and-junk-food-loving boy."⁴ These were the qualities that led novelist Toni Morrison to call Bill Clinton "our first black President. Blacker than any actual black person who could ever be elected in our children's lifetime."⁵ Ta-Nehisi Coates has emphasized that Morrison didn't intend to compliment

Clinton for being "sufficiently soulful" to count as black so much as to welcome him to the powerlessness that even wealthy and prominent black Americans so often experience when they interact with the police and the courts.[6] Morrison did write that Clinton endured a sex scandal that saw him "metaphorically seized and body-searched"[7] and "treated like a black on the street, already guilty, already a perp."[8] "The message was clear," Morrison wrote of Clinton's impeachment—and it was a message all too familiar to black Americans: "No matter how smart you are, how hard you work, how much coin you earn for us, we will put you in your place or put you out of the place you have somehow, albeit with our permission, achieved. You will be fired from your job, sent away in disgrace, and—who knows?—maybe sentenced and jailed to boot. In short, unless you do as we say (i.e. assimilate at once), your expletives belong to us."[9]

Coates explained that Morrison was speaking about the *treatment* of black Americans (this is what America *does* to black people) rather than speaking about attributes inherent in black Americans (this is how black people *are*), but I still see some essentialist thinking in her description of "almost every trope of blackness: single-parent household, born poor, working-class, saxophone-playing, McDonald's-and-junk-food-loving boy from Arkansas"[10] and the way it equates black identity with poverty, junk food, and single moms. Such essentialist thinking awarded Bill Clinton an honorary blackness (even if Morrison was, as Coates put it, "welcoming him into a club which should not exist"[11]), while Barack Obama's critics claimed he was not black enough. Ben Carson argued that Obama was "raised white";[12] Cornell West claimed Obama grew up "in a white context."[13] Obama, however, believed himself to be black enough that he said, "If I had a son, he'd look like Trayvon,"[14] which is to say he'd look like what a racist vigilante wanted to see as a threat.

Obama had a black father and a white mother, and was raised by white grandparents, but that did not make him something less than black. No wonder Earl Sweatshirt—born during President Clinton's first term—says he grew up "too black for the white kids, too white for the black."[15]

White people have long joked about black people being cooler than whites; at its worst, it's a way to indulge in racial essentialism while seeking to sound like we only mean to envy black cool. At its best, my joke about my sweater and glasses is a joke at my own expense, but the danger, of course, is that the joke traffics in the same essentialism that has blamed the violent deaths of black kids on their attire. The same pundits who'd spent the Nineties scoffing at the street gangs that shot each other over their clothing's colors now defended a neighborhood-watch vigilante for shooting a black teen who'd stepped onto his turf wearing a garment he considered a threat. George Zimmerman shot seventeen-year-old Trayvon Martin to death, and Fox News hosts blamed his black hooded sweatshirt: Geraldo Rivera said, "I think the hoodie is as much responsible for Trayvon Martin's death as George Zimmerman was";[16] Bill O'Reilly said, "Trayvon Martin died because he looked a certain way and it wasn't based on skin color . . . he was wearing a hoodie and he looked a certain way. And that way is how 'gangstas' look."[17]

Even a rapper joined the chorus against clothing. Wu-Tang Clan's RZA—who's made millions selling Wu-Wear hoodies and songs full of gunshots—said, "When you think about some of the brothers who are being brutalized by the police, you also got to have them take a look, and us take a look, in the mirror, at the image we portray. I tell my sons, you don't have to wear a hoodie. Button up your shirt. Clean up. It's the image that we portray that could invoke a fear into a white officer, or any officer."[18] The Internet responded with a meme of a suited black man hanged from a tree in a lynching; the caption read "#TellRZA I Was

Wearing a Suit." Martin Luther King Jr, Malcolm X, and Medgar Evers all wore suits, yet still all got shot to death. Eric Garner was wearing a white T-shirt and khaki shorts when police placed him in the chokehold that killed him. Alton Sterling was wearing a red polo shirt and khaki shorts when police shot him. "Is it logical," asked retired police detective Richard Greelis, defending the killings of Sterling and Philando Castile, "that a city police officer treat a young man dressed and acting out like a gangster exactly the same as he would treat a young white man dressed like a 'prepster?'" Logic tells you that the police would use more caution with the gangsterish black man based on experience."[19] But neither of the men who'd just been killed by police had dressed *or* acted the way Greelis described. I can't judge RZA's advice to his son—I'd tell my son the same thing if I were him. But of course we can't truly trust that black men dressing more professionally would hinder racial profiling and halt police shootings. RZA and Greelis are blaming the victim the same way the rape apologists say a woman in a short dress was asking for it. Button your shirt, they say, or the cops might mistake you for the bad kind of black.

•

Hip-hop tells us being black doesn't mean only one thing, except when it does: Open Mike Eagle, with his glasses and cardigan, raps on *Dark Comedy*, with its double-entendre title, "Fuck you if you're a white man that assumes I speak for black folks. Fuck you if you're a white man that thinks I can't speak for black folks."[20] Mello Music Group's website introduces *Dark Comedy* with an Oscar Wilde quote: "If you want to tell people the truth, make them laugh. Otherwise, they'll kill you."[21] There's some truth in Mike's joke, which riffs on the stereotype of the angry black man yelling "fuck you" at the white man no matter which attitude he takes toward black art. But if the white listener can't win in this situation, think about the black rapper—one man, an individual—who gets told he makes black people look bad.

Hip-hop has so come to represent black America that the two have been rendered synonymous in the minds of people who don't care to look for much depth in either. In my book *Is Hip-Hop Dead*, I wrote about an incident in Tempe, Arizona in 2006, when Sergeant Chuck Schoville pulled over two young black men for littering and offered to let them off if they'd rap for him: "No littering ticket," he said, "if you two just do a little rap about—what do you want to rap about today, littering?"[22] They rapped for him and he let them go without a ticket, but with these parting words: "You know I'm right."[23]

"You know why you say I'm right," Officer Schoville asked the two men who'd shrugged and met his request to rap about littering, "Because I have a gun and badge. I'm always right. Okay?"[24] *I'm always right*, said a man who was so clearly wrong.

After viewing the video of Sergeant Schoville interacting with the litterers, Reverend Jarrett Maupin of the National Action Network remarked, "It's important for police officers to realize that black people do not speak hip-hop. We're not all rappers and thugs and gangbangers."[25] Dr. Charis Kubrin—professor of criminology, law, and society at UC Irvine—has dedicated her work to fighting such stereotypes as they manifest in the courtroom, where rappers often see their lyrics presented not as artistic expression, but incriminating evidence of a violent lifestyle; Kubrin wants to change this perception of rappers as criminals who chronicle their felonies on songs. As for the impression Kubrin herself makes, Kelly Puente of the *OC Register* writes, "Even Kubrin concedes she doesn't look like a typical fan. As a white scholar in her forties, she garners snickers in the courtroom when she's introduced as an expert witness in rap music. 'The defendants have even laughed at me,' she says, with a chuckle."[26] Forty-five seconds into her 2014 TED Talk, Kubrin identified herself as a rap music scholar, then paused to feign disbelief, to act out her audience's shock at the mismatch between the scholar on stage and her subject. She motioned to herself, to her silk blouse, and asked, "This doesn't look like a rap music scholar?"[27]

It reminded me of my own dumb joke about my sweater and glasses, reminded me that Masta Ace wore his glasses during his roundtable discussion with Rider students, then removed them — like Clark Kent switching to Superman—for his concert that followed the talk. Looking for the "typical" rap fan, or rap music scholar, or rapper leads us down a dangerous path. We shake our heads at Sergeant Schoville's clumsy and racist assumptions that young black men are ready and willing to rap. We can't turn around and chuckle along with Kubrin and me.

It's important to realize that black people do not speak hip-hop, said Reverend Maupin, *nor are black people all rappers.* Rappers and rap critics, though, often slip into a similar essentialism. They don't want hip-hop to lose its basis in black culture like other forms of music did, so in defending hip-hop as black people's property, they sometimes present black people as intrinsically closer to hip-hop. I assign my students Bakari Kitwana's chapter, "Erasing Blackness," which points to the "growing trend among mass audiences to expunge Blackness from hip-hop,"[28] both in the university classroom and in the record store. Kitwana writes that he fears "the emergence of white critics (far removed from the culture) farther out ahead in the field than Black critics (closer to the culture)."[29] The concern is valid, but it's the parentheses that give me pause. They seem to assume that black skin equals proximity to hip-hop, which seems uncomfortably close to the assumption that Sergeant Schoville made.

Being black doesn't mean only one thing, said hip-hop, *except when it does.* "Black people do not like ice skating or winter," Prince Paul told *MTV News,* in explaining the name of his comedy rap group, Negroes on Ice, a collaboration with his son Paul Jr. "So the title is pretty ironic. We kinda both came up with the name Negroes on Ice and just laughed and laughed about it . . . Like, people see the name and they're interested but then it's like, 'Wait, should I be seeing something like this?'"[30] *MTV News* even put the group's name in quotation marks—"Prince Paul and Son are 'Negroes on Ice.'" That's not a punctuation error; it's scare quotes to distance MTV from Paul's use of the term Negroes.

I wanted to bring Paul and Paul Jr. to campus together for a conversation on hip-hop across the generations, but the younger Paul was away getting his own college education at Clark Atlanta University. So his dad came alone and brought me a Negroes on Ice T-shirt—asked ahead for my size and everything. "Am I gonna be able to wear that," I asked him.

"Yep," he said. "I got mediums."

My concern was not the shirt size but the fit of a white man wearing a garment that said Negroes on Ice, so I was relieved to see the shirt didn't sport the group's name. Smart marketing, I told Paul—and he grinned—but leaving off the name may have been more of a grand joke on his white fans, as everyone who saw me wear the shirt asked questions. The group's logo—a clip-art figure-skater sporting an Afro and "N" medallion—prompted supermarket cashiers to ask, "What's on your shirt?"

"It's a band."

"What's the name of the band?"

To say the band's name to a white cashier seemed all kinds of wrong. To say the name to black cashier is what Lord Jamar might call pushing it too far. So I hung the shirt back in my closet.

In the era of Black Lives Matter, Paul joined J-Zone and Sacha Jenkins to form a new group called SuperBlack, which spoofed black militants and released a T-shirt that read, "I'm not racist. Some of my best friends are Super Black." The shirt seemed to—hilariously—dare white listeners to wear it, and to revel in our discomfort in sporting a statement typically made by white people defending having said something racist. The group's name reminded me of the note Fran Ross provided her reader in her 1974 comic novel *Oreo*. Placed beneath her chart labeled Colors of Black People, the note read: "There is no 'very black.' Only white people use this term. To blacks, 'black' is black enough (and in most cases too black, since the majority of black people are not nearly so black as your black pocketbook). If a black person says, 'John is very black,' he is referring to John's politics, not his skin color."[31] Thus, in a new era of black protest, hip-hop presents SuperBlack—three middle-aged rap veterans poking fun at the college-age activists.

I didn't buy that SuperBlack T-shirt, or the one with the hooded Klansman pointing his finger, Uncle-Sam style, to say, "SuperblacKKK wants you!" I congratulated myself for drawing this line, for teaching and writing about Prince Paul's music rather than wearing his T-shirts. Context was key, I told myself. A T-shirt doesn't come with a backstory —I can't exactly stop strangers and say, *No, it's okay. Prince Paul himself gave me this Negroes on Ice shirt when he came to my class as a guest speaker.* But in class I can begin the semester by addressing my race and my distance from the culture that created hip-hop. In fact, the more years I've spent teaching Hip-Hop and American Culture, the more time I find myself spending on the question of what the hell *I'm* doing teaching it.

There was a moment, early on, when I told myself my work could stand on its own and any attention to my own identity only distracted from the topic I was writing about. It didn't take me long to realize that a white hip-hop scholar *has* to address the role of white critics in relation to black art, but I did find some logic to my initial reluctance—I was a white person, writing about white people writing about hip-hop. I studied the self-rationalizations other white scholars gave for their involvement hip-hop. I studied disclaimers like Adam Krims' "Any claim I could make to hip-hop authenticity would be preposterous. So I do not make it. My connection to rap music and hip-hop culture is that of an ardent fan, someone whose musical life has been saturated by rap music since (roughly) 1990, who is at times a rap performer (as instrumentalist and producer), who is both a producer and a consumer, but who is by no means close either to hip-hop's original cultural existence or to rap's current source of authenticity."[32]

Krims earned a PhD in musicology and wrote a book that studied hip-hop's musical structures, yet he opened by acknowledging that he hadn't lived a life closer the ones celebrated by rap musicians. Knowledge doesn't come from familiarity alone, but professors have tended to approach other cultures with a sense of intellectual superiority, as if the knowledge *they* value isn't as good as the knowledge *we* value—as if the strength of street knowledge is no match for book-learning. This is why Krims leads by humbling himself: *I'm a musicologist,* he says, *an outsider; I may be looking at hip-hop entirely wrong.* But, as the first scholar to design a music notation system to map hip-hop's complex sonic layers of beats, samples, and rhymes, he was looking at it with a valuably fresh pair of eyes.

These disclaimers were everywhere. Crispin Sartwell—the same professor who listed his lust for black classmates on his rap-cred résumé—wrote, in the introduction to his book about black autobiography, "Any book about African-American writing by a white man is, obviously, problematic. I cannot hope to escape the possibility that some of what follows—or even all of it—is racist . . . what follows is written in the *anxiety* that it could be interpreted to express racist attitudes."[33] I'm a white man writing about black authors, he says, so I'm afraid my book will be racist. There's some logic to that anxiety: as a white man in America, I benefit every day from the legacy of racism and the way it's been so built into our social institutions and into our consciousness—racist thoughts inevitably enter my mind. But stating that inevitability in his intro is nothing more than an attempt to buffer his book with the caveat that he was *already worried* he might be racist. If you find something racist, well, he was already worried about it, so he's given himself an out. It's a professor's version of the age-old conversational trigger-warning, *I know this is going to sound racist, but . . .*

•

I found that white people involved in hip-hop remained convinced they were doing it better than the other white people involved. A white Harvard student, Dave Mays, founded hip-hop's pre-eminent magazine, *The Source*, yet campaigned against putting white rapper Eminem on the cover. "Oh, did he look upon other white folk with deep suspicion,"[34] wrote Selwyn Seyfu Hinds, a black writer and editor at the *Source*. Hinds wrote that Mays was quick to scorn "'these white boys running around like they hip-hop,' a comment that could encompass anyone, from writers, to fans, to music industry executives."[35] Hinds wrote that Mays displayed an unbelievable degree of "authority and presumption," as a white Harvard grad going so far as to suggest that the young, black writers Hinds hired were too "bourgie."[36]

When Hinds commented on such presumptuousness coming from some of the white people involved in hip-hop, his *Source* colleague Jon Caramanica responded, "It's like a sliding scale. As a white boy in hip-hop, you gotta have someone on the scale below you. First, it's all the corny white kids, then the ones new to hip-hop. The ones trying really hard. Clearly you're cooler than that. But then you start measuring yourself up to the black kids, thinking surely you're cooler, more hip-hop than the ones who don't seem to wear hip-hop on their sleeve, the ones who you perceive as corny. Then you start thinking you're more hip-hop than they are."[37] But the sliding-scale is not an apt metaphor— Caramanica and Dave Mays aren't advocating for write people to pay what they can afford. Instead, they seemed to imagine a sort of *Kinsey* scale for blackness. Based on how well they can be—or *appear* to be— hip-hop vs. how much they're willing to listen.

I found an uncomfortable niche writing about white people and their relationships to hip-hop. I published an article in *Critical Studies in Media Communication*—where professors write for professors— about the strategies white rappers use to convince us we should allow them to rap. There was immersion: the Beastie Boys had rap's first platinum-selling record, but they were sponsored by Russell Simmons and Run DMC. There was imitation: Vanilla Ice's fake bio. Then there was inversion: Eminem claimed that being white in the wake of Vanilla Ice's downfall made it even harder for a white rapper to make it than it was for a black rapper. Immersion, imitation, and inversion: the three I's. "Man," said Traum, half-joking, nodding his head at the breadth of my knowledge of this one small corner of hip-hop. "You should teach a class on white rappers." But I responded, "It's not a good look for me." I didn't want to become the white guy who studies white rappers, but I saw it happening. A&E invited me to share my expertise on camera for their Vanilla Ice *Biography* episode. The manager of an up-and-coming white rapper emailed to ask if I'd like to schedule an interview. I had to stop and reconsider if a white professor should devote two chapters of a seven-chapter book—or one week of a twelve-week semester—to white rappers. I'd always believed it would be irresponsible for me not to address the role of my race in my subject matter, but now I risked pegging myself as Mickey Hess, white-rapper expert, which seemed far too insular and self-obsessed. I needed to reassess my approach.

Seven

PROFESSORS AND RAPPERS

Having fallen too far down the white-rapper rabbit hole, I declared I would write *with* rappers instead of just writing about them. I got Masta Ace and Jeru the Damaja some money to write a foreword and afterword to my edited collection of professors writing about rappers. (Ace and Jeru met every deadline; I had to chase down and threaten the ethnomusicologists.) I visited the Beatminerz—Mr. Walt and his younger brother Evil Dee—at their childhood home, where they still live in Bushwick, Brooklyn, and got the scoop on their neighborhood's hip-hop history, from the old school—"We had a guy who used to say the same line at every block party, how some Puerto Rican guys beat him up with a baseball bat"[1]—to the impending gentrification—"I sit on my step and there's cats skateboarding by," Evil Dee told me. "Now it's more diverse here. The neighborhoods are getting better, so I'm not mad at that, but back in the day it wasn't like that."[2]

"It's different now," added Mr. Walt. "A lot of whites are buying property out here. Used to be, back in the days, the white people would only go to Park Slope and Greenpoint. Everything else was predominantly black. Now I look at Bed-Stuy and white people are walking around and they're talking to everybody and everybody's cool. The money is coming in."[3] The Beatminerz spoke with me as the New Jersey

Nets were moving to a new home stadium on Brooklyn's Flatbush Avenue. They sounded excited for Brooklyn, even as they worried it might no longer be the Brooklyn they knew and loved. This was the attitude I'd seen rappers take toward hip-hop itself; they were happy to see hip-hop become a worldwide cultural force—and happy to see rappers get rich—yet they remained convinced that the very possibility of making a living from rap music was what ruined rap.

I can't argue I was much different from a hipster on a skateboard, visiting Brooklyn to interview rappers for a book written for professors by professors. It was important to me to get the voices of rappers into a book about rap music, but at the same time, I can't deny that doing so benefitted me by making my book look so credible that even rappers would contribute. I'm reminded of the boardroom scene from Spike Lee's *Bamboozled*, as the white television exec Mr. Dunwitty and his "media consultant" Myrna Goldfarb, with her PhD in African-American studies from Yale. ("Continue, oh great niggerologist," quips Damon Wayans' character Pierre Delacroix.) Embarking on production of *Mantan's New Millennium Minstrel Show*, Dunwitty and Goldfarb strategize to staff the show with African-Americans: "I need a black grip, a black gaffer, a black PA . . ." In their thinking, the more black people the show employs, the better it will weather accusations of racism. The more rappers' names you can put on a professor's book, the more credible that book becomes.

As fraught as reaching out to rappers could be, I felt it still had to be better than the alternative of writing in isolation. I started to wonder if rappers were even aware of the attention professors were giving them. Back home in New Jersey, I read "Black Female Identity and Challenges to Masculine Discourse in Rah Digga's *Dirty Harriet*" in the academic journal *Popular Music and Society*. "Congrats!" I tweeted to Rah Digga, who tweeted me back with a question mark. She had no idea the article existed. I had to use my database access on campus to download and send her a copy. "I know I've been mentioned in things but not of that magnitude . . ." she responded. "I thought you were making a joke." Professors were writing about rappers and not even informing the rappers. The whole endeavor felt as clinical as shoving a beatboxer into an MRI machine.

"Don't push it too far," said Lord Jamar. There was the problem of academics being presumptuous about how we fit into rap's world, and then there was getting too comfortable with writing our rap books in isolation. I was guilty myself. I was once scheduled to appear on a Baltimore Book Festival panel with KRS-ONE, a prospect I found more frightening than thrilling. He was a hip-hop purist, while my book argued for the value of a lot of the rap he wrote off. He wouldn't even like the way I use the terms rap and hip-hop interchangeably. Rap is something you do, he's said, while hip-hop is something you live, meaning hip-hop is a culture and rap is a commercial product: "When 'Rapper's Delight' sold two million records in 1979," he told an interviewer, "all the attention was placed on rap music as a selling tool, not on hip-hop as a consciousness-raising tool, as a maturing of the community. When hip-hop culture got discarded for the money to be made into rap product, we went wrong right there."[4] He's right about the commerce vs. culture at the heart of the debate, but if we're talking about terminology, I'd note that "Rapper's Delight" begins with the term "hip-hop," and rappers—for the most part—have been using the terms interchangeably in rhymes ever since, so I do too.

KRS-ONE wouldn't like my disputing his terminology. The author of a few books himself, he said only hip-hop's practitioners were qualified to write about it: "How you gonna critique somethin' you ain't even doin'?"[5] It sounds like pure hip-hop ego, but remember the poet Ezra Pound's advice to writers, which I myself have clung to in the face of a bad review: "Pay no attention to the criticism of men who have never themselves written a notable work."[6] For me to sit on a panel and argue with KRS-ONE would be to push it too far, and I knew he'd out-debate me into the dirt. This was a man who'd once pushed pop-rappers PM Dawn off stage so that he could play some real hip-hop. At a Stanford University Hip-Hop Conference, he called activist and journalist Adisa Banjoko "a fraud," "an enemy to our culture," and "an FBI agent in disguise."[7]

"What I wanna do," said KRS-One—the rapper who'd founded the Stop the Violence movement—"is jump across the table and beat your fuckin' ass."[8] If he'd say that to Banjoko, a black rapper-turned-journalist, I hated to imagine what he might say to me. It cannot be good for a hip-hop scholar's career to have his ass beat by KRS-ONE. When he canceled at the last minute, I breathed a silent sigh of relief.

•

I thought a lot about the first impression I made. Traum Diggs introduced me to his roommate, the computer scientist/poet Nnamdi Osuagwu, by telling him 1) I grew up in Kentucky, and 2) I really know my hip-hop. Nnamdi studied me for a moment. "So you've read about hip-hop in books," he said. "I was *there*." He and Traum were there, as teenagers in Brooklyn, for the emergence of some of the best hip-hop to come out of New York. I had read books about it. But I'd also *written* books, I wanted to add. I felt the impulse to defend myself, but I let it go. I was talking to a man who witnessed, from his front stoop, the golden era of hip-hop during the same years he saw personified Chicken McNuggets rap in a McDonald's commercial. He was right—I'd never gain that perspective, no matter how many books I read *or* wrote.

Plenty of critics are outsiders who don't come from the culture they write about. My department's Shakespeare specialist is a Korean professor who grew up a lot further from Shakespeare than I did from Big Daddy Kane. But Shakespeare comes from the culture that did all the looting, and the claw marks from the hip-hop culture vultures are still fresh. So many outsiders made money from caricaturing rap, so it's hard to convince a stranger that I'm the exception. I don't know if Nnamdi read my books or not, but something convinced him to invite me to join him on stage for his book release in South Philly, where he read poetry and I read a short piece about the old-school rap duo Nice & Smooth.

Nnamdi and Traum came to my readings too. Of all the guest speakers I've brought to campus, Traum is the one with whom I became closest. We first met on the campus of SUNY Rockland, where we were both panelists on a hip-hop forum hosted by our mutual friend, Dr. Shamika Mitchell. Traum was a music journalist. I was a professor. The other panelists were a campus radio DJ and a record-label employee. We discussed rap for an hour on stage, but Traum never mentioned he was a rapper. He never mentioned he'd opened shows for Talib Kweli and Pharoahe Monch, even when those names came up in the discussion. It wasn't until after the talk ended and the audience left that he'd slipped me the flier for his mixtape release show at Club Fluid in Philly. I showed up and stood next to Nnamdi in the front row.

Traum grew up in Brooklyn as a whiz kid; he was taking high school classes by the time he was twelve years old, and left Brooklyn when he was sixteen to major in journalism at Temple University in Philly.

His older brother earned his PhD in education down in Alabama, but Traum chose rap over grad school. He had interviewed countless rappers for magazines and published a chapter in a book for writing teachers, but hip-hop remained his passion. His mixtape was only a precursor to the album—his first official album—*Major Journalism*. He was working on it relentlessly.

Hip-hop had taught Traum, same as me, that if you just kept rapping you'd someday succeed. I didn't rap, but I remember fixating on the Q-Tip line, "The aim is to succeed and achieve at twenty-one"[8] and finding motivation to succeed at writing by that age. When I was twenty years old I wrote a book and people smiled the way they'd smile at a child's drawing; those who didn't dismiss it so easily seemed to fear for my future the way you might fear for a grown man who still played make-believe. Despite the discouragement, I kept writing. I wrote and wrote so that I could one day get a job that included writing. I kept going to school until I earned enough grad-school credits that I could teach writing part-time at colleges and use that income to put myself through a PhD program. I commuted between community college campuses, teaching more classes as a part-timer than the full-time professors taught. I wrote a memoir, *Big Wheel at the Cracker Factory*, about my teaching jobs and the colleges' grand scheme of staffing courses with low-paid part-time instructors, even as tuition skyrocketed. I made money from that system even as I criticized it. I paid for grad school with the money I made teaching, knowing the whole time that landing a full-time, tenure-track job was a crap shoot because all the jobs had been farmed out to adjuncts. During the week, I took classes until ten at night and started teaching at 8 the next morning. On weekends I drove hours to Chicago or Cleveland bookstores to read out loud from my books, hoping enough people bought one that I could cover the gas money home. Traum chose making art over going to grad school; I was convinced I could do both.

Finding a job as a professor meant being willing to move anywhere in the country. I applied for thirty jobs, from Maine to Southern California, and got called for ten interviews. I interviewed for a position at a college in Rochester, New York, where an older professor—a white woman, a Princeton alumna—told me she and her husband have a name they call rap music when they hear it coming from a passing car. "We call it Fucka-Fucka-Mothafucka," she said, in a voice that might fit a cartoon gorilla. Then she challenged me to tell her how hip-hop was any different from Nazi Germany—she'd looked up the lyrics to a 50 Cent song, she said, and found his treatment of women appalling. (I wonder what she'd say to a student who condemned all poetry after reading only the SparkNotes to *Leaves of Grass*.) This was the same campus where another faculty member, walking me down the hallway to speak to a class, told me, "We don't usually have this many African-American students." It was a statement of fact, delivered matter-of-factly, but did he mean to say *Too bad* we don't usually have this many African-American students, or *Don't worry*, we don't usually have this many African-American students? I was invited to dinner at a department member's house, but I told her I'd rather just go back to the hotel. I didn't get the job.

When professors with PhDs make such ignorant comments, I know we're not educating people the way we should. The poet Claudia Rankine describes a conversation in which one of her colleagues tells her "his dean is making him hire a person of color when there are so many great writers out there."[9] The comment implies, of course, that the greater writers might not get jobs because the jobs have to go to black writers like Rankine. The conversation ends with the colleague trying to back away from his comments and Rankine left wondering, "Why do you feel comfortable saying this to me?"[10] Rankine got a job she didn't deserve, her colleague implied. The long-overdue push to hire more black professors has made being black an advantage, but this conversation shows how that advantage is almost instinctively turned into a disadvantage. *You didn't earn this job,* Rankine's colleague suggested. *You were lucky to get it.* Lucky like the white men who got every professor position for the first two hundred years universities existed in America. Lucky like the 78% of professors who were white in 2013.

I was lucky to get a job. Every professor is. Universities have replaced their professors with so many part-time instructors hired on a course-by-course basis that the part-timers now taught 70% of the college courses nationwide.[11] A professor retires and the administration replaces her with a rotation of part-timers at a fraction of her salary and benefits. Capitalist efficiency: state governments cut funding to universities, so universities spike the tuition *and* cut their teaching costs. Tenure-track professor positions become rarer and rarer. More than 300 people applied for the position I got at Rider. It is entirely possible that the hiring committees saw the hip-hop publications on my CV and assumed I was black. In an era ostensibly dedicated to diversity hires, I could be inadvertently passing for black by virtue of my subject matter. The academic journals to which I submitted my articles for blind peer review might have read "hip-hop" in the title and assumed I was a black professor. I would like to think my work stood on its own and that the peer-review process worked as it was intended to work, but if it's true that we must read a white scholar writing about black culture differently than we'd read a black scholar writing about black culture, the reviewers were denied a key piece of information in not knowing that I am white.

Blind review, in this case, would be *too* blind to see a white author's cultural blinders that skewed his vision of hip-hop.

Blind review is designed to prevent judgments based on the identity of the author rather than the quality of their work. When a journal sends me an article to review, I don't see the author's name, so I can't make subconscious assumptions about their gender or racial identity. Creative writing professors are anomalies among university faculty in that the university-run literary journals that publish short stories, essays, and poems somehow skirt the accountability of blind review. This design proved problematic in 2015, when white poet Michael Derrick Hudson submitted a poem under the name Yi-Fen Chou. It was more than a *nom de plume*; Hudson had published several poems under his own name, but admitted in his biographical note in *Best American Poetry 2015* that the poem in question had been rejected forty times under his real name before he got it published as Yi-Fen Chou. "As a strategy for 'placing' poems," he wrote, "this has been quite successful for me."[12] The push to publish more writers of color led a white poet to simply pretend he was Chinese. Hudson's "strategy" sounded a lot like the aggrieved white nationalists crying that minorities sought to erase their culture or even replace them in society. Such resentment came from an obnoxious sense of entitlement that had Hudson telling himself his poems were good enough to get published, if it weren't for the Affirmative Action office giving away his space on the page to any Chinese-American poet who came in off the street. By publishing Yi-Fen Chou, the journal *Prairie Schooner* confirmed his suspicions. By anthologizing the poem despite Hudson's revelation of his deceit, *Best American Poetry* set them in stone.

White men, who had written most of the American literature that had been published and celebrated and taught in classrooms, worried that readers were getting tired of hearing their stories. Many of them, like Hudson, saw the push for diversity and inclusion as a sort of exoticism that made a book or a journal more appealing by virtue of including non-white, non-male, non-cis, or non-straight authors. Things got more complicated when white men wrote from the perspectives of black characters, as Michael Chabon did in his 2012 novel *Telegraph Avenue*. When asked about cultural appropriation, Chabon responded:

> I understand it politically. I understand the historical context, completely. Artistically, I don't understand it at all. Because if I can't write from the point of view of a black woman nurse-midwife, then I can't write from anybody's point of view. That's why I do this. I use my imagination to imagine myself living lives I don't live and being people who I'm not.[13]

No one had suggested Chabon, a fiction writer, was not free to use his imagination; the problem was that his defense spoke more to his sense of entitlement to have all identities available for use in his novels and less to the right of the "black woman nurse-midwife" to speak for herself. White writers, after all, had been using their imaginations to depict black lives for centuries. They'd made the nurse-midwife a stock character called the Mammy way back when black women weren't allowed to learn to read or write, let alone publish a book. The question was not whether or not Chabon had America's permission to write from the perspective of a black character—he clearly did. Harper Perennial published his novel. The *New York Times* lauded it. Barnes and Noble and Amazon sold it. The question was what was the *effect* of his having written it, and what were those companies doing to publish and promote black authors?

Studying the reviews of Chabon's *Telegraph Avenue*, Tanner Colby observed, "For all his skills as a novelist, Chabon's whiteness must be reckoned as a disability when it comes to writing about race, an asterisk next to his name. Either he's crazy for wanting to 'go there,' or, like a toddler learning how to walk, he is to be applauded just for getting in a few good steps before the inevitable stumble."[14] So the critics on one hand said *God bless Chabon for trying and failing* and on the other said *How* brave *of this white man to speak about race.* Colby challenges such notions of cultural ownership: "'White person tackles race,'" he writes, "shouldn't have to be such a big deal."[15] The line reminds me of the white, grandfatherly stand-up comic Joe Pera—red cheeks, glasses, stammer—who joked that at a wedding reception he stood up and clinked his wine glass and announced, "And now I will tackle race." *Tackling* seems like too violent a metaphor. Again, our language leaves the white commentator either commendably brave or lamentably stupid: the issue of race is running full steam and we catch it and drag it to its knees (whites conquer race). If we aren't tackling race, we're stepping foolishly into a field full of land mines (race conquers whites). I can't separate politics from aesthetics as easily as Chabon does. When black artists who aren't politically driven get criticized for doing nothing for the plight of their people, white writers can't simply step in and claim to be talking art, not politics.

The separation of art from commerce is compelling, but the idea that the artist can stake his claim on any and all materials that he can use to make art may not sit well with the rappers who've been sued over sampling. Prince Paul told my class that he's still getting sued twenty-five years after the release of De La Soul's platinum album *3 Feet High and Rising*. The legal fees and fines have eaten up most of the money the group made from the album, and their example has steered other producers away from the sampling that distinguished so much of the golden-era hip-hop. In sampling's heyday, De La Soul sampled everything from Johnny Cash to the Turtles to NYC mayor Fiorello LaGuardia. The album is so notoriously thick with samples that when record labels sue another artist they often add De La's name, just in case, and Paul has to pay a lawyer and go to court to prove that he *didn't* sample the music in question. So lawsuits and politics do affect art and constrain creativity. Hiring lawyers to clear samples got so expensive that the labels began to tell rappers they could sample only the music the label already owned. Sampling still happens in hip-hop, but we'll never see another major-label album that samples the way Paul did on *3 Feet High and Rising*. It would be far too expensive to make.

Hip-hop's sampling lived and breathed by taking culture new places that got too expensive to visit, yet hip-hop felt uneasy about being taken on a trip of its own. With the history of the minstrel show hanging over America's head, it's a very different thing for a rapper to sample a rock song than for the Pillsbury Doughboy to don gold chains and rap in a crescent roll commercial. "Just grab a wiener filled with cheese/wrap it up. It's sure to please." I risked crossing that line myself by writing short stories that sampled snippets of Nobel prize speeches and rap interviews and used them as dialogue between novelists and rappers: Left Eye from TLC attends a backyard barbecue at Hemingway's house the day before he commits suicide; William Faulkner speaks on the act of artistic creation at a high school assembly where De La Soul is accused of plagiarism. Shock-G and Isaac Bashevis Singer debate artistic careers and retirement as the New Year's Eve countdown approaches. I asked Traum to beatbox while I read that Shock-G and Singer story out loud at a book signing in Philly. I hadn't anticipated the flaw in the design: a short story is a lot longer than a rap song. I had Traum up there beatboxing for twenty minutes straight, yet he waved me off when I offered to pay him for helping me out on stage, even though when parking in front of the bookstore he'd grazed someone's car and had to leave a note on their windshield.

Our reading got a good response, and Traum said he had fun, but I still felt uneasy about it in retrospect. I'd invited him to close out the show by performing one of his own songs—"I might spit a few bars if it feels right," he'd said, but in the end he changed his mind. Had Traum—the humblest rapper I've ever met—selflessly chosen not to steal my spotlight, or did the mood in the room not feel right? Did the crowd seem more novelist than rapper? Despite Traum's reassurances, I was left with the nagging anxiety that he'd felt as out of place beatboxing at Brickbat Books as he would beatboxing in an MRI machine.

•

Traum was recording and touring like crazy, driving from Philly to Austin, Texas for the South by Southwest festival, and to Atlanta for A3C. He had a near-miss with Tommy Boy Records, the label that launched De La Soul. He took pride in having earned his underground stripes, even as he dreamed of getting signed by a label. I knew how he felt; having worked with academic and literary presses, I'd never seen my books on the shelves at Barnes and Noble. I developed the desire—common among professors—to be read by people besides other professors.

I didn't like the books on those shelves any more than Traum liked Top 40 hip-hop. When I saw a book about Ol' Dirty Bastard, one of my favorite rappers and the man to whom I'd dedicated my doctoral dissertation, I experienced what I can guess is a hint of what Nnamdi felt when he met me. That should have been my name on that book, I thought, staring at the author photo of a young white woman who'd never before written one piece about hip-hop. If I felt robbed because I wrote about rappers before she did, imagine how Nnamdi and Traum felt when they saw those rapping Chicken McNuggets.

I was as hard on those popular authors as anyone. In fact, it was complaining about them that led me to my next book deal. I told Traum I'd read Jaime Lowe's *Digging for Dirt: The Life and Death of ODB*. Lowe was fresh out of a Sarah Lawrence MFA, interviewing Dirty, fresh out of prison. She'd landed a book deal counting on interviews with him. They set up a meeting but he canceled. She spent weeks working to reschedule, then described Dirty as "impatient and sort of dumbfounded" by her questions (e.g., "You were in jail. What was that like?"). Dirty stopped taking her calls and when she tracked him down he said, "I did an interview with you already." Then Dirty died and Lowe was left to finish the book by interviewing those who surrounded him—Wu-Tang members, his widow, his mother.

Many of the people she interviewed voiced their displeasure with the finished product. Dirty's mother Cherry Jones called for her son's fans to boycott the book, "as none of the proceeds are going to [his] children *and this author's motives and intentions seems to be in the vein of disgracing my son's legacy.*"[16] Dirty's A&R Dante Ross joined in the criticism of Jaime Lowe: "She is uninformed. It reads like she discovered the culture of hip-hop last week and her connection to Dirty appears nonexistent . . . To put it bluntly, this book sucks."[17] To me as a fan, Lowe's greatest transgression was comparing an Ol' Dirty Bastard concert to a racist freak show: "There was something wrong in the air, like we might as well have been at the Bronx Zoo a hundred years ago marveling at the pygmies on display, in cages."[18] She was right that racism did exist in that room full of young Manhattanites watching a man just freed from a prison psych ward rap on stage, but Lowe was unable to counter those echoes of the minstrel show by painting a portrait that could recover Dirty's humanity.

Dirty deserved a better book, and I knew I could write one. I asked Traum to introduce me to Buddha Monk, Dirty's right-hand man. Buddha toured the world performing beside Dirty all the way from his first appearance on *Yo! MTV Raps* to the final concerts before his death. Much of the writing about Dirty—including Lowe's book—includes interviews with Buddha Monk, but no one had ever given him a platform to tell his whole story. Traum had met Buddha when he helped film one of his music videos, so I asked him to put me in touch. "How do you think Buddha would feel about co-authoring a book about Dirty?"

"I'll vouch for you," Traum assured me. "He'll be able to tell you're coming from the right place."

Eight

"WHERE WE ARE IS WHO WE ARE"

I have lived in two of the most maligned places in this country. The difference is that Kentuckians know they are being made fun of, while people in New Jersey seem to have no clue. The proximity to Manhattan somehow leads them to feel more urbane and sophisticated than the rest of the country. Somehow they watch late-night TV talk shows and believe only the New Yorkers are laughing at them. My Haddonfield neighbors assume they're better educated and more cosmopolitan than Kentuckians, so they've convinced themselves racism is a Southern phenomenon. The citizens of New Jersey—a state so socially progressive as to foster the slums of Trenton, Newark, Paterson, and Camden—figured a Kentucky boy would have some shocking stories of Southern racism.

The racism I've heard expressed in conversations in New Jersey is more coded than crude. My Kentucky neighbor never shied away from using the word *nigger*, but my New Jersey neighbor found a way to say the same thing without saying that word itself. He warned me not to go to the Cherry Hill Mall too late on the weekend: "I like to get out of there before it gets too dark, if you know what I mean."

"I sure do," I told him. "My mom has night blindness."

He cocked his head, puzzled that I hadn't picked up on his racist pun.

Such comments confirmed my own prejudices about the people of Haddonfield, a wealthy white town just a few miles from the decaying black and Hispanic city of Camden. "Aren't they all Republicans," my friend had asked, and I couldn't get his accusation out of my head. My wife and I took our baby daughter for a stroll, and I saw signs of Republicans everywhere. Could be anyone, really: this old man reading the *Trenton Times* in the coffee shop; the young, suited woman in line at the bank; the ponytailed toy-store proprietor with the scrawled signs on the front door: *No food or drink; No unaccompanied minors.* Don't let the ponytail fool you. He's probably a reformed hippie stuck with the career choice of his idealistic younger self; his hairstyle hasn't caught up to his politics. With election season still months away, no one had party-affiliated signs on their lawns. All I had to go on was stereotypes.

A decade of higher education in urban Louisville flattened my accent, but the people of New Jersey can tell I come from the South. They can smell it on me like ragweed and biscuits. I've known some friends who became decidedly more Southern after they moved away from the South: accents thickened, love of grits cemented as being from the South became a parlor trick or a calling card. The novelty of Southernness that had escaped them in the South drew them to perform a version themselves for a Northern audience, the way an American tourist might charm Europeans with his cravings for ranch dressing or peanut butter. But in embracing in themselves an endearing specimen of the Southern, they soon might find themselves defending the aspects of the South that made them want to leave in the first place.

What will people picture when they picture Kentucky? Our cause célèbre, the woman who refused to marry two men? Or Wendell Berry, our poet-saint? I once saw Kentucky's native son Muhammad Ali—gray-haired and shaking with Parkinson's—shopping with his wife at

3:00 AM in a Louisville Wal-Mart; he posed for pictures, did a sleight-of-hand card trick, still sharp despite his advanced Parkinson's, still in there somewhere. I sat ten feet away as Louisville's mayor presented keys to the city to Hunter S. Thompson and Johnny Depp—both Kentucky born. I used to take pride in schooling my Los Angeles friend on the celebrities born in Kentucky—never mind that they left, never mind that they graduated high school and drove straight to the airport without so much as a backward glance.

America clings to its stories of transformation, but we can't see the potential in the people who have yet to transform. I was Southern until I wasn't. My dad was a Republican until he wasn't. Better to start out a Republican than become one: voting Democrat until you've made some money is like being a straight-edge teetotaler till you turn twenty-one—you weren't taking a moral stand, you were just too timid to talk grownups into buying you beer. We take up arms against excess until we can access it ourselves, and then once we gain it we cling to it. The more you have, the more you worry you'll need. Rich people want to protect what they have, and poor people want to protect their belief that they, too, can become rich. With identities so fluid they can take a man from rags to riches, how can I fret over living in a town of Republicans? My eighty-four-year-old neighbor told me she'd lived in Haddonfield for sixty years. She and her husband were one of the first Italian families to move to a town that is now plenty Italian. "Back then," she said, "*We* were the Mexicans."

Politicians push to send the Mexicans back to Mexico and build better fences to keep new ones from coming in. In the same campaign speeches, they gain ground from stories of their own immigrant grand-parents. They like their success stories finished, their books closed: young immigrant gets a job at a floor-mat factory, where he works himself to death so that his kids can one day express pride in factory work without ever having to resort to it. But when it comes to the plot trajectories of modern-day immigrants they can't see past the exposition.

•

Having wanted for so long to move away from Kentucky, I was surprised to find myself defending my home state to my neighbors in New Jersey. There's something healthy about hating the place you came from; nothing could be more American. Haddonfield teenagers probably scoff at the delusions of grandeur in the town-sponsored T-shirts that read "London, *Paris*, Rome . . . *Haddonfield!*"

My new neighbors were kind enough, certainly. Two different couples welcomed us with homemade banana bread. But the storefronts downtown gave me pause. "Rich people," I muttered. Jewelry store, antiques store, jewelry store, antiques store, a store that sells nothing but olive oil, then a place you can trade your excess money for handmade bars of soap. Your money or your life, say the muggers, but don't we make that decision every day when we get up to go to work? No matter the luxury items for sale downtown, Haddonfield's holy grail is the gratification of keeping one parent home. No greater luxury than time with your children. Yet the families with stay-at-home moms begrudge the two-earner families their larger houses: "We could have a bigger place, but we'd rather have my wife home with the kids." I moved to a wealthy town and they still resent rich people. There is always somebody richer. Poorer, too: a stay-at-home mom complained to me about welfare moms: "Most of them don't even want to work," she said.

All reasoning is rationalizing. We only find what we're looking for. My friend wants to affirm his decision to live in Philly, so he looks across the river at Haddonfield and sees boring and privileged Republicans. I want to affirm that I've made the best choice for my daughter, so I see pristine playgrounds. But I want the playgrounds without having to look like what he sees. I can afford a house in an expensive town, so when friends congratulate me on having bought a house in Haddonfield I qualify it by saying, "But it's a really *small* house."

What began as a rationalization became an obsession. I developed house envy. I bought a house I could not even truly afford, and it took me only a few months to start wishing I could buy a bigger one. This is how they get us. The mortgage brokers and real estate agents know what they're doing. "Buy a house in the best neighborhood you can afford," they say. "You don't want to have the best house on the block." This advice so that we will constantly look out our windows and want more than we already have.

•

In 1979—before anyone had made money from rapping—Sugarhill Gang rapped about owning a Lincoln Continental and a color TV. In 2000, Ghostface Killah rapped about wearing a bracelet the size of a trophy—a solid-gold eagle that stood six inches tall on his wrist. By 2017, Royce da 5'9 was rapping about his granite countertops, Pusha T was rapping about his remote-control blinds, and Techn9ne was posting pics of a new desk he'd bought. 2 Chainz rhymed, "Marble countertops, see-through fridge/$3000 for the microwave. Touchscreen stove, lil bitch!" If 2 Chainz really paid three thousand dollars for a microwave, it sounds like *he's* the bitch. But my point is that our ideas of success can change.

My wife and I bought a house to get access to a good school and we found out that across town there's an even better school. Our neighbors are hermit crabs. The family who sold us our house moved two blocks away to a bigger house, and a year later down the street to a slightly bigger one near a slightly higher-scoring school. We're convinced we've brought our kids to the best possible town, and we did so in the best possible way. We were lured by standardized test scores to a town so child-focused that we set off New Year's fireworks at 9:00 PM so no children miss bedtime. We want our kids to experience the kind of childhood we believe Americans had in the past, when kids could roam without fear and one parent's salary could feed a family.

The town is quaint, but the past wasn't better for everyone. A local maid service advertises "hardworking, honest, European women." A league of Liechtensteinian ladies arriving by boat, banding together to keep America clean? No! They mean *white* women. The same people who used to rely exclusively on black housekeepers now don't want them in their houses for pay.

I question if I am imagining things—if I have studied racism for so long that I see it where it doesn't exist. I see black writers voice a similar concern. In his 2016 essay, "How to Make a Slave," Jerald Walker depicts himself as a man who comes to question having "taught himself to see race in everything"[1] and had "lived in communities with drugs, gangs, crime, bad schools, police brutality, and the collective view that white people were and would always be racists."[2] Having made himself a slave to this view and hoping to save his sons from that same fate, he tells himself that the only way to become a good father is to: "give yourself a fighting chance by ending your subjection to race."[3] Camille Dungy's 2016 poem "Conspiracy (to breathe together)" opens with the narrator carrying her baby in a sling she worries white people might find "quaintly primitive":

I walk every day with my daughter and wonder
what is happening in other people's minds. Half the time
I am filled with terror. Half the time I am full of myself.[4]

These black narrators second-guessing their fears seems like the logical evolution of the concept of double-consciousness, developed by W.E.B. DuBois in the waning days of the nineteenth century to describe the psychological effects of being regarded as less than human. The self-perception of black Americans, he wrote, was tainted with the ever-present reminder of the way society looked at them. Hard to develop a strong self-image when you're still seventy years away from being allowed to eat in the same room as white people.

But that was 1897 and this is 2018. Now that white people get fired for spouting slurs at work, it's much easier for a writer like Walker or Dungy, above, to buy into the argument that she's just being paranoid, that a society that embraces racism now exists only in the past—or only in her head. Double-consciousness took such a hold that the paranoia lingers long after overt racist finally meets with a backlash, even if that backlash makes a black American worry that things are better now and he's the one who just can't let go of this feeling of being looked down on. "Being black," writes Carvell Wallace, "and thinking about race all the time, means that there's a moment where you start to worry that you're just making things up, imagining racial problems where none exist."[5] Black Americans like Walker and Dungy and Wallace worry that they've been so traumatized by racism that they're seeing things. Meanwhile, white Americans convince themselves that their thoughts and inclinations are not racist.

Racism is not make-believe: from the beginning of America's history, whites designed stereotypes of blacks to justify our country's treatment of them. We must accept and admit that such prejudices exist in our minds, rather than convince ourselves they belong to the South, or the past, or the trailer park, or the Republicans. We have to stop outsourcing racism by villainizing the versions that exist outside our immediate experience and rationalizing the ones that play out in our circle of friends. In a Louisville bar I once watched a man introduce an old friend to his coworker. They shook hands, but after the friend departed the coworker made a prejudiced comment. Shaking his head in disbelief that his coworker dared defame his friend based only on his physical appearance, the man exclaimed, "Well, sure he's a skinhead, but he's a real good guy!"

I hate him because he hates other people is ultimately an untenable position, but I will not grant that a racist skinhead can be a good guy. Not a lot I can do with a skinhead. Seems a losing proposition to give him a chance. Say I was able to set aside my better judgment and get to know the man underneath the symbolism of his hairstyle. We'd sit together on a bench and engage in a friendly talk about race in America and share pink cotton candy and what would people say—there goes Mickey Hess, so open-minded he's friends with the skinheads?

No, it's avoid him or argue with him, and no one's winning that argument. But avoiding a confrontation with the lost causes only gets you so far. Not all racism manifests so overtly—not all racists wear uniforms—yet I find myself secure in my prejudice against who's probably racist. When I hear a CEO make a hateful comment, it's hard not to blame businessmen and not the business*man*. Does a police uniform signify racism to me? Does gray hair and a walker? To steer clear of people who act or speak in a hateful manner is one thing, but it gets trickier if you start to avoid people who *look like* they might think that way. Judging racists on their appearance alone was a result—intended or unintended—of the political correctness that took hold of this country when I was in high school and college and taught us it was not to our benefit to make racist jokes in front of people we weren't certain would laugh. White people who took pride in their college educations decided what the racists looked like and talked like and made sure not to look or talk like them. If this more enlightened class of white people had something racist to say, they said it behind closed doors. Like gentlemen. But whites hiding their racist inclinations could be scarier to a black person than whites shouting slurs. "As a black person" writes Lincoln Blades, "there's nothing I appreciate more than white people being upfront and honest about their problematic beliefs."[6]

Political correctness hid problematic beliefs; it was rooted less in the desire to avoid hurting feelings and more in the fear of repercussions from black people. White people had come up with so many ways to fear black people; political correctness was only the latest one. During slavery whites feared a revolt. After emancipation they feared revenge. White men dreaded having to share, so they decided black men were bloodthirsty animals after their land and their women. Whites taught their children to fear blacks as a way to justify the brutality of chattel slavery and lynchings. Decades and decades later, when black Americans began to publicly reject whites' treatment of them, whites depicted them as marauding protestors after their schools and their water fountains. Once black Americans won the long fight for desegregation, whites said their true power came from the bigger things they could take away from whites: our elections, our cleaner and better-paying jobs, our hard-earned admission into elite universities. Now, finally, black Americans could cost whites our social status—they could take so much from us; all it took was one bad joke. Whites came to fear black indignation, black protest, black litigiousness.

From the beginning of America's history white people had designed stereotypes of black people to justify our country's treatment of them. White people used black people as farm machinery, so they convinced themselves they were less than human. Then, forced to let them go, white people told themselves blacks were vicious chained animals, suddenly freed. Spreading the fear that the freed slaves were coming to rob us or rape our women made white people feel okay about lynchings. The fear was real and it created a vicious cycle: whites had kidnapped, imprisoned, beaten, raped, and killed the people they now begrudgingly invited to stay in their country as guests. We'd scared ourselves to death of them, so we had to scare them right back by hanging one from a tree and setting his body on fire so the rest of them saw what we were capable of. We'd scared them to death of us, but we didn't want to look like the bad guys, so we had to make up reasons to keep terrorizing them with impunity.

Slave patrols evolved into police departments. During Reconstruction, the police were taught it was their job to protect white people from black people; their actions taught black children it was the policeman's job to find a reason to arrest black men so they can put them on a chain gang and turn them back into slaves via convict-leasing. It was easy to turn them back into slaves; whites made laws against them looking at whites the wrong way. Whites wouldn't hire them for jobs so they had no money; then whites came up with a law against standing around with no money, called it *vagrancy*. Without money, blacks would turn to crime, whites rationalized, so they put them in jail as a pre-emptive strike. Thrown in jail for having no money, black Americans couldn't pay court fees or fines, but an upstanding white man could step up and volunteer to pay and let them work off the debt on his farm. Sometimes a crowd tortured and hanged a black man and then shot guns at his dead body.

Whites had used guns to take everything black people had. In the Sixties, the Black Panthers began to brandish their own guns in public. They recognized there was power in being feared, so they stood together holding guns in public places such as the steps of a courthouse. Bearing arms was their Constitutional right, after all. The sight of them told the police, *Look, we have guns too, and we are watching what you do with yours.* The symbolism inspired children who grew up to make music that relied on this power of a black man with a gun. They put guns on their album covers, in their music videos. They wrote songs about shooting people and being shot, and missing close friends who'd been shot to death. Some of them dressed like revolutionaries, but more of them dressed like street criminals. They dressed like criminals, so the police stopped them in case they were. One had drugs on him so they sent him to prison. They took his shoelaces and belt so he couldn't use them to hang himself. When the man came out of prison he left his sneakers unlaced and his pants sagging. He liked the look: it told people he'd been to prison. Kids liked the way the musicians dressed, so they started to dress that way too. They weren't rappers *or* criminals. Some of them didn't even listen to rap. The police had always dressed the same, more or less. They wore uniforms so you could know who they were and either tip your hat or run, given your inclination. They'd been killing black men long before hooded sweatshirts or sagging pants. They'd been trained to be scared to death of the very people whose homes they invaded to snatch drugs, so they drew their guns and kept their fingers on the triggers.

Given power and impunity, the police became predators. Officers from the NYPD Street Crimes Unit wore T-shirts printed with the Hemingway quote, "Certainly there is no hunting like the hunting of man, and those who have hunted armed men long enough and liked it, never really care for anything else thereafter." This wartime mentality extended to the unit's motto: We Own the Night. The mission? To venture into crime-ridden neighborhoods and seize guns. The Street Crimes Unit formed in 1971, then in 1994 Mayor Rudy Giuliani told them to get more aggressive. By 1997, Police Commissioner Howard Safir had nearly tripled the size of the Street Crimes Unit to 380 officers patrolling New York City for guns.[7]

"Just because you're paranoid," sang Nirvana's Kurt Cobain, "don't mean they're not after you." Friends and family of Ol' Dirty Bastard have often remarked on his paranoia, which had the uncanny tendency to play out in reality. He was convinced the cops were out to get him long before the NYPD Street Crimes Unit pulled him over and opened fire. Dirty was convinced the FBI was watching him long before his fans saw his fears confirmed with the release of the FBI's files on him and the rest of the Wu-Tang Clan. We didn't know until after his death that when Dirty sang what sounded like a joke line—"FBI, don't you be watching meeeeee"—the FBI was actively watching him. On Martin Luther King Jr. Day, 1999, two plainclothes officers from the Street Crimes Unit followed Dirty through Brooklyn in their unmarked car. Dirty had been robbed and shot nine months earlier on his cousin's couch in the Brevoort Projects, so when he saw a car tailing him he tried to lose the car. In turn, his erratic driving gave the police cause to force his car off the road and approach with their guns drawn, yelling "Get out of the car!" Dirty did not have a gun. He held his empty hands out the window and pled *don't shoot*, but the police saw a black male driver and the gun they suspected he had, despite his empty hands in clear sight. Dirty saw two white men in street clothes, pointing their actual guns at him. "If you don't get out of the car," they're reported to have said, "we're gonna blow your damn head off."[8]

Having so recently been shot because somebody wanted his necklace, Dirty froze. The officers claim he pulled a gun and began firing at them, but investigators found no weapon and no shell casings, and paraffin tests proved neither Dirty nor his passenger fired a gun. The day after a Brooklyn grand jury ruled that Ol' Dirty Bastard should not face the charges against him, four officers from the Street Crimes Unit fired forty-one bullets and hit the unarmed Guinean college student Amadou Diallo nineteen times, killing him. They mistook his wallet for a gun.

I think of Madvillain's brilliant song "Strange Ways"—the first verse set in the drug war and the second one set in Iraq. Verse One presents the police officer "paid to interfere with how a brother get his money"; Verse Two presents the oil tycoons who tricked America into a war against Saddam Hussein: "Obviously, they came to portion up his fortune." Our leaders sent us into Iraq by pretending Saddam Hussein had weapons he never had, same as they've tricked us into believing black men are carrying guns. When you stole the land you built your country on, and stole the people you enslaved to build it, you'll worry every day that someone is coming to steal it from you.

•

In the years before my wife and I moved north, we bought a house in Louisville's Germantown neighborhood. We moved in and installed an alarm system, thereby introducing ourselves to our new neighbors by saying, *Hello, we fear you*, or, worse, *Fear us. We have some nice things in here—don't try to rob us or the cops will come.* Either way you phrase it, our message was clear: we are different from you. We came in and announced we were different in a neighborhood proud of its roots. We marked an unwelcome transition, neighbors told us in coded speech: we've lived in these houses for generations, they said; they didn't speak German themselves but they missed the way their grandparents used to speak it in the corner liquor store where these new Iraqi owners don't even speak English. Yet the block was adorned not with the red, black, and gold of the German flag, but with Confederate flag tattoos that made me feel a vicarious discomfort for the one black family, who lived at the top of the hill. The tattoos, for the most part, peeked from underneath the rolled-up sleeves of rap T-shirts, but they negated those shirts so decisively.

My alarm system made it easier to sleep at night until it malfunctioned and its blaring siren ripped me from the depths of my dreams. The only thing worse than the false alarms was the fear of another one coming. I'd lie in bed half afraid of the shouting in the street outside, half-anticipating the terrifying scream of my own security system. The alarm was somewhat more reassuring when I wasn't home; it did its job one afternoon when some kids tried to pry open the lock on our back gate, but more often it just caused me to rush home from work for a false alarm. Nobody who lived on our street flinched. I'd screech the car to a stop and leap out; neighbors would nod a hello and state, "Your alarm's goin' off again." The noise was so familiar that if somebody had wanted to rob our house the alarm would have given them the perfect cover.

I gentrified Germantown. I moved in and bought a cheap house and sold it for more money a couple years later. A couple years after that, I returned from the Northeast to visit friends and could barely recognize my old neighborhood. My fourth-generation Germantown neighbors lamented that their people no longer spoke German; I complained the old dive bar I'd loved was now a dive in its décor alone.

Could Germantown weather hipster gentrification or would it lose its identity like Paristown up the street? Things change: in the few years since I moved away, real estate agents came up with a whole new part of Louisville and named it NuLu; in the 1800s Germantown was best known for floods and malaria; nearby Irish Hill was called Billy Goat Hill until the Micks moved in and ran out the goats. How proud we Americans used to be of our ethnic isolationism, of our pockets of neighborhoods named for ancestral countries my generation had never seen. Being American came to subsume it all to the point that being German-American doesn't mean much anymore. We used to name neighborhoods for the people who'd settled them or the business those people engaged in. The Germans lived in Germantown. Or in Butchertown, where they worked slaughtering cows and where in 1855 some anti-immigration activists killed dozens of those no-good Krauts to keep them from voting.

But that's the past, all the past. To stand in Louisville and say *Germantown* already means something different than it did when I lived there only a decade ago. I am a New Jerseyan now, a Haddonfielder, and anxious about what that might mean. *Republicans.* One offhand comment from my well-meaning friend and I moved to Haddonfield with my mindset tainted by the silly idea that a whole town could think one way. True, the common denominator among friends I've made in Haddonfield is the age of our children—but that seems like at least as legitimate a basis for friendship as our liking the same music or politics. My wife and I made friends with the other parents we saw pushing strollers, the other parents lingering by the doorway as we dropped our daughter off for her first day at preschool. *Were* they Republicans? I met two Brazilian brothers. I met a man from Bolivia who'd married a woman from Norway. I said hello to my white neighbor's black nanny, who he'd told me lived in North Philadelphia. Making conversation and not knowing any other facts about her, I asked what part of North Philly she lived in. She stiffened. "I live in Center City." In her mind, it was a slight, a microaggression. In her mind, I had assumed that because she was black she must live in impoverished North Philly rather than wealthy Center City. Did her boss really not know where she lived? Did I mishear him? Or did I hear him say Philly and somehow unconsciously translate it to North Philly?

"Where we are is who we are," says Miss Moore in Toni Cade Bambara's short story "The Lesson." Having gone to college and returned to her old neighborhood, Miss Moore feels it is her responsibility to teach her neighbor's children that they live in the slums and drive home her point about inequality by taking them on an excursion to see the unbelievably expensive toys at FAO Schwarz, just about three miles away from their homes in Harlem. One child, Sylvia, refuses to play along and "give that bitch the satisfaction"[9] by telling Miss Moore what she wants to hear: "'Where we are is who we are' Miss Moore always pointin out. But it don't necessarily have to be that way, she always adds then waits for somebody to say that poor people have to wake up and demand their share of the pie and don't none of us know what kind of pie she talkin about in the first damn place."[10] By the end of the story, young Sylvia has stolen a fistful of dollars from Miss Moore, a cab driver, and even her partner-in-crime Sugar. We last see her hanging back, letting Sugar win a footrace while she pockets the four dollars they'd promised to split and blow on potato chips and ice-cream sodas. Sylvia refused to admit to Miss Moore that she learned anything from her lesson, but as Sugar runs ahead the reader sees Sylvia admit that she needs to "think this day through," because "Ain't nobody gonna beat me at nuthin."[11]

"Where we are is who we are," Miss Moore always said, but a more accurate lesson might be where *they* are is who they are. Our thinking about each other is clouded by our impressions of neighborhoods we've no more than driven through with our doors locked, the reverse of Bambara's scene that depicts young Sylvia looking at the expensive toys through the window of FAO Schwarz, but feeling out-of-place going inside. Segregation in the United States is no accident, but a consistent and deliberate process of keeping "them" out of "our" neighborhoods. A world away from Sylvia and Miss Moore, I sat at a preschool picnic with the upstanding Haddonfield parents, white and wealthy and not at all shy about talking about race. Culturally speaking, I was a world away from Sylvia and Miss Moore, but geographically I was only five miles away from Camden, New Jersey, where an overwhelming 40% of residents live below the poverty line and only 4.44% of residents are white. In Haddonfield, by contrast, a miniscule 2.82% of residents live below the poverty line and only 1% of residents are black. Haddonfield is 93.6% white, although my eighty-four-year-old white neighbor told me it used to be "better." "I mean, I'm all for diversity," she said, "but there is such a thing as *too much* diversity."

I talked to the one black dad at the picnic—he told me that years ago he'd narrowly missed becoming the one black member of the inaugural cast of MTV's pioneering reality show *The Real World* because the casting director felt he was not black in the right way, or not black *enough*. We watched kids shoot foam rockets into the sky and race tiny electric Jeeps while the adults talked about who we were, where we came from, and what brought us to Haddonfield. My wife left her purse on the kitchen counter and while we were in the back yard eating miniature cupcakes one of those goddamned Republicans sneaked inside, opened her wallet, and stole forty dollars.

Robbed! By the parents of my child's classmates. By the very people with whom I'd traded commiserative smiles as we dropped our kids off for their first-ever day of school. This never happened to me in Louisville's Germantown. This never happened to me in Philly. Never mind the standardized test scores and murder maps; my personal threat meter registered reddest in colonial Haddonfield. The intimacy of the crime rattled me more than the audacity. I'd lost forty dollars before. My cable company charged me that much for an unjustified late fee and never responded to my complaints; I railed against them but I still send those crooks money. But with the Haddonfield preschool parents, I found myself asking what kind of people would do something like this?

This is how it begins. We blame the person standing closest; we warn our friends not to hang out in Haddonfield. Soon enough people who have never even driven through Haddonfield come to bristle at its mention—"Watch your wallet! My friend warned me about that place."

When I announced my plan to move from Louisville to Philadelphia, a friend's father asked me, "You think you can stand them people up there?"

On my first trip to scout apartments in New Jersey, a bartender drank a shot of bourbon with me. "Welcome to the Northeast," he said, slamming his glass on the bar. "I think I'd kill myself if I had to live in Kentucky."

His comment stung. As much of my childhood as I'd spent dreaming of leaving Kentucky, by the time I'd finished college and grad school in-state I'd fallen in love with the city of Louisville. I still dreamed of living in a bigger city with more writers and rappers in it, but let's just say central New Jersey was not at the top of my list; no grad student dreams of landing a job in a suburb of Trenton. I shrugged off the bartender's comment, wondering why we come to take such pride in the place we live, to the point that we're scared to death of living in a state, a region, or a part of town that we've never even deigned to visit.

Nine

SIT DOWN—CENSORSHIP, GRANDSTANDING, AND SHUTTING YOUR MOUTH

"Is it my place to give my two cents," asked Macklemore. "Or should I stand on the side and shut my mouth?" Hip-hop, a music genre that flourished in the Nineties with black men fighting censorship, had finally ceded the stage to a white man asking what it was ok for him to say. The lyrics above come from "White Privilege II," where Macklemore questions if a white man should join in chanting "Black Lives Matter." Plenty of other white folks had asked themselves that question and decided the answer was no, so they'd taken to chanting All Lives Matter instead. They pretended they couldn't hear the parenthetical *too* at the end of Black Lives Matter, but it was there, and they knew it was there. Putting it on the T-shirts and picket signs would have sounded too supplicating, but there was no denying it hung there unstated, its absence making the point even stronger. Throughout the history of this country, it's been a societal given that white lives matter, so there's no reason to hold up signs stating that. That's why the people who believed the slogan Black Lives Matter expressed an anti-white sentiment countered with their own rallying cry of All Lives Matter, because if white people went around holding signs that said White Lives Matter, there'd be a parenthetical *Only* at the beginning.

Black Lives Matter was already saying All Lives Matter. They were saying it to a country whose Constitution designated "free Persons" from "all other Persons" and where the young male descendants of those "other Persons" were still, more than 200 years later, nine times more likely than the descendants of the "free Persons" to get killed by the police—so likely, in fact, that around 1 out of every 65 young black men who died were killed by cops.[1] Outside of that all-important context, the phrase "All Lives Matter" sounds like it could be a corollary (plus one) of the rallying cry from just a year earlier: "We Are the 99%" Did the unity of the 99% vs. the 1% give way to the separatism of Black Lives Matter vs. All Lives Matter, or was the unity never there to begin with? I am not laying our longstanding division at the feet of this recent movement—politicians have strategized to divide us for centuries: during the American Revolution the British army turned colonists against slaves and slaves against colonists;[2] in the decades after the Civil War Northern carpetbaggers moved South to get freed blacks to vote against white southerners; in 1960, President Lyndon Johnson said, "If you can convince the lowest white man he's better than the best colored man, he won't notice you're picking his pocket. Hell, give him somebody to look down on, and he'll empty his pockets for you."[3] Nixon's aide John Erlichman later admitted Nixon had declared war on drugs in order to continue a campaign against black people in a country that would no longer (or more likely wanted to *look* like they would no longer) accept attacking them on the basis of color alone:

> We knew we couldn't make it illegal to be either against the war or black, but by getting the public to associate the hippies with marijuana and blacks with heroin. And then criminalizing both heavily, we could disrupt those communities. We could arrest their leaders, raid their homes, break up their meetings,

and vilify them night after night on the evening news. Did we know we were lying about the drugs? Of course we did.[4]

Lee Atwater, a member of Ronald Reagan's administration, described the Republicans' process of making racism more "abstract":

> You start out in 1954 by saying, "Nigger, nigger, nigger." By 1968 you can't say "nigger"—that hurts you, backfires. So you say stuff like, uh, forced busing, states' rights, and all that stuff, and you're getting so abstract. Now, you're talking about cutting taxes, and all these things you're talking about are totally economic things and a byproduct of them is, blacks get hurt worse than whites.[5]

So the war on black people wages on, masquerading as a war on poor people.

In the simplest terms of Us vs. Them, I've spent a good part of my life resenting people who were born with money—for the head start and safety net it gave and continues to give them—so surely I can understand a similar attitude toward people born with white skin, particularly when they don't appear to think much about the advantages it gives them. Macklemore, though, devoted a nine-minute song to thinking about what advantages he got by being white. Aesthetically speaking, "White Privilege II" was not a good hip-hop song—the vocals smacked of bad coffee-shop spoken word. It didn't reach nearly as many plays on my phone as better-sounding but mindless songs about gunshots and car upholstery, but I did play it for my students in class. Had hip-hop in the university created a two-tier system of songs we enjoyed versus songs we discussed in class? Not necessarily. Anti-Iraq War songs like

DM and Jemini's "Bush Boys" and Madvillain's "Strange Ways" ranked high on my playlist, same as Wise Intelligent's "Mr. Rocket Launcher," which confronted the binary opposition of gangsta versus teacher—"fallacy of common knowledge: he's too hood to be a prophet." Why did it take a white rapper to (re?)open the discussion? Aren't *all* hip-hop songs about white privilege?

Kris Ex at *Pitchfork* wrote that because Macklemore's white, he's going to get much more press for speaking on these topics than some black activists who've spent their careers speaking about them: "He's going to get an inordinate amount of attention for speaking out. He's going to be vaulted to a level of authority in this country's high-profile discussions on race that's taken DeRay McKesson a lot more marching, organizing, and tweeting to achieve."[6] But attention didn't grant authority—reporters certainly wrote about Macklemore, but Ex's own article title labeled the song "a mess," an assessment which was not far out of step with the other reactions. Justin Charity at *Complex* called it "literally the whitest song ever recorded,"[7] which doesn't exactly paint Macklemore as an authority on race.

Charity did commend Macklemore for his "tireless," "thankless" crusade of self-interrogation. "What should a white ally be?" asked Charity. "How should they sound? When should they speak and to whom?"[8] "What, in practice," asked *Vulture*'s Rembert Browne, "is a white person actually supposed to do, and how are nonwhite people supposed to respond?"[9] On one hand, it would have been easy not to say anything—and no one was exactly clamoring for Macklemore to tackle white privilege. If anything, his press team seemed overeager to win the approval of black journalists: Browne wrote that, "A handful of people were sent early streams of the song by Macklemore's reps. I don't know everyone who got a stream, but none of the people I knew who did were white. It was clear what was happening."[10] Gene Demby, host of NPR's *Code Switch*, wrote that, "Prior to the song's launch, his press people repeatedly reached out to me and a few other folks in 'the race space,' urging us to cover it. His PR folks felt a little thirsty for coverage—as is the wont of press flacks—but given the subject matter, it all seemed a bit short on self-awareness. *Hey, black people who write about race stuff all day! Macklemore's got some incisive thoughts on white privilege, and you're gonna want to hear them!*"[11] The press campaign seemed to suggest the song was a self-serving attempt to attract the attention of black journalists. Was the song nothing more than a publicity stunt, or an attempt for a white rapper to earn a black journalist's stamp of approval? Was Macklemore hoping for headlines like "White Person Gets It" or "White Person Acknowledges Racism"?

Demby saw self-indulgence where Ex saw "self-sabotage."[12] Demby, even while feeling uncertain about Macklemore's press push, granted that Macklemore was earnestly wrestling with his position as a white rapper, even if he couldn't figure out who he was rapping to: "Outside of the catharsis for Macklemore, though, it's not clear just who the song is *for*."[13] Macklemore isn't telling black people anything they don't already know, and it's doubtful a nine-minute rap song is going to convert a white racist. Ex, in labeling the song self-sabotage, suggested Macklemore was bringing up contradictions his fans had never considered: "It's hard," wrote Ex, "to listen to this song and not hear the targeted destruction of a pop base."[14] Did Macklemore feel so earnestly conflicted about his participation in hip-hop that he set out to lose fans? If the goal truly were self-interrogation, couldn't it be done in private, just Macklemore and his mirror? Did it need to become the first single off his new album?

"You've exploited and stolen the music," Macklemore accuses

himself. "The culture was never yours to make better / You're Miley, you're Elvis, you're Iggy Azalea." By saying, "make better," Macklemore isn't bragging about his rhyme skills but addressing the *white savior* complex. It's an old trope in movies like *Dangerous Minds*, where a white teacher enters a high school populated mostly with black and Latino students and liberates them—or their thinking, at least—from the limits of the ghetto. But does rejecting that trope mean that white artists, teachers, and thinkers should only engage *un*critically with black or Latino culture? Hip-hop was never Macklemore's to make better, yet here he was trying to challenge hip-hop's homophobia. Here he was suggesting white rappers should think more about white privilege.

Iggy Azalea didn't appreciate the way Macklemore so casually name-dropped her as an avatar of cultural appropriation. Talib Kweli, in turn, didn't like the way Iggy took the song as a personal attack rather than a challenge to rise to the occasion and take herself to task: she'd made money from hip-hop, but what had she done for black people? "So you want me to use my platform as a pop / rapper," she asked Talib, "to become a social activist or else I'm a shitty person." Certainly, a very few rappers were activists. "Where was Jay-Z when Sean Bell was killed?" asked my fellow panelist at Mercer County Community College. Talib was on the front lines at Ferguson, but the vast majority of his rap peers were not. Did white rappers bear a greater responsibility to engage in social activism than did black rappers? Were they not allowed to speak unless they had a record of activism?

Jesse Williams, in his impassioned BET Awards speech in 2016, would appear to say the answer is yes: "If you have a critique for our resistance, then you better have an established record of critique of our oppression. If you have no interest in equal rights for black people, then do not make suggestions to those who do. Sit down."[15] Criticisms abounded that Black Lives Matter protestors should be more polite, because activists speaking in the name of that movement often stopped speeches in progress and demanded to speak. "I like protesters," said former President Bill Clinton in a heated exchange with Black Lives Matter protestors who interrupted his speech in Philadelphia, "but the ones that won't let you answer are afraid of the truth."[16] Clinton's commitment to equal rights for black people is, of course, marred by the mass incarcerations of black people during his two terms. I can't disagree with Jesse Williams about a balanced record of critique, but at a campaign rally in Seattle, Black Lives Matter protestors snatched the mic from Bernie Sanders—a long-serving senator with an established record of critique of the oppression of black Americans—the way KRS snatched it from PM Dawn, the way Ol' Dirty Bastard snatched it from country singer Shawn Colvin when she was accepting the Grammy for Song of the Year.

As willing as so many white people were to stay silent on the issues black people faced, nothing riled them more than seeing a hateful speaker shut down. In 2017, UC-Berkeley shut down a speech by an alt-right apologist. In 2014, Rutgers students occupied an administration building to protest the selection of former Secretary of State Condoleezza Rice as commencement speaker. Two years later, President Obama's commencement speech criticized the students for having prompted Rice to back out: "If you disagree with somebody," said Obama, "bring them in and ask them tough questions."[17] But, as the Rutgers protestors had already pointed out, commencement speeches don't come with a Q&A session. President Obama seemed to envision a courtroom-style direct examination, with Rutgers students taking Rice to task. If such a forum existed, there might be less need for mic-snatching.

"Bring them in and ask them tough questions," said Obama, but the rapper Nelly backed out of a bone-marrow drive in honor of his sister after he learned that students from Spelman College's Feminist Majority Leadership Alliance planned to confront him about the misogyny of his music video for the song "Tip Drill." Women criticized the video not only for the gyrating bodies of black women—familiar from rap videos from artists ranging from Big Daddy Kane to Tupac to Paul Wall—but because Nelly went so far as to swipe a credit card down the crack of a woman's butt. The image became emblematic of hip-hop's treatment of women. Protestors asked Nelly to take part in a campus-wide forum on misogynist imagery before his bone-marrow drive would take place; they posted signs that read, "We Care About Your Sister, But You Have To Care About Ours, Too." Rather than sit down for a conversation with the women, Nelly canceled his concert; William Jelani Cobb—a hip-hop scholar and a history professor at Spelman—described the move as, "tantamount to saying 'shut up and give me your bone marrow.'"[18]

Years after canceling his bone-marrow drive, Nelly blamed the student protesters for his sister's death from leukemia, telling *The Huffington Post*, "I don't have my sister. And I doubt it if half of those girls are still campaigning for what they quote, unquote took advantage of that opportunity for."[19] As for the fact that Nelly himself canceled his appearance rather than speak with protesters? "The only thing I would have did different," he said, "is kick somebody's ass."[20] A rapper denied college women an opportunity to ask him tough questions about his harmful portrayals of women. Given a few years to think over his decision, he came to regret not harming them physically.

Nelly, as I finish this book in 2018, is facing sexual assault accusations from two women. A decade ago, he joined a BET panel discussion on hip-hop and misogyny; the four men on the panel barely let the two women talk. Men were represented by the older generation—the jazz critic Stanley Crouch and scholar Dr. Michael Eric Dyson—as well as the younger—rappers T.I. and Nelly. Throw in Jeff Johnson as moderator and you have a five to two man-to-woman ratio. The video plays for a full three minutes, in fact, before a woman speaks, and another four minutes before a woman speaks again. The panel included former *Source* editor-in-chief Kim Osorio and the model and actor Melyssa Ford, who at one point in the discussion described her role on the panel as watching the cars speed past while trying to merge onto the highway. "Why can't women be looked at as intellectuals?" asked Osorio.[21] Because it won't sell records, T.I. and Nelly agreed.

The mission of selling records didn't exactly invite the men to come off as intellectuals either, yet Dyson had carved his niche as "the hip-hop intellectual," as his book's cover proclaimed. He went full intellectual as he took Nelly to task using Marx's terminology: "When you swipe a credit card down a woman's behind, it shows the relationship between slavery—where women were sold on an auction block for crass commercialism—and her ass, which now becomes the commodity to be consumed."[22]

Nelly, flabbergasted, went full *anti*-intellectual and asked, "How is it that an eighteen-year-old girl who probably just got out of high school said *that* by looking at the TV?"[23]

But the college-age women of Spelman had said that, whether they'd used Marx's terminology or not. One student, senior Nikole Howard, displayed an intellectual condescension of her own when she told *Today* that the women in Nelly's video "have to demand respect, but I doubt these women even thought they were being disrespected. It makes me sad, makes me realize how much work we have to do to educate women."[24] College: saving women from credit-card swipes since

1833. As for Dyson's auction-block imagery, "That's your interpretation," T.I. told Dyson. "Not theirs."[25]

"What were you doing," Nelly asked the middle-aged Dyson, "up at 2:00 AM watching uncut videos?"[26] Nelly's strategy sought to distance Dyson from hip-hop's audience, to out him as a schoolboy interloper, the way Eminem's character B. Rabbit taunted Papa Doc in *8 Mile*: "I know something about you: you went to Cranbrook—that's a private school." Dyson, in fact, graduated from Cranbrook, which he's described as "one of the most highly esteemed private schools in the country."[27] Yet he wrote about how he regrets squandering, initially, the opportunities his teachers gave him: "I didn't go to college until I was twenty-one years old," writes Dyson. "I had been a teen father, lived on welfare, and hustled several years before furthering my formal education."[28] Even with that balance to his experiences—and even though his book opened with a foreword from Jay-Z and ended with an afterword from Nas—was hip-hop simply not made for professors?

"Let's not overcomplicate the situation," said Kim Osorio, who'd moments before lamented that hip-hop doesn't show women as intellectuals. "It's great to look at this as an intellectual conversation, but what are the kids listening to right now? Are they going to listen to T. I. and Nelly, or are they going to listen to the intellectuals?"[29]

Anti-intellectualism certainly wasn't the brainchild of hip-hop. College campuses had been accused of becoming so dedicated to political correctness that students and professors sought to stifle learning by censoring speakers or texts that challenged the campus's notion of the correct way to speak. Politicians, like former Arkansas governor Mike Huckabee, framed this campus mission as hypocritical, classist, and anti-religious. Huckabee had taken to using "Ivy League" as a slur during speeches. "I was on the campus of Yale," he said. "They always feel like, well, this dumb conservative Christian hick is gonna come. Can't wait to eat *him* alive . . . I went to Cornell to speak . . . there were about 100 kids protesting my being there. All in the name of tolerance and diversity, of course."[30] Had "tolerance"—a buzzword on campuses—come to include refusing to tolerate *in*tolerance? Huckabee, after all, once referred to Jay-Z as Beyonce's "pimp."[31] He laughed at gender identification: "Now I wish that someone told me that when I was in high school that I could have felt like a woman when it came time to take showers in P.E. I'm pretty sure that I would have found my feminine side and said, 'Coach, I think I'd rather shower with the girls today.'"[32] When Rider invited Huckabee to speak on our campus, my English department colleague Matthew Goldie led the protest: "Gov. Huckabee has been invited to a place that encourages students' intellectual growth. His views would not be leading to constructive intellectual debate. Rider as a whole encourages tolerance and diversity. Gov. Huckabee represents the opposite."[33] Huckabee argued that our promotion of "tolerance" mean that to uphold our own standards, we had to tolerate the jabs he took at the groups underrepresented in politics and higher education. According to his view, defenders of free speech ought to be out there promoting America's long-cherished tolerance of intolerance.

•

My first political cause was the free-speech campaign led by hip-hop. I scoped out Pirate's Cove, the arcade in the Somerset Mall, looking for a community-college student over eighteen who'd take my money to Sound Shop and buy 2 Live Crew's *Banned in the USA*, Ice-T's *Freedom of Speech . . . Just Watch What You Say*, or other albums they would not sell to the underaged. C. Delores Tucker, a civil rights activist who'd marched with Dr. Martin Luther King Jr, declared war on gangsta rap: "Rap music is wonderful," she said, but the corporate record labels "perverted it" by selling the image of young black men as "thugs and rapists."[34] Rappers proudly called themselves pimps on records, but Tucker argued the rappers were in fact the ones being whored: "The pimps in the entertainment industry who distribute gangsta rap are major contributors to the destruction of the African American community."[35] She silenced no rappers, but she rendered Time Warner record executives mute at a stockholders meeting when she challenged them to read aloud from the rap lyrics they sold on CDs.

At fourteen years old, I saw Tucker as an old and out-of-touch Church Lady trying to silence the rappers I loved. Did I grow up on the wrong side of this fight? I listened to hip-hop for thirty years before I ever considered censoring it. My daughter was far too young when I learned not to watch a new rap video for the first time with her sitting in my lap. I should have previewed Killer Mike's "Reagan," which depicts the cowboy president of my youth as a bloodthirsty antichrist smuggling guns and drugs even as he declared war on crack cocaine in black neighborhoods. Crucial history, but too much too soon? The police, as she knew them from books, were smiling finders of lost puppies. She was too young to have that image shattered by cartoon cops cracking the heads of black kids. "What is that red stuff coming out of him when they hit him with their sticks?"

Yet I censored a book: *David Gets in Trouble*. She laughed at the drawing of David pulling a cat's tail, and—ignoring the cautionary tale of his punishment by time-out—she pulled our cat's tail. David was such a bad influence that my wife and I considered giving the book to Goodwill, but our daughter loved it so much that we settled for gluing the cat page closed. Now she has no interest in reading the story, only in peeling the pages apart.

I didn't foresee myself censoring books; it just doesn't jibe with my job as an English professor. If I will resort to censorship to protect my child—or my cat—am I okay with being lied to? America's leaders said they weren't listening in on our phone calls. When we caught them, they said they were just trying to keep us safe. Catching them gave us the satisfaction of being right: those fuckers, I *knew* they were lying. If not for confirming our suspicions, what victory is there in uncovering the truth? The lies came out, but what happens next? Nobody's going to jail. I'm not renouncing my citizenship. The cycle repeats. They'd lied before, after all: waged war under false pretenses; tortured enemies to get them to tell us the truth. When these lies came out there was no coup d'état, no mass exodus from the US. Am I comfortable despite being lied to, or am I comfortable precisely because I am lied to, despite the nagging question of what else they're keeping from me?

•

While Reagan's administration was secretly meeting with drug traffickers to make the Iran-Contra gun deals he'd later pretend to forget, our government started putting warning labels on music that talked about drugs and guns. Record stores would no longer sell the youth an uncensored album, so I scoped out the Somerset Mall arcade looking for someone over eighteen to send into the Sound Shop in my place. Ashamed of myself, initially, I sneaked my ill-gotten Eazy-E cassette into the house and hid it, unopened, in the top of my closet, until curiosity got the better of me: what could it possibly say?

I already owned the censored version. Mom bought me K-Mart

cassettes pocked with dead air where the cursing would have gone, or with lines rerecorded and tempered by the rappers themselves. Eazy-E recorded an edited version of his song about raping a woman at gunpoint until the discovery of her penis so killed the mood that he—or the character he was playing—had to shoot him rather than rape him. In the uncensored original, Eazy rhymed, "stuck the gat up his leg, all the way up her skirt / cause this was one faggot that I had to hurt." The censored version changed *faggot* to *sissy*, which rendered rape and murder suitable for selling at K-Mart and harmless to sensitive ears.

Eazy's group N.W.A. turned the dirty words backward. Thirsting for truth, I took apart the cassette tape and reversed the reels so that it played garbled, warbled nonsense punctuated with *bitch* and *motherfucker*, which is what rap's critics tend to say it sounds like anyway. But N.W.A's *Straight Outta Compton* was distinctive among censored rap albums in that one song, rather than being overdubbed with silence or backward curse words, was simply left off. The only way to tame this song's message was to cut it entirely. I pulled the unopened, uncensored tape from behind the hand-me-down sweaters in the top of my closet and stared at this song on the track list: "Fuck tha Police," the most emblematic anthem of protest rap.

"Fuck tha Police" frightened parents. So did Body Count's "Cop Killer" and Paris's "Bush Killa" and "Coffee, Donuts, and Death." Policemen weren't pleased. Corporations dropped rappers from their record labels. Graphic violence got equated with militancy, then with racially-charged commentary, to the point that the record label shelved KMD's sophomore album "Black Bastards," because of its cover art: a black Sambo figure in a hangman's noose. Was it a government conspiracy—or was it just business—that shifted rap's politics to a mindless hedonism hardly worth censoring? Was any spirit of protest still there?

So many rappers lost their record deals in the wake of songs like "Fuck tha Police" that they learned to sneak politics into songs that appear mindless on the surface. The second verse of a song about car upholstery tells the story of a man born in a New Orleans charity hospital who asserts, "I gotta die with money cause I wasn't born with it." What's more American than a poor man bent on becoming rich?

When professors wrote about rap music they tended to criticize much of it but praise the things said by a handful of rappers—the sons of professors, many of them—who rapped about biased sentencing and overcrowded prisons while the other rappers, with their nonprofessor parents, got shot and imprisoned and wrote songs celebrating those events as rites of passage. Theirs was a terrible message, as unjustifiable as an earlier generation's telling boys that joining a war would make them men.

Some rappers we called thugs and some revolutionaries—we pitted the two images against each other to make it appear these were the only options available, as if there were nothing else a young black man could be. Revolutionary or thug, we said, choose your brand of criminal. It wasn't always easy to tell one from the other, although interviewers spent a lot of time asking rappers which brand they were and hoping they'd say something critical of the other variety. Plenty of rappers saw through this strategy; plenty of them exploited it to keep their names in the news and their records on store shelves. I write songs that make money, said the thugs. I write songs that make people think, said the revolutionaries. I see what's going on clearer than you do, they each said, I am better than you are at business. The thugs—and sometimes the revolutionaries, too—wrote songs about how they'd made so much money from rap they'd become businessmen, the worst kind of criminal there is.

•

CEOs sell us stereotypes. Women in rap videos dress and dance the way men want to see them dress and dance; male rappers leer at them in a manner white people once used to justify murdering black men, whether the black men had really leered at a woman or not. I pay good money so I can be entertained by songs about a ghetto I've never lived in.

My mother was certain rap music was a bad influence, but I played the Geto Boys for my little sister and she came out fine. She grew up to be a campus minister who spells out curse words when she's quoting them, even in a crowd of adults. If rap music did not harm my sister—if I make *money* writing about rap music—can I justify keeping it from my daughter? In the car, in the early months of my daughter's life, I broke my car stereo forcing the volume down to silence the filthiest few seconds. Beaten, I turned to the tactic of allowing explicit content in a language I did not understand. She and I became huge fans of German rap, in particular a white kid, Lance Butters, who raps wearing an Ironman mask.

She came to love Lance Butters so much—and know so little of comic book superheroes and their blockbuster movies—that she believed her favorite rapping Berliner had a huge U.S. following. The blockbuster *Ironman* movie had just been released, and there was Lance Butters imagery everywhere. She was four years old, at the playground, excited to meet a little boy in an Ironman T-shirt. She ran to share her enthusiasm for songs like "Halt Die Fresse" and "Auf Deutschrap," but then walked back to me grinning and shaking her head: "Daddy, that boy doesn't even know who he has on his shirt."

Can I get on board with censorship when Viacom-owned MTV

and BET censor words like "work" and "supply"—good capitalist words—when a rapper uses them to talk about selling drugs, while we can hear Viacom's billionaire owner live and uncut, taped in a phone conversation bribing a journalist to rat out his source? I sought to protect my little daughter from the cunnilingus rhymes of Azealia Banks, but is she truly more dangerous than the women pantomiming orgasms in shampoo commercials? Is it all somehow empowering? Maybe my plan backfired. Maybe she can curse like a German sailor. What was I censoring, exactly, showing her rap was a white European in a superhero mask?

I returned to the militant rap of Trenton, New Jersey's Wise Intelligent. No cunnilingus rhymes, but what did my daughter make of his discussion of the prison-industrial complex? What did she make, on our way to her Presbyterian preschool, of a line like "White Jesus on your chain can't save you"? I grew up in a time when cursing still felt revolutionary: 2 Live Crew took its dirty nursery rhymes all the way to the Supreme Court. Those battles behind us, we buy *Thug Kitchen*, a best-selling cookbook full of foul-mouthed recipes; we buy a mock bedtime story for frustrated parents called *Go the Fuck to Sleep*. Both books, written by white authors, smacked of minstrelsy, even as they emphasized the fact that hip-hop has so changed the cultural landscape that swearing's become as passé as smoking. All the trouble parents and politicians took to keep bad words out of my music and blur marijuana leaves on rappers' shirts in the videos, and this is where we've come: swearing reduced to a pedestrian gimmick, weed nearly legal after all these years. The children of my daughter's generation will stare, puzzled, at Nineties rappers with their finally unblurred pot leafs and wonder what they thought was so revolutionary. Might as well rap wearing Marlboro T-shirts.

•

Censorship triggers the evil of our imaginations. Place a black bar over something and we envision the worst. When I was a child my mom bought me two rabbits from Mr. Hargis, a man Daddy knew. "Where did you get the bunnies?" my cousin Debbie asked.

"Jim Hargis," Mom told her.

"Does he raise them to sell as pets?"

"Well," Mom said, "I'll tell you later what he raises them for, but I don't want to say it in front of Mickey."

I was no rabbit expert, but I did know they were known to reproduce quickly and frequently. I knew the expression *fuck like bunnies.*

Today, as a grown man, I understand that Mr. Hargis raised rabbits for meat. And Mom was right—this would have upset me. But for years I went around thinking this old man kept rabbits so he could watch them fuck, like bunnies.

Information was kept from me and my mind chose the dirtiest possible explanation. And anytime that Hargis fellow would stop by the body shop, I would think, "Here comes that old pervert."

•

The news told my parents rap music was filthy, so they heard filth even where there was none. Dad was sure Salt N Pepa said not "Push It" but "Pussy." Mom was sure EU's dance hit was not named "Doin Da Butt" but "Do it in the Butt." When I spoke up in my music's defense I was drowned out by my own stereo playing Luther Campbell shouting about a woman licking his ass. In Alabama, a record-store owner was arrested for selling an adult man a 2 Live Crew album. Stores had sold plenty of 2 Live Crew records before that one, so why arrest that man at that store? "We'd sold hundreds of thousands of records to black people at black record stores," wrote Campbell in his 2015 memoir *The Book of Luke*, "and no cop or judge ever said shit about it. Nobody cared if we were corrupting young black minds with our evil jungle music. But the day some white teenager got caught with a 2 Live Crew album, that's what started the whole shitstorm right fucking there."[36] The white comedian Andrew Dice Clay, a contemporary of Campbell's, sold records as nasty as 2 Live Crew's *As Nasty as They Wanna Be*, and no one was being arrested. But Dice was a white man, while Campbell describes 2 Live Crew as "black men coming across the color line talking about sex. We were black men in the company of whites, and we'd forgotten to lower our heads and shuffle away."[37]

Was 2 Live Crew being punished for speaking to white listeners? "We told the truth about life in the ghettos," wrote Campbell, "and we were selling a ton of records to white kids. Rap was doing what school busing and affirmative action and these other things failed to do: it was integrating the culture."[38] I wouldn't write off the Civil Rights Movement quite as quickly as Campbell does here, but I can't deny that my first lesson in the fight for free speech came from Luther Campbell and his 2 Live Crew, who brought kids of all creeds and colors together to listen to:

> Abraham Lincoln was a good old man
> Hopped out the window with his dick in his hand
> Said excuse me, lady, I'm just doing my duty
> So pull down your pants and give me some booty

I can find no historical evidence of this episode from the life of our sixteenth president (nor does it appear in the Constitution's list of presidential responsibilities) but I watched 2 Live Crew make history fighting for the right to make dick jokes. The professor and literary critic Henry Louis Gates Jr. testified in court that they were, in fact, joking— working within a tradition of African folktales and African-American literature that included boastful exaggeration not meant to be taken literally. When 2 Live Crew said, "Lick it till your tongue turns doo-doo brown," they didn't exactly mean to tell women to go out and do so. Sure, said Dr. Kimberlé Williams Crenshaw, the black feminist scholar best known for introducing the theory of intersectionality, but should black women stand in solidarity with black male rappers even as they told women to lick their assholes? "As a Black feminist," she wrote, "I felt the pull of each of these poles, but not the compelling attractions of either. My immediate response to the criminal charges against 2 Live Crew was ambivalence: I wanted to stand together with the brothers against a racist attack, but I wanted to stand *against* a frightening explosion of violent imagery directed at women like me. My sharp internal division—my dissatisfaction with the idea that the 'real issue' is race or that the 'real issue' is gender— is characteristic of my experience as a Black woman living at the intersection of racial and sexual subordination."[39] If the whole thing was a joke, she suggested, it sure wasn't funny.

•

Excusing a hateful comment as a joke allowed Americans to see hate speech as a big misunderstanding that could be solved by sitting down and having a talk. Radio host Don Imus said he was only joking when he called the Rutgers women's basketball team "nappy-headed ho's" and New Jersey's governor suggested they all just sit down together and talk it out. Whether or not we took these lyrics as a threat or a joke, their effect was to remind women of the place men had kept them for so many years. These lyrics were another instance of hip-hop chanting *Pimps Up, Ho's Down*, as T. Denean Sharpley-Whiting titled her 2008 book about the ways women engage with a hip-hop culture that is, at its core, misogynist? In 2007, Snoop Dogg, the rapper who first chanted *pimps up, ho's down* (or its variant "G'z Up, Ho's Down," at least), came to the defense of the Rutgers women's basketball team after Imus called them ho's. As for the names rappers called black women, Snoop claimed, "It's a completely different scenario. We're not talking about no collegiate basketball girls who have made it to the next level in education and sports. We're talking about ho's that's in the hood that ain't doing shit."[40]

"I will be fucking you. You will be sucking me then licking my asshole," said 2 Live Crew, but it's okay—they were saying it to women who never planned to go to college.

"I never said it was Shakespeare," said Gates, although Sharpley-Whiting quotes him telling 2 Live Crew's prosecutors, "The greatest literary tradition in English literature . . . people such as Chaucer and Shakespeare . . . has always included a lot of lewdity."[41] Decades after Professor Gates testified, a policeman arrested him for entering his own home, just a few blocks from Harvard's campus. He'd returned from a trip and had to force open his stubborn front door. The policeman couldn't charge him with breaking and entering—it was his own home after all—so he arrested him for disorderly conduct, for getting upset that he was being cuffed by the cops in his own living room. President Obama said, "I think it's fair to say, number one, any of us would be pretty angry; number two, that the Cambridge police acted stupidly in arresting somebody when there was already proof that they were in their own home, and, number three, what I think we know separate and apart from this incident is that there's a long history in this country of African Americans and Latinos being stopped by law enforcement disproportionately."[42] Tradition was no excuse. Shakespeare and Chaucer wrote lewd books, goes the logic, so 2 Live Crew worked within a rich literary tradition of asshole-licking; American police departments were fortified, after the Civil War, to keep the newly freed black Americans from taking anything from the original "free persons," so the police 150 years later upheld that tradition with Gates. President Obama invoked the fact of the disproportionate stopping of people of color, but then he apologized for saying it—thus upholding the tradition of presidents refusing to acknowledge that fact.

President Obama apologized for having broken with tradition by criticizing a police officer. Cambridge's mayor called Professor Gates to apologize for his treatment by the city's police. With all that apologizing, people looked at the arresting officer, expecting he might join in. "There are not many certainties in life," said Sergeant Crowley, "but it is for certain that Sergeant Crowley will not be apologizing."[43] Still, President Obama suggested the three of them sit down and talk through the whole thing over a beer. But sitting down for the sake of civility just didn't set things right in these instances where one side was so clearly wrong. Gates sat down with Sergeant Crowley. The Rutgers women's basketball team sat down with Don Imus. Every November, Americans sat down to dinner to commemorate the idea that Native Americans had once sat down to dinner with the pilgrims who effected their genocide.

Ten

WHO WILL TELL HIP-HOP'S STORY?

Buddha Monk and I sat down to dinner at Houlihan's, where I pitched my idea to write a book about Buddha's dead friend. I wanted to write a book that painted a three-dimensional portrait of Ol' Dirty Bastard, the man other writers had turned into a caricature. Much of the writing about Dirty ends up at the poles of minstrelsy (his performance was all a show) vs. insanity (he couldn't help acting the way he did), neither of which leaves much room for his humanity. Dirty cemented the public's perception of him with his career-defining stunt, when he took MTV cameras along on his infamous limousine ride to pick up his food stamps. It was 1995, and President Clinton had vowed to end welfare as a way of life and "make it a path to independence and dignity."[1] By taking pride in his food stamps, Dirty seemed to embody so many of hip-hop's contradictions: his critics saw him reinforcing the stereotype of the black welfare cheat; his Bed-Stuy neighbors cheered for him, waving their own food stamps in solidarity because Dirty had gone on TV and made government assistance something no one had to be ashamed of. In the *MTV News* footage, Dirty stepped out of the limo wearing a sky-blue hunting cap and took his wife and three kids into the welfare office. He asked if the cameras were rolling, then said, "The people that want to cut off the welfare, man, I think that's terrible. You know how hard it is for people to live without nothing. You owe me forty acres and a mule anyway."[2] Never mind that Dirty pocketed just $375; he was Robin Hood. He was a newly famous rapper, making money for the first time in his life, stepping out of a limousine to ask Americans the question, "Why wouldn't you want to get free money?" But more than anything, Buddha assured me, Dirty did it because he thought it would be funny.

But who was laughing, and why? Dante Ross, the white man who'd signed Ol' Dirty Bastard to his record deal at Elektra, said, "To a lot of people who deem themselves politically correct, I think Dirty became their minstrel show. He was as close as they could get to the ghetto and watch someone totally dissolve as a human, while sitting far enough back to laugh."[3] Dirty was shot once in a street altercation, shot twice more when robbers broke into his cousin's house, then shot *at* by the NYPD with his hands held out his car window and no weapon in his possession. No rap fan would categorize Dirty's lyrics as conscious, or woke, or political, yet Dirty got the brunt of the social conditions that the woke rappers critique. He embodied a larger trend; across hip-hop's history, the rappers getting shot at by the cops and thrown in prison haven't tended to be the rappers writing songs about police brutality and the prison industrial complex. Dirty's arrest record became the subject of jokes, like Chris Rock's "On this day in hip-hop: August 19, 1999, Russell Jones a.k.a Ol' Dirty Bastard was *not* under arrest. For a period of at least twenty-four hours, the Wu-Tang rapper didn't break a single law."[4] Dirty's rap sheet included a litany of charges for drug possession, gun possession, and terrorist threats, culminating in his arrest in California for wearing a bulletproof vest as a felon, a law since overturned as unconstitutional. He spent two of the last three years of his life in prison, then died in the studio from a lethal combination of cocaine and the painkiller Tramadol, two days before his thirty-sixth birthday. We love to see a celebrity self-destruct, but we bring to mind a whole different history when a white fan watches that process play out for a black celebrity. Can white fans ever truly be certain that we didn't gawk at Dirty in a different way, or for different reasons, than we gawked at Amy Winehouse or Anna Nicole Smith?

To view Dirty's career as a mere extension of the minstrel show is to reduce the complexities of who he was and what he was saying. His pride in the ghetto was a stand of solidarity with his neighbors, even as outsiders paid money to see Dirty's show. But if Dirty's antics weren't all just part of the act, did they stem from genuine mental illness? Dream Hampton wrote, "I'm not sure Ol' Dirty articulated with any clarity his politics on welfare reform. It's pretty bananas to expect clarity from hip-hop's self-proclaimed drunken bastard, I know. The question is, can insanity be revolutionary if it lives within the Black body of an unpredictable crazy motherfucker? If our nuts can't be trusted, can they be dismissed?"[5]

"Dirty wasn't schizophrenic," Buddha told me. "Dirty was paranoid, but getting shot a couple times will do that to a nigga." Buddha maintained that Dirty's career was not some kind of extended and misguided publicity stunt, that there was a real person the press didn't see— or didn't want to show. "Dirty was a loving brother, a caring friend, and a very supportive father to his kids. Even on his bad days, no matter how bad he was, tomorrow would come and it was hard to stay mad at him, because that's just who he was. It wasn't a character. It was him."[6] Drug abuse took its toll on Dirty, Buddha admitted, but it was the prison sentence that led to his death. The authorities took a man who'd been shot in two separate attempts on his life and placed him in with the general population at a maximum-security prison. When he told the guards the other prisoners were threatening him, he ended up dosed with Haldol for his paranoid delusions. "They fucked him up," Buddha said. "On that psychiatric ward type shit. They shot Dirty up with some of the craziest drugs. He wasn't even himself when he came out."

I knew Buddha Monk was protective of his friend's legacy. He'd been burned by writers before, and I needed to convince him I was the right person to work with. I broached the subject of Jaime Lowe's biography of Dirty, the book that my friend Traum Diggs and I had found so lacking, the book that Dirty's mother had called for her son's fans to boycott. "She clowned us," said Buddha, shaking his head. "She got Dirty's lyrics wrong. She misquoted me. She didn't do justice to Dirty's story." There was more to be written, and Buddha was ready to give it another try. "I want to set the record straight. I want the true story to come out. Hess, I would love to work together on a book, man," he said. "I got the stories and you got the writing skills." Buddha had the connection to Dirty and hip-hop, and I had the connection to the university and the publishing industry. But was I so different from Jaime Lowe? I had published other books about hip-hop, which she had not, but I was no less white and even more entrenched in academia. Despite my close collaboration with Buddha, it was a challenge to bring Dirty to life on the page. Buddha was too close to Dirty to want to risk tarnishing his friend's legacy, but my life experiences were too far from Dirty's for me to tell his story without my own perspective somehow intruding.

"I just want Dirty's legacy to be preserved," said Buddha. "And I want my credit too." The credit that Buddha wants has tended to go to Dirty's cousin the RZA, the undisputed mastermind behind the Wu-Tang Clan and executive producer of Dirty's solo albums. "They gave RZA credit for everything," Buddha said. "There was tracks that RZA talked to Dirty about on the *phone* but left me with the hard work of recording. And, yeah, my name's in the liner notes but I didn't get the recognition or the royalties I deserved. It wasn't my name on the checks. But, hey, that's the music business."

"Wait till you see the publishing business," I warned him, half-joking. "It's the same thing with less money to fight over."

Buddha shook his head. "Yo, I ain't worried about the money," he assured me. "Money's nice, but honestly I just can't wait to get this book published. Who else could tell this story the way I can? My friendship with Dirty was deeper than most people know. Ol' Dirty Bastard and Buddha Monk were together all the time. In the studio, on the road, just chillin together, but let people tell the story and Buddha Monk's name gets left out. People always want to put their own spin on the story or try to tear Dirty down instead of preserve his legacy. But if my man Traum vouches for you I know I got nothing to worry about."

•

We started working. I taped and transcribed Buddha's stories. I turned the tapes into text and the text into prose. "Oh my God," said Buddha when I called him to tell him I'd got us a contract with a publisher. "I'm gonna be an author. I'm gonna call my mom! You need to come up to my place and stay with me for a few days and we'll really get this book off the ground."

"Sounds good," I said. "Brooklyn's an easy trip."

"Oh, shit! I meant to tell you, Mickey. I ain't living in Brooklyn no more. I moved to Worcester, Massachusetts. I met a very lovely lady up here. But you can come up and stay with me and my girl in Worcester. Stay for a few days and get drunk and I'll talk about Dirty while you record it. We got plenty of room. I'll do all the cookin."

But I did not go to Worcester. When I called Buddha to take him up on his invitation, his only response was a text that read, "Today is Dirty's bday. Please leave me alone." Dirty died on November 13, 2004, two days before his thirty-sixth birthday. During the weeks surrounding those anniversaries, Buddha becomes unreachable. He suffers from a mix of grief and survivor's guilt that he could have stopped Dirty from taking the drugs. Dirty's death hit Buddha so hard that he moved to Switzerland and stayed almost five years; he felt like he had to get out of New York, where he'd spent so many years with his friend. European rappers sought him out on the strength of his production credits on Wu-Tang and Ol' Dirty albums. He took selfies on ski slopes, got his forearm tattooed with the face of an Albanian national hero. He was either processing, or avoiding facing, the death of his close friend.

The end of Dirty's life is one of the saddest stories in hip-hop. Famous for just over a decade, he spent five of those years in rehab and prison, where by all accounts he stayed clean and attended his drug treatment program. Prison doctors prescribed antipsychotics which caused him to gain over thirty pounds and become stiff and lethargic. In his initial post-prison interviews, he doesn't even look like himself. Dirty said the hardest part of parole was staying off drugs, which he called "the only thing that makes me enjoy myself, because life is boring." Months out of prison he stopped taking the psych meds and rediscovered cocaine. That was the beginning of the end. But even though Buddha admitted to these facts, he'd balked at calling Dirty an addict when I'd used that term during our first conversation at Houlihan's. "Dirty wasn't considered an addict," he'd said. "He knew he still had to go to work and handle his business."

I'd backed off the topic at Houlihan's, and I left Buddha alone after the anniversary of Dirty's death. But weeks later, when I checked back in, he said it still wasn't a good time to get together and work on the book. He had a lot of family stuff happening so it wasn't a good time. Dirty's sister was dying so it wasn't a good time. I kept pushing for interviews, over the phone if nothing else. It took patience. Buddha was easily distracted. "Just double-checking," I texted. "We're on for a phone interview tomorrow at noon?"

"For sure, big bro."

But when noon came there was no answer. I left a voicemail, then another one. Hours later, Buddha finally called back. "Yo, what's up? You've been calling me like crazy."

"We're on for an interview, right?"

"Sure, of course." Buddha coughed. He yawned. "I just woke up."

"Should I call you back later?"

"Nah, man. I'm up now. Let's talk." He talked about groupies. "Dirty was known for not showing up when you booked him to play a show," Buddha told me. We'd roll into town, Dirty would meet a girl, and if the chick was bad we'd wind up staying for two or three days."[7]

"Did Dirty's wife know about the other women?" I asked.

"Yeah, I mean, she knew. She was cool with it as long as he didn't put it in her face."

"He told a judge he had thirteen kids," I prodded.

"Yeah, he had a few. I don't know the exact number. He was a good dad. He loved taking the kids to Coney Island to ride the Cyclone."

"But didn't he also get taken to court over unpaid child support?"

"Yeah, I mean, I don't really want to take the book that direction. People have already written plenty of things trying to tear him down. I want to show people the side they don't know."

"That's exactly what I want to get into the story," I said. "The contradictions that made him a real, three-dimensional person. I mean, in the course of three months he was arrested for attempted assault on his wife and named Citizen of the Week by *Time* magazine."

"We can show both sides. It's just, yo, this book has to come out right if it's got Buddha Monk's name on it."

Buddha started to disappear on me. We scheduled phone interviews but they did not happen. Sometimes he'd text me to reschedule. Sometimes he just wouldn't answer his phone. I began to set aside a two-day window for the process of getting Buddha on the phone and recording an hour of interview. The phone tag was more tedious than the transcription. Buddha would trail off mid-story and abruptly shift from talking to me to talking to someone else in the room. "Hang on, I got to deal with my nephew. Will you please shut the fuck up? I'm on a book right now. I'm writing a book. I'm sorry, Mickey, we're going to have to do this another time. I got to get off the phone."

I knew Buddha was easily distracted, but I worried that he was avoiding me because of the questions I'd asked. I feared I was becoming one of the writers that Buddha couldn't trust, that I had pried too deep, too soon, with my questions about Dirty's court cases and child support. When I asked about Dirty's demons, had Buddha heard me asking, *Was Dirty a stereotype? Was Dirty the kind of black man that white people find entertaining because he confirms their prejudices?* From the moment I first pitched the book idea, Buddha had welcomed me so warmly that I'd seen myself as a very different creature than Dirty's first biographer. *I'm doing this book right,* I had told myself, *Me and Buddha are cool.* Now I was coming to the realization that Buddha had once been cool with that first writer as well.

I'd told myself that the solution to my dilemma was co-authoring with a rapper, but now I feared I was relying on the same optics of reconciliation as Professor Gates and Sergeant Crowley sitting down for a beer. My name and Buddha Monk's were on a book together, but Buddha mistrusted me and I was growing frustrated with his unavailability. When I talked about working with Buddha, I heard myself echoing the old pattern of put-upon writer meets recalcitrant star. Gay Talese may have launched this genre in 1966 with his legendary *Esquire* profile, "Frank Sinatra Has a Cold," for which Sinatra refused to be interviewed. "I may not get the piece we'd hoped for," wrote Talese, "but perhaps, by not getting it—and by getting rejected constantly and by seeing his flunkies protecting his flanks—we will be getting close to the truth about the man."[8] Musicians are uniquely confident that people will wait all night for them—fans do at their concerts, after all. Writers working with musicians get stuck in the same limbo as the crowd calling for an encore. The relationship between bard and patron was never built on equality; Talese just made complaining about our patrons a part of the story. His literary descendants include John Jeremiah Sullivan—who tracked down the reclusive reggae star Bunny Wailer[9]—and Ta-Nehisi Coates, who went for a ride with the masked rapper MF DOOM.[10] Much as I love reading those pieces, I didn't want to find my place in their lineage. I wanted to get back on track and get closer to the truth about Ol' Dirty Bastard by getting Buddha to address his friend's contradictions.

But when I could get Buddha to answer his phone he spent less time talking about Ol' Dirty Bastard than he did asking how soon our checks would arrive.

"When are they gonna send us our money?"

"They said give them six weeks."

"How long has it been?"

"Five weeks?"

"Nah, it's been way longer than that. Do they mean six weeks since they sent us the contract or six weeks since we signed? They're tellin' us this is the way contracts work, but I've signed contracts before. It don't take six weeks to get paid. When they start saying stuff like that, it's a sign that shit is about to go downhill. Listen, I think you should just write me a check for my part and then I'll mail you my check when I get it, because I can't keep waiting around like this. This is ridiculous."

When it wasn't check talk it was small talk. "How you been, man? I been crazy over here. Working on music, family stuff, all that mess." I'd chase him for two weeks and never pin down an interview, but he'd text me to say, "Please tell your wife I wish her a Happy Mother's Day."

"What's the rush?" he asked when I complained. "We got plenty of time to get down these stories by the deadline. I don't just want to get this book done. I want to get it done *right*. It seems like you just want it off your plate."

Stood up one afternoon for a phone interview, I gave up and went to a Haddonfield coffee shop to grade some midterm exams. I'd barely made it through the first one when Buddha called. Inspiration had struck, and he was ready to talk. I rushed to my car. I've learned by interviewing rappers that a car's interior comes close to replicating the conditions of a recording booth, so I sat, parked on the street by the coffee shop, and I called Buddha back.

"Growing up where Dirty and I did," he said, "it breeds a mistrust of the system. It's easy to think the world's out to get you when you growing up in a place where you see other people got so much and you got so little. Where the cops seem like they're out to get you instead of protect and serve."[11] Buddha never doubted Dirty. The man said the cops and the government were out to get him, and Buddha took his friend at his word. He sees a particular prescience to Dirty's line, "In a G Building, taking all types of medicine . . . ," which he sang years before a judge sent him to the G Building, otherwise known as the psychiatric ward at King's County Psychiatric Hospital in Brooklyn. Jailed and institutionalized in the wake of the unsolved murders of Tupac and Biggie, Dirty told *Vibe* magazine he saw a larger conspiracy at play: "I think the government is tryin' to set a nigga up."[12]

"Dirty spent two months in the G Building," Buddha told me as I sat, listening over the phone, in my car. "They prescribed meds that caused him to gain over thirty pounds and become very lethargic and zombie-like. Dirty didn't commit a crime that required being sedated. That was their way to silence him."

I lurched forward. "Shit, Buddha. Hold on a minute. Somebody just hit my car."

"See? I'm telling you," he joked. "People don't want this story told. You got to put this in the book—you're sitting here, working on a book about Ol' Dirty Bastard and your car gets hit. I'm telling you. They're *still* trying to shut us down."

·

It wasn't just the government Buddha mistrusted. He complained about the rappers who'd screwed him out of record deals, out of production credits on songs, out of royalty payments. He complained about being left out of liner notes and interviews. "Let the magazines tell the story, and somehow when I'm not around and the cameras are rolling, Buddha Monk's name gets left out—how many times have you seen the name Buddha Monk in a magazine?" Buddha wanted the credit he felt he'd been robbed of, yet given this platform to tell his own story of the role he played in the life and music of Ol' Dirty Bastard, he would not sit down and focus. Buddha railed against Dirty's first biographer for misquoting him, but now faced with the opportunity to set the record straight he pawned the work off on me: "You're a good writer, man. You know what you're doing. Just read all the old magazine articles about Dirty and make it sound like the way I'd say it."

Buddha's proposition was problematic on several fronts, not the least of which was the prospect of a white professor given license to write in the voice of a black rapper. The consensus among creative-writing professors held that white authors had abused that privilege in past decades when white-written words in black mouths had tended toward minstrelsy. Even in ostensibly anti-slavery texts like *Uncle Tom's Cabin* and *Huckleberry Finn*, white authors wrote dialect that seemed to mock black speech more than attempt to capture it on the page. Having Buddha there to sign off on my work didn't excuse me from that legacy. Even when writing from my taped conversations with Buddha, I had to ask myself how many times a book about Ol' Dirty Bastard—who named an album *Nigga Please*—should include the word *nigga*? These considerations were common for interviewers. Traum Diggs had transcribed so many dozens of rap interviews he said he could no longer bring himself to type the phrase *Know what I mean*. My friend Jonathan Menjivar once worked as an editor on NPR's radio program *Fresh Air*, where the producers placed a limit on the number of *uh*s or *um*s in the final product—enough to make the guests' voices sound human and not robotic, but not enough to make them sound hesitant or inarticulate. *De-umming*, his co-worker dubbed it. What verbal tics could I justify leaving or cutting from Buddha? I had hours of his speech on tape, which I could use to replicate his diction and cadence. But should those sections, written by a white author, contain none of the *niggas* that peppered the rest of the book? I wanted to include them to match Buddha's voice from the tapes, but I didn't want to risk making Buddha sound like a stereotype.

I wanted to capture the way Buddha and Dirty spoke. Buddha described the way Dirty made up his own words—like *pupperize*: to turn a man into a puppet—which he claimed his record label was doing when they asked him to show up for interviews. "That was his Ebonics for the day," said Buddha, laughing. "I had a dude I met in Italy tell me he learned English listening to me and Dirty rap. Our English is broke as fuck on those records. How the fuck you learn English from us?"[13]

Buddha's voice told the story, but I wrote the scenes from Dirty's life for which Buddha was not present. When Buddha disappeared on me, I spent my time researching the prison where Dirty was held and the antipsychotic he was prescribed. I researched the NYPD Street Crimes Unit that fired shots at an unarmed Ol' Dirty Bastard less than two weeks before they shot and killed the unarmed student Amadou Diallo. I studied police reports and eyewitness accounts. I interviewed Dirty's widow Icelene Jones. As the administrator of her late husband's estate, Icelene sought to rein in unlicensed use of his image and control who told Dirty's story. She filed a cease-and-desist order when Wu-Tang Clan announced an Ol' Dirty Bastard hologram would perform with them in concert. She filed an injunction to halt the premiere of an Ol' Dirty Bastard documentary Dirty's cousin Raison Allah had filmed without her approval. Raison planned to commemorate Dirty's birthday by screening his film at the Brooklyn Academy of Music, but Icelene's lawyers shut down the screening with a last-minute cease-and-desist order. To add to the chaos, Dirty's cousin and fellow Wu-Tang Clan member, RZA, spoke to the audience via Skype: "I can't see how a lawyer can stop culture from being spread . . . I can't see how a lawyer, who never met [Dirty] personally, can stop this film from being shown to the public."[14]

"Any likeness," Icelene explained. "Any music, they need to come to me. I'm so accessible. I'm easy to contact. I just want to make that understood. I'm a nice person. It's just that people are doing things without my knowledge."[15] She was perfectly nice to me. She told me stories about her teenage romance with Ol' Dirty Bastard and his grief over the miscarriage she suffered when they were just sixteen years old. She told me he once threw a computer at her. She insisted that no matter how many kids Dirty told a judge he had, the only ones anybody knows for sure are his are the three kids he had with her. She was protective of her husband's legacy, but she wasn't power-hungry and she certainly wasn't money-hungry. In the years since Dirty's death she had gone back to school and earned her nursing degree. She bragged about her two daughters going to college and her son Young Dirty Bastard following in his father's footsteps as a rapper. I asked her what she was doing today, as in at this point in her life, but she took my question literally. "What am I doing *today*? Well, if we had some money we'd go eat some Jamaican food." I tried to get the publisher to buy some never-before-seen family photos from Icelene, but they never came to terms on the money. Mine was a weak effort compared to the foundation the author Rebecca Skloot set up to give money to the descendants of her book's subject, Henrietta Lacks. Not nearly as good as Shea Serrano, author of *The Rap Yearbook*, handing out hundred-dollar bills to fast-food workers and thrift-store shoppers.[16] She wanted her due as the widow and the best I could do was a few hundred dollars for some photos.

The book needed Icelene's perspective, but Buddha wasn't happy I'd called her. "Listen, this is *my* book, Mickey," said Buddha. "This is *my* friend we're writing about. Why are we even trying to talk to Popa Wu? What are you doing calling Icelene?"

Yet despite his possessiveness over Dirty's story, Buddha made good on his promise to introduce me to the only man who could tell us the story no one had told before. "Listen," Buddha said, "I'm not trying to say you fucked up the book. And I know I've been hard to get hold of. But you have to understand I got all kinds of other shit going on with family and all that, and I have to put my music first. But, listen, I'm going to make this up to you. Just wait til you see what I have for you. I'm gonna bring you the story nobody knows—I'm gonna get you the dude who hid Dirty from the cops during that missing week."

The missing week. I'd been asking about it since the first time I spoke to Buddha. In all the published accounts of Dirty's life, no one had been able to pin down just where he was and what he was doing in between two of his most infamous moments. He'd escaped court-mandated rehab in California and showed up onstage with the Wu-Tang Clan in New York. Wu-Tang introduced a surprise guest and Dirty rushed out and did two or three songs and told the crowd, "I can't stay on the stage too long tonight. The cops is after me. The whole fucking world's after me."[17] And he disappeared. He made it offstage, all the way through the venue, and past the cops out front. Six days later he was arrested in Philadelphia in a McDonald's parking lot. No one had ever written about what happened during those six days. This is the story Buddha Monk promised to bring me. In a book full of stories told by Dirty's close friend and right-hand man, this missing week Buddha promised me would be the key piece of the puzzle, the one to take our book from great to amazing.

•

Traum Diggs and I met Buddha in the parking lot of the Palmer Inn in Princeton, New Jersey. In his passenger seat sat a man wearing Army fatigues and majestic dreadlocks. He was K-Blunt, an MC from the Wu-Tang affiliate Zu Ninjaz, and a stranger I best knew for harboring felons. Yes, it was K-Blunt who helped hide Ol' Dirty Bastard when he was on the run from the cops. It was K-Blunt in the driver's seat when Dirty was finally apprehended at that Philly McDonald's.

The receptionist didn't like the looks of us. She looked at Buddha, then me, then back at Traum and K-Blunt, trying, maybe, to determine the connection that led the four of us to share a hotel room. "I need a credit card on file for incidentals."

Buddha looked straight ahead. I waited for him to speak but he didn't speak. He was the one who'd spend the night in the room before he drove back to Worcester in the morning, but I shrugged and gave her my credit card number. "Is that cool?" Buddha asked me.

"Yeah," I said. "Just don't steal any towels." It was a bad joke. Not because hack comics had told jokes about bad airline food and stolen hotel towels for decades, but because I was a white man warning a black man not to steal something. I worried I'd offended him, but in the room he boasted about all the shoplifting he and Blunt had done, in their late thirties, while recording the Brooklyn Zu's album in Orlando: "Beer, licorice, deodorant, whatever, we need it all!" He shifted gears. "Okay, Professor, I'm all yours. We're gonna get these stories recorded and get this book written and get the rest of our money. We got us a hotel room. We're gonna drink some liquor and tell some stories, and oh, shit, I almost forgot. Smell this." He produced a baggie of marijuana and offered it to Traum.

"Goddamn," Traum exclaimed, and took a second deep sniff. I bit my tongue, thinking of my credit card on file and the threat of a

$300 cleaning fee for the non-smoking room. Let it go, I told myself. Buddha has brought you a surprise guest, and the man's name is Blunt. There will be smoking in this room. Buddha stuffed the weed back in his satchel and led into his reminiscences the way he usually did—he remembered nothing so clearly as being forgotten. Busta Rhymes never did the song he promised Buddha he'd do with him. RZA didn't give Buddha the production credits or royalties he was owed. Buddha spent long nights in the studio working on production for Dirty's album, but in the liner notes the credits read "Produced by the RZA, Recording Engineer: The RZA, Mixing Engineer: The RZA featuring the RZA."

"The problem with this industry," Buddha said, "is that the cameras are just focused on getting Busta Rhymes and not panning out to the whole team. They want superstars. But who's helping that scene come together? Same thing with Dirty. I bust my ass all night to get a song right, and we walk out the studio door and who's getting all the fame? Dirty. He's getting all the star traction and nobody really realizes. Nobody asks, *how did you do this song? Who did you work with on it?* They just see the star as the genius. Dirty wasn't like that. Dirty would always be like, *This is Buddha Monk, this is my brother, he be doing all the producing.*"[18]

Buddha told us Dirty cost him a record deal when he didn't show up as promised for his meeting with the label execs. Dirty didn't show up to film his cameo for Buddha's music video, but when they were home from tour he stopped by Buddha's place and handed him some money.

Buddha and Blunt agreed that they just couldn't stay mad at Dirty.

"I still can't believe he's gone," said Buddha.

"I can't believe it's been almost ten years," said Blunt.

"I remember staying up all night in the studio ordering pizza with broccoli. That was Dirty's favorite—broccoli pizza. We must have ordered a hundred of those." Dirty was their friend and they missed him. He'd been in bad shape, Blunt said, when he walked out of the rehab facility in California. He flew to New York and called Blunt from a payphone asking him to help sneak him out of the city. His face was all over the news. Blunt had him well hidden in New Jersey until Dirty insisted on taking a ride into Philly, where his arrest at McDonald's on Gray's Ferry Avenue sent him to prison for over two years. "He just had to have a damn fish filet sandwich," Blunt said, shaking his head. Dirty was wanted by police on both coasts, yet insisted on leaving the safety of rural New Jersey to ride with Blunt to a car shop in Philly. The trip went smoothly until Dirty insisted they stop for a McDonald's Filet-O-Fish. Blunt tried to rush him, Dirty took his time going inside to order his sandwich, use the restroom, and even try to get a girl's phone number. When he was back in the car and ready to head home, two police cruisers pulled up and blocked Blunt's car. Dirty handed the officer a fake ID, but she recognized him from the posters on her son's wall. She and her partner pulled Dirty and Blunt out of the car and took them to the station for booking. "How did you know we were at that McDonald's?" Blunt asked.

"Well, a cashier called the radio station and said she just sold Ol' Dirty Bastard a fish filet sandwich."[19]

I had read almost every word printed about Ol' Dirty Bastard, and these were the stories no one had told. They weren't Buddha's stories or Blunt's stories or Icelene's stories—they worked together to tell Dirty's story. The only way to get to the truth was to step back from the tug-of-war of whose story it was to tell and let the true story emerge by letting each other speak. I was not above wanting my own credit as well. I frowned when the publisher listed the book's authors as Buddha Monk with Mickey Hess, rather than Buddha Monk *and* Mickey Hess. I had no problem with Buddha's name coming first. I went into the project with second billing—of *course* Buddha's name would go first—but after all the work I did without Buddha, I couldn't accept a *with*. I would never disregard the fact that it was Buddha's book more than mine, but I didn't like feeling dispensable. I'd worked hard for that *and*. I'd earned that *and*. Let the people tell the stories, Buddha had said time and again, and Buddha Monk's name gets left out. Now I knew how he felt.

I finally went to Worcester. The day after Christmas, the book finished except for my introduction and Buddha's afterword, I went to Buddha's house on Pleasant Street and immediately spilled an entire beer on his living room carpet and he pointed and laughed like he was delighted to see it happen. I brought him a Christmas present: a fifth of Kentucky bourbon. I met his girlfriend Atlantis Price, the daughter of a jazz musician and a civil rights activist. I met Buddha's little blue-and-white parakeet, named—I kid you not—Patience. I met the teenage rapper, King Fresh, who Buddha took in after his mom moved out of town. "He's been living with us for two years now," Buddha explained. "We make it work as a family." Atlantis fried some fish and we ate dinner in their living room with their Christmas tree lit and their stockings hung and by the end of the night we had finished our book. "Thank you," said Buddha. "I needed to tell this story, and without you it would not have been possible."

On the tenth anniversary of Dirty's death, Buddha and I held our book release at the Billie Holiday Theater in Brooklyn, a few blocks from where Buddha and Dirty grew up, a few blocks from the corner where Dirty once helped lift a burning car off a four-year-old girl. Dirty's sister Monique stood up and introduced herself. I met Dirty's daughter Taniqua, her husband Shamiel, and Dirty's little three-year-old grandson Noah. I met Buddha's mom and uncle. I sat back while

Buddha held forth in the Q&A, telling better stories than the ones he told in the book. I patted his back, awkwardly, when he began to weep, wailing, "I just miss my brother Dirty so much right now." The publisher got Buddha and me booked on *The Ed Lover Show* with Ed Lover, the legendary *Yo! MTV Raps* host I used to watch every afternoon after school, and the man who introduced me to more hip-hop than anyone. It was a dream come true. Ed posed for pictures with Buddha and me. He rapped along with the Wu-Tang song he was playing on the air— pausing to point out the genius in Dirty's lines before he introduced us, his special guests. "We're here with Buddha Monk and Mickey Hess," he said. "And I was glad to see Buddha Monk's name on the book, because honestly I don't know if I would have read it if it was just Mickey Hess."

He was right, much as it hurt to hear. I couldn't let my ego get in the way. I remembered when Buddha and I sat down together and called Dirty's mentor Popa Wu, but he'd balked at giving an interview, asking the same question Icelene had asked when I first contacted her: "What if I want to write my own book?"

"Well," replied Buddha. "You need to get you a professor."

I was a medium, a conduit to the bookstore shelves. I was a white author who'd never met Dirty and was sure I could tell his story better than his first biographer, a white woman who'd barely met him. Imagine the tense emotions between his best friend, cousin, and widow, all fighting to tell the story—*their* story—of the man they knew. But in the end it wasn't their story either; it was Dirty's story, and his story was a microcosm of hip-hop's, with rappers, professors, and critics fighting over who got to tell it and how.

Eleven

REVISIONIST HISTORY

It wasn't so much that Americans forgot their history as they chose to remember it differently. In preparation for the town tricentennial, Haddonfield removed its welcome signs from each end of town. Aha, I said, they're updating the logo. I had long looked askance at the drawing of a white pioneer woman offering a basket of food to three Native Americans, one of whom strokes his chin as if to say, *Hmm, I don't know about this, guys* . . . But new signs went up and the logo remained the same. Weeks later, on a walk, my wife and I found the old signs in the trash behind Public Works. They looked like perfectly good signs, so why replace them? My wife, always quicker than me, noticed the old sign's "Settled in 1682" would have hit the three-hundred-year mark decades ago, but the new sign switched to "Founded in 1713." With the change of a verb and a date, these Republican bastards got to celebrate two tricentennials. Might as well make it all up. Whether you call it settling or founding, people were already living here before Elizabeth Haddon moved in and named the place after herself.

Haddonfield outlawed alcohol just after the Civil War, yet the town's historical markers commemorate revolution-era bars: the Indian King Tavern, where the state of New Jersey ratified the Declaration of Independence; Gibbs Tavern and Smithy, where drunks molded hot metal into shoes for horses. After a hundred years of drinking and founding taverns, Haddonfielders apparently woke up hung over, took a good look at themselves and their misshaped metalwork, and said, "Okay, boys, this is ridiculous. We ain't getting a lick of work done . . . horses running around barefoot . . . I hate to say it, by God, but we've got to quit bringing beer into town." In order to drink hard liquor, my friend Rob and I had to walk across the border to a neighboring town. Our town's pretend tricentennial clouding his judgment, Rob convinced himself that a young hipster's old-timey moustache was a fake. The idea of a man's cultivating such a moustache struck Rob as sillier than wearing a toy moustache to a drinking establishment. "Only one way to find out," I told Rob. We watched the man stroke his waxy handlebars. "Walk over there and try to yank it off him."

My town won't let me drink and my state won't let me pump gas or shoot fireworks. What kind of state won't let a man brandish sparklers on the Fourth of July? Worse, this town so in love with its Revolutionary War history let a man open a British gift shop where I can spend my money on Union Jack T-shirts and official Guinness pint glasses for the beer they can't sell me. Right here in Haddonfield, along the very road where the Continental Army used to round up and imprison the enemies of liberty (deserters, British loyalists, and the like), a British flag flies today.

The American Revolution happened a long time ago, of course. A British flag flying today in America doesn't mean what it meant in the 1700s. What a difference a few hundred years makes. We'll buy trinkets from a local Anglophile, but in a less expensive town near ours, a high school suspended a student for flying a Confederate flag. I find it briefly reassuring (after all, my wife and I had once considered moving to that town) then not reassuring at all. The student told his local newspaper that, sure, he can see why some people might see his flag as a symbol of hate and oppression. But he said he didn't mean it like that, he didn't mean it the way it looked.

•

Haddonfield infants wear onesies advertising the elite universities that educated their parents and grandparents in buildings named after old racists. They wear Ramones and Run DMC onesies with no choice in the matter, their parents using children's apparel as a beacon to draw in other parents who share their nostalgia. We push strollers past each other with a wink and a nod and congratulate ourselves that our town's high-schoolers aren't flying Confederate flags. It didn't happen in Haddonfield, we tell ourselves, but have we just traded the overt for the insidious? At the playground at the end of our street, I saw a child wearing an AIG soccer jersey. AIG—a prime player in the subprime mortgage crisis, was so brazenly crooked it paid its CEOs bonuses with funds from the government bailout. AIG's CEO told the news he felt victimized by the public outcry: "everybody out there with their pitchforks and their hangman nooses," he said, "sort of like what we did in the Deep South."[1] This from the corporation whose mortgage-backed security scams hit black borrowers disproportionately hard. In fact, AIG settled a racial discrimination suit to the tune of $7.1 million, with $6.1 million in restitution to the black borrowers they scammed and $1 million in funding to "organizations that provide credit counseling, financial literacy and other educational programs that target blacks."[2] After the bailout and the bonuses, Manchester United found a new sponsor for its soccer team and removed the AIG logo from its jerseys, but the AIG logo is still out there on the throwback jerseys worn by fans who shrug and say *I don't know anything about subprime mortgage scandals; I just like watching millionaires kick a ball around.*

In the rock-paper-scissors of where to raise one's daughter, does AIG shirt beat Confederate flag? Your money ended up in my pockets, said the AIG CEO, and you came after me the way white people used to chase down black people. It was white men who terrorized black men with nooses and burned women at the stake. Yet when criticized, white men in positions of power were quick to cry *lynch mob* or *witch hunt*. It was tempting to detach words and symbols from history, the way TV did the Confederate flag in my childhood. I used to play with a little orange racecar with the Confederate flag painted all over it. I didn't know what those stars and bars meant any more than my daughter knows the Ironman action figure I bought her isn't the German rapper Lance Butters. My favorite childhood TV show *The Dukes of Hazzard* was set in Georgia, but I was proud to learn a town near mine was named Hazard, Kentucky, proud to carry my embossed metal lunchbox depicting the show's pair of rambunctious cousins and their car with the Confederate flag on its roof. I was proud that a man who lived in Science Hill once drove a tour bus for Waylon Jennings, who sang the *Dukes* theme song my whole second-grade class knew by heart: "Just some good old boys," it went, "never meaning no harm."

When elementary school taught us the Civil War it was hard not to see the Rebels like the Duke Boys: noble and misunderstood underdogs. Even while the same lessons taught us Abraham Lincoln was a hero for freeing the slaves. Even while we rooted for Harriet Tubman and her underground railroad. The slaves were the ultimate Cinderella story, and we loved them for that, same as we loved the Confederacy for having endured such a crushing defeat. We were second graders in a country born of rebellion and proud of it: how could we not root for the Rebels? I stayed up late to watch the melodramatic TV miniseries *North and South*. I was thrilled to see the tattered Confederate dollar my grandmother was embarrassed to see I'd found in an old box of keepsakes in her attic. I played Civil War with my cousins and I always wanted to be the South. I loved the gray of their uniforms, the stars of the stars and bars. These symbols hold power for a young white man in the South: you grow up told it means one thing, and it's hard to let that thing go and accept that it means something else.

I don't know what happened to my Granny's Confederate dollar after she died, but if I had it today I would treasure it. I wouldn't fly it from my pickup truck, but I would treasure it. I treasure the Lance Butters T-shirt my daughter bought me for Father's Day, one of the first gifts she bought for me with her own money. She and I know it's Lance Butters no matter if the tag says Ironman, but what will other people see? If someone comes up to me and says, "I'll have you know Ironman kidnapped and murdered my great-grandparents," I'm not going to tell them, "To me it's not Ironman. It's just a German boy in a mask."

"And if that weren't enough," they might add, "a generation later a group of men wearing Ironman T-shirts beat my grandfather to death because they said he looked too long at a white woman. They dragged my father to death behind a pickup truck, and they burned down my sister's church. Maybe not every man who wears an Ironman shirt is a killer, but seeing that symbol rattles me so bad I don't know whether I want to run or fight or just stand here shaking my head."

In reality my Lance Butters shirt seems to announce I am a particular type of grown man who wishes to discuss comic-book superheroes with other grown men—which could not be further from the truth. But no matter how much I try to protest I have no knowledge of comic-book lore—or any desire to learn it—once these guys get started I find myself trapped. I've never worn a Confederate-flag shirt, but I imagine it might spark conversations just as fanatical. I could say it means whatever I want, but that doesn't change the fact that it already meant something.

.

In line at a Haddonfield Starbucks, I wore a Rider Black Student Union T-shirt. A white man standing in line behind me said, "I hope they got a *white* student union too." Okay, one, it tends to make people uncomfortable when a group of white folks comes together to celebrate being white. Two, I am a white man wearing the shirt, so how exactly does it exclude whites? Three, the Black Student Union formed in response to "Nigger Night," a fraternity hazing tradition in which white pledges wore blackface and played slave to their prospective brothers.[3]

There was a popular song about a misunderstood T-shirt—in 2013, twenty years after Rider shut down Nigger Night, Brad Paisley's "Accidental Racist" made an attempt to shrug and say, *I'm just a simple old country boy. I don't understand such sophisticated issues as race relations.* When he puts on his Confederate flag T-shirt, he sang, "the only thing I meant to say is I'm a Skynyrd fan." But that doesn't sound like an accident; to say I know this offends you, I know what it means to you, but it means something different to me . . . that's not accidental. It's purposefully defiant. "Purposefully Defiant Racist" just doesn't have the same ring to it, I reckon, but there's nothing accidental in the actions the song describes. If a man's willing to wear a symbol he knows people see as racist, he's willing to be mistaken for a racist. It doesn't matter how he personally interprets the symbol. The swastika existed long before the Nazis adopted it, but I'm not going to print one on a T-shirt and hope I get the chance to explain my intentions to people.

"It ain't like you and me can rewrite history," sings Brad Paisley. "It ain't like I can walk a mile in someone else's skin."

LL Cool J, in his guest verse on Paisley's song, responds as if the necklace he wore carried the same history as the flag waved by the Southern states who sought to preserve slavery: "If you don't judge my gold chains, I'll forget the iron chains."

"Racism is a lot of things," wrote M. K. Asante in an open letter to LL Cool J in *The New York Times*, "cancerous, insidious, learned, dangerous, destructive, dumb, vicious, institutional—but not accidental. Neither is your idea of forgetting 'the iron chains.' Forgetting our collective past, no matter how good, bad, or ugly those narratives may be—is mutually assured destruction. We must study our past, remembering, as Maya Angelou put it, that 'history, despite its wrenching pain, cannot be unlived, but if faced with courage, need not be lived again.'"[4] Whether or not a person sporting it on his T-shirt wants to pretend to forget it, the Confederate flag stands for slavery. So do the flags of Great Britain, Portugal, The Netherlands, and the United States. We like to limit our sense of America's associations with the slave trade to the South because the Confederacy is dead and gone, problem solved. The Northerners get to think *we won, get over it, get a load of this hick and his vestigial flag.* Never mind that Kentucky entered the Civil War neutral and spent most of the war under Union control. Never mind that New Jersey didn't let go of its slaves any sooner than the states in the South. The further into the South—and the past—we can push slavery, the more we can convince ourselves it has nothing to do with us, we can pack all that history inside one flag and bury it somewhere.

I've seen Confederate flags fly in New Jersey, a state that once fought a war against the people who waved that flag. I've seen Confederate flags fly in West Virginia, a state literally formed by breaking away from the Confederacy. Facts don't faze us. After my dad died, I took an electric Gibson guitar he'd left in the body shop. It needed extensive, expensive fretwork before it would be playable, so it stayed on a shelf in my basement. I never touched it, but it was my dad's. A decade later I'd moved that guitar from Kentucky to New Jersey and never had it repaired. It stayed in my basement and I took it out of its case and looked at it whenever I rediscovered it in the process of moving from apartment to apartment to house. When I had a guitar-playing houseguest I'd present it to them. *Look at my dad's guitar.*

Once, when visiting Kentucky, I described the guitar to my cousin Matt. He cocked his head and said, "Why, that's David Gooch's guitar."

Matt told me David Gooch had hired Daddy to repair his guitar. Daddy died and the guitar went missing so quickly that David assumed somebody stole it while we were at the funeral home. Daddy didn't live long enough to do any work on the guitar, and he certainly never played it, but even after learning its actual origins, I refused to give back the guitar.

I stole a guitar simply because I believed it had belonged to my father. When presented with facts to the contrary, I still could not let go of the story I'd invented, or the meaning I'd attached to that guitar. Can Americans return to an earlier greatness when our very story of that greatness was shaped from theft and lies? Black Americans have long been erased from our nation's history, but that effort may be no more about erasing the contributions of black people than it is about erasing the crimes of whites.

White Americans have felt so entitled to steal any aspects of black culture that it took me a long time to understand what was not mine. When I was a teenager, the glossy, gatefold inserts from rap cassettes tried to sell me fashion accessories: my *Niggaz4Life* cassette included an order form for N.W.A. beanies and sunglasses; the Jungle Brothers included an address to order Jungle Beads—items my mother assured me were not meant for a white child in Kentucky. But weren't they? "Black kids buy the records," said Ice-T, "but the white kids buy the cassette, the CD, the album, the tour jacket, the hats, everything."[5] Fifty percent of his sales, he claimed, came from white fans.

Choosing my own shirts was problematic in that Aunt Linda brought me perfectly good hand-me-downs from my older cousins, while I picked ones Mom found too expensive and controversial. Standing beside her in the young men's section of JCPenney, I held up a Homey the Clown T-shirt. Homey was an *In Living Color* character created by Pryor's old partner Paul Mooney and played by Damon Wayans, the comedic genius whose other characters mocked gay men and the physically challenged. Homey, a scowling black parolee in a clown suit, performed at children's birthday parties but skipped the balloon animals to launch into lessons about how The Man was trying to keep Homey down. Mom narrowed her eyes at the cartoonish black face smeared with clown make-up. "I don't think you're supposed to wear that."

So I wore my older cousin's white polo shirt that proclaimed "I Love Hilton Head Island," although I'd never in my life gone there. I could not swim and avoided situations where I'd be expected to take off my shirt. But I knew that Hilton Head was where the rich kids at my school went for their beach vacations. They tended to pair their souvenir shirts with our school's athletic insignia, as if to say, *Look at us: we take pride both in where we've been and where we've come back to.* Nodding at my shirt, one of our beach-loving athletes asked me, "You go down to Hilton Head?"

"Oh yeah," I replied, in a tone that said *Of course, doesn't everyone?*

"Which resort?"

"Oh, you know. Down by the beach."

"Well, they're all by the beach," he said, grinning. "What's its name, though?"

"Beach . . . Haven?" I suggested, hoping he didn't know better. "It's one a lot of people don't know."

"Do any scuba diving down there?"

"Sure did."

I tried to sneak through the lunch line at school without standing next to any of my friends; I didn't want them to hear me say I was on Free Lunch—even the ones who were on Free Lunch themselves. My friend Chad once picked up an empty food stamp booklet he saw in the back seat of our car. I saw him see it. He saw me see him see it. The booklet didn't say food stamps; it said Food *Coupons*. I sat there devising a scheme to explain how my family wasn't poor but just members of some thrifty money-savers club, but it never came to that. Chad was a good enough friend that the entire car ride he didn't look at me or the food stamps. He didn't even look like he was trying *not* to look.

•

All that time I spent trying to look richer than I was, rappers spent trying to look poorer. In 1993, Bo$$ rapped about drive-by shootings and body bags; she said she didn't give a fuck—not a single, solitary fuck—but her dad told the *Wall Street Journal* she actually gave so much of a fuck that she'd studied ballet and piano and spent three years in college.

Her mother, a church deacon, added, "We were sending her money whenever she asked for it."[6]

Newspapers loved to take down rappers. Never mind that Bo$$ had already revealed—on Track One of her album, no less—everything her parents revealed to the *Wall Street Journal*. Never mind that she bookended her album with answering machine messages from her parents telling her they raised her to know better than make gangsta rap. When rappers wrote songs about poverty, reporters scrambled to find any shred of wealth in their upbringing. When rappers showed stacks of money in their videos, reporters and rappers alike scrambled to assure us it's not really their money, they're not really that rich. It felt good to expose a fraud.

Journalists and rappers alike ferreted out the ballet lessons rappers hid—Jay-Z showed us an old picture of Mobb Deep's Prodigy in a leotard. There was nothing wrong with ballet, necessarily. Rappers didn't hate the arts. These skeletons in rappers' closets spoke less for achievement than advantage: taking dance classes was less of a problem than having been able to *afford* dance classes. Studying hard in a private school was less of a problem than having been able to *afford* private school. Rappers were supposed to start out with nothing, then get rich and buy lots of things so that everyone knew.

Journalists loved to make rappers look like liars, but the courts were perfectly happy to take rappers at their word. Rappers swore they were telling the truth, so it was convenient to put rappers in jail for the things they said in songs. In 2012, Killer Reese rapped, "I'm not bragging, I'm confessing";[7] just months later, his group King Fantastic tweeted a mailing address to use "if you would like to send Reese money in prison."[8]

Even amateur rappers saw their lyrics used against them in court: a police officer pulls a man over and finds a little marijuana in the glove compartment, so he enters into evidence the notebook he finds in the passenger seat—a notebook filled with the man's rhyming fantasies of being a cartel kingpin. It's hard to imagine a poet or novelist being arrested on similar charges, yet Erik Nielson, a professor at the University of Richmond, has identified hundreds of cases of rap lyrics being entered as evidence: "What prosecutors have found," he told PBS, "is that when they can introduce rap lyrics as evidence, particularly in situations where they don't have strong evidence otherwise, they are still able to secure convictions."[9] We love to say it's all fake until we can get something out of believing it's real.

•

Rappers didn't like when white people tried to look blacker. Russell Simmons recalls first meeting the Beastie Boys, who he'd make rap's first white superstars: "They were wearing shiny red sweatsuits and doo rags on their heads. They had talent, but they came across as the worst sort of blackface band. It was like they were making fun of black people. A lot of people thought they were racist, that they were putting down black culture. I taught them how to fucking walk and how to fucking talk. I convinced the black community that they were real."[10] A black man taught three white men to walk and talk like white men in a way that black audiences found convincing; or at least he convinced them that his white rappers weren't trying to steal or mock some stereotypical notion of the way black people walked and talked. Black rappers remained cool with the Beastie Boys even as Vanilla Ice crashed and burned trying to mimic black rappers. "You know why I could fuck with them?" asked Q-Tip. "They don't try to be black. They're just themselves."[11]

Rappers didn't like when black people tried to look whiter: "Miss blue eyes, how'd you do that?" asked Paris in 1990; quit getting nose jobs, said Digital Underground in 1992. Even the white rappers in 3rd Bass joined in, in 1990, when they claimed on "The Gas Face" that the devil himself schemed to get black people to put in blue contact lenses and straighten their hair. Beyonce, two decades later, sang, "I like my baby hair with baby hair and Afros. I like my Negro nose with Jackson Five nostrils."

Hair was a big deal. In 2015, America found out the NAACP chapter president Rachel Dolezal was really a white woman who'd fooled us by doing her hair like a black woman. She even gave a talk at Eastern Washington University—while people still believed she was black—about the power of black hairstyles. Whatever color she was, Dolezal was by many accounts doing some good for black people until her parents told a reporter she was really a white woman. Hounded by reporters and fired from her job teaching Africana studies at EWU, Dolezal finally admitted she was born white but had come to *identify* as black. As for her hair? "This is a weave," she said. "And I do it myself."[12]

"Where'd you get that nigger haircut," classmates asked my white friend Chris, when he came to ninth grade with his hair in the lopsided Gumby cut that was popular in early Nineties rap videos. Our classmates laughed at him so hard that he claimed he'd fallen asleep in the barber's chair, that no matter how much he loved rap he would never of his own volition walked into that barbershop and asked for a black person's haircut. Our classmates were not offended by his cultural appropriation but by the idea that a white teenager would deign to wear his hair like someone he was so clearly *better* than. Why, they wondered, would he want to look anything other than white? The motivations of my classmates were different from those of Dolezal's critics. For Dolezal's critics, her hairstyle was *black*, and thus noble and worth defending as property. For my classmates, Chris's hairstyle was *black*, and thus undesirable and ridiculous. Each situation reinforced the wall between white people and black hairstyles, whether the critics were white or black, whether they were motivated by protecting black culture or protecting white culture. Chris came to school the next day with his head shaved down to the skin. He, like Dolezal, had done it himself.

At its worst, policing hairstyles reinforced separation between the races and fostered resentment from white people who just couldn't understand the concept of something not being theirs for the taking. At its best, it protected black culture from further pillaging by whites and told the ancestors of slave-owners that they didn't get to sport dreadlocks without risking rebuke. Slaves brought from Africa didn't even get to keep the names their parents gave them, yet so many whites felt slighted that they could no longer say the n-word in public. White people seem to revel in a particular martyrdom when denied the right to use the word with impunity. Black artists had taken a common name whites called them to dehumanize them and made it the riskiest word a white American could say. Black rap stars broadcast the word to an extent matched by no pop culture genre before it, yet made clear the word was now the exclusive property of black Americans. This genius strategy balanced censorship and overuse along racial lines, and thus defeated the contradictions of earlier calls by white people to defuse the word simply by refusing to censor it.

In the early Sixties, Lenny Bruce proclaimed, "It's the suppression of the word that gives it the power, the violence, the viciousness. if President Kennedy would just go on television, and say, 'I would like to introduce you to all the niggers in my cabinet,' and if he'd just say 'nigger

nigger nigger nigger nigger' to every nigger he saw . . . til nigger didn't mean anything anymore, then you could never make some six-year-old black kid cry because somebody called him a nigger at school."[13] Bruce didn't adopt his anti-censorship stance simply for the sake of one joke; in fact, he ruined his life fighting to free the words an American was restricted from saying on stage. But his joke missed the mark in that Americans had already tried what he suggested—white people already went around saying that word with impunity, and six-year-old black kids still wept.

Black journalist Belva Davis recounts hearing Bruce open his act with this joke at the jazz club Basin Street West in San Francisco. "I was shocked speechless," she wrote, "which I suppose is what Bruce intended."[14] Davis interviewed Bruce after the show and found him combative when she asked how he could use such a hurtful word onstage just for its comedic shock value. Bruce, she wrote, "pretty much said that he didn't care if he hurt anybody because that was his act, baby—take it or leave it."[15] In her 2012 memoir, Davis looked back at Bruce's act in the newer context of black comedian Chris Rock and the legions of black hip-hop stars who'd made the word so much a part of their acts. "I would argue," she wrote, "that a half-century after Lenny Bruce thought he was disarming the word, it has lost none of its lacerating power to wound."[16]

Thirty years after Lenny Bruce made his joke, rappers had rebranded the word and given it a new swagger. In 1991, when I was sixteen years old, I sat in my Kentucky bedroom and listened to the gangsta rap group N.W.A. use the word "nigga" sixty-four times in one song, "Niggaz 4 Life." The song ended with Eazy-E sing-songing, to the tune of an old Dr. Pepper jingle, "I'm a nigga, he's a nigga, she's a nigga, we some niggas, wouldn't you like to be a nigga too?" In 1993, when asked about rap's frequent use of the n-word, KRS-ONE predicted, "In another five to ten years, you're going to see youth in elementary schools spelling it out on their vocabulary tests. It's going to be that accepted by the society."[17] But two decades later, America's first black president said the word in a podcast interview and the pundits gasped. "Racism," said President Obama. "We are not cured of it. And it's not just a matter of it not being polite to say 'nigger' in public. That's not the measure of whether racism still exists or not. It's not just a matter of overt discrimination. Societies don't overnight completely erase everything that happened 200–300 years prior."[18] Celebrating America's progress in politeness risked confusing that one word for all the history it symbolized, yet the scandals and sanctions over that single word also fostered, in some small part, an unprecedented deference on the part of whites: after all those decades of requiring submissive yessirs from black Americans, there was finally one thing white Americans were not allowed to say.

Hip-hop was part of a tradition of obliterating the word by foregrounding it so much in black texts that it lost its impact when spoken by whites. In 1964, the comedian and civil rights warrior Dick Gregory named his autobiography *Nigger*, writing that people had called him that word so much as a child that he thought it must be his real name and Richard was just what they called him at home. "We're ready," he wrote in his introduction, "to change a system where a white man can destroy a black man with a single word. Nigger. When we're through, Momma. There won't be any niggers anymore." Fifty-two years later, in 2016, the University of Seattle suspended white Dean Jodi Kelly for recommending Gregory's book to a black student. Gregory—who was close friends with Malcolm X and who'd been beaten and arrested with Dr. Martin Luther King Jr. in Birmingham, Alabama, in 1963—wrote in Dean Kelly's defense, arguing that the campus's black student group had diffused its objective of a more diverse curriculum by focusing so much attention on one dean recommending one book: "Ya'll black folks need to learn who your true oppressors are," he wrote. "The Dean, who had read my autobiography, gave good advice. I contacted Dean Kelly directly. I wanted to make sure she didn't disrespect the title of my book by using it to be a closeted bigot. I will be eighty-four years old this year, and I have battled true racism, and, trust me, this ain't it."[19] A closeted bigot, resentful that white people were not longer allowed to say a word they'd given so much power—might keep a copy of *Nigger* on hand as a prop, as a device to use a slur against black students without having to say the word herself. Gregory had "battled true racism," overt and violent and vicious racism, but he didn't mean that the true racism remained in the past. A little over a year after he responded to the University of Seattle students, he spent his last week alive in the hospital, as news channels showed footage of the white nationalist march on Charlottesville, Virginia. He died five days after the anti-racist counterprotestor Heather Heyer, who was killed when a racist sympathizer drove his car into the crowd of people standing up against racism. It was 2017, fifty-three years after Gregory used his book's intro to promise his mom that he and the Civil Rights movement would obliterate the word "nigger," and the President of the United States described the white nationalist movement that descended on Charlottesville as including "some very fine people" that the press treated "absolutely unfairly."[20]

In 2007, a decade before the funerals for Heather Heyer and Dick Gregory, the NAACP held a funeral for the word "nigger."[21] But the word roared back from its grave. Nas, in the spirit of Dick Gregory, planned to use the word for the title of his 2008 album: "You see how white boys ain't mad at *cracker* 'cause it don't have the same [sting] as *nigger*? I want *nigger* to have less meaning [than] *cracker*," he told *MTV News*. "We're taking power [away] from the word."[22] What Nas called "sting," Dave Chappelle called "venom": "I'm gonna have to say," Chappelle told *Inside the Actor's Studio* host James Lipton, "that if used incorrectly, the venom's still there." History shows that it is impossible to de-fang a word that white Americans used for so long to dehumanize black Americans—a word that was used as mobs of whites murdered more than 4,000 blacks between 1877 and 1950.[23] As for the question of why white people in 2018 can't say the word without risking rebuke, don't forget that white people had their turn. They invented this word and the hate that it carries. Now any attempt by a black person to reclaim the word as the sole property of blacks fosters resentment among whites who feel it's only fair they get to say it with impunity as well. But the rights of the speaker (to freedom of speech) don't trump the rights of the listener (to freedom from hate speech). Think of it this way: if you're holding a snake that's killed more than 4,000 people since emancipation and continues to let cops kill with impunity—but you're sure it's now been de-fanged, or it's bitten so many people its venom has worn out—would you toss it to a stranger? Would you toss it to a descendent of the people it killed?

•

I grew up hearing racist jokes, so I saw *In Living Color* as an extension of the jokes my dad's friends would tell in his garage. Homey the Clown was funny to me because I'd grown up on jokes about black ex-convicts stealing hubcaps, not because I understood, in any sense, that Homey's creator Paul Mooney was making a joke *about* those old jokes. Blackness, for the white adults I'd heard tell jokes, was a punchline in itself. So I stole jokes from black comedians I watched on TV and repeated them at school. In 1990, I was fifteen years old and *nigger* was the funniest word I'd ever heard. Play a Richard Pryor album and tell me I'm wrong. *That Nigger's Crazy* and *Bicentennial Nigger*—copies of copies passed down from longhaired uncles, handed off in school hallways same as Geto Boys cassettes. I taped *In Living Color* every Sunday, snatched snippets from *Blazing Saddles* and used them to relentlessly prank-call my white friend's white dad:

"Hello?"

"Up yours, nigger."

"Excuse me?"

"Aw, that uppity nigger just hit me on the head with a shovel."

"I think you might have the wrong phone number."

I was a black comedian's nightmare, the reason Pryor came home from a tour of Africa in 1980 and swore he'd stop using the word. The reason Chappelle walked away from a fifty-million-dollar contract for his show that kept the word funny in 2006. Chappelle said he quit because he could no longer tell if his white fans were laughing in the right way, or for the right reasons. I would like to say I was laughing at the sheer absurdity of racism, at the juxtaposition of an anachronistic term with a politically-correct society, at calling a white man a nigger. But I was fifteen years old and my thinking was not that sophisticated. I was making fun of my classmates, the ones I thought I was better than, the real live versions of the white characters who were the rednecks and fools and buffoons in the comedy series and rap-album skits that I loved so much. TV and music made racism so laughable that it became instinct for me to snicker when I saw it in real life. At school, when the AC went out, a classmate announced, "Boys, I'm sweating like a nigger on election day." I laughed, and as far as he knew I was laughing with him, laughing at the wit and humor of his offhand remark, which I'd repeat for my younger sister in a fake country accent and with a smug sense of superiority.

My sense of humor was shared by my friend James, who had moved to Kentucky from Cincinnati and was as amused by the farm-boys as I was. It was the humor of self-defense—the joke was that we were so much smarter, so much more cultured and forward-thinking than the other folks where we lived. A classmate in a John Deere cap thought it was funny to write a slur on the back of his notebook—*Fuck U, Niger*—but I thought it was funnier that he misspelled it and walked around all day looking like he hated an African river. James and I told ourselves we were laughing on an ironic level, but we were still laughing after that level peeled away. Still, anytime somebody suggested I was laughing at racist jokes as opposed to laughing at racists, I told myself they just didn't get it.

My childhood idols the Beastie Boys spent their career trying to live down the misogyny of their first album, *Licensed to Ill*. "When we're talking about women or whatever," said Beastie Boy MCA in 1987, "we're creating a fantasy, so far-fetched and overboard that the 99 percent of people that understand it understand that there is such a thing as humor, such a thing as parody."[24]

"The only thing that upsets me," added Mike D, "is that we might have reinforced certain values of some people in our audience when our own values were actually totally different. There were tons of guys singing along to 'Fight for Your Right' who were oblivious to the fact it was a total goof on them."[25]

But the obliviousness went both ways, according to Ad-Rock. "Then we had our *become-what-you-hate* moment. We were making fun of a frat-boy mentality, and suddenly we were the thing we were making fun of."[26]

I would like to say my jokes were victimless. After all, seeing a black person in Pulaski County during my childhood was rare. I might as well have been telling jokes about Martians. But then Christina moved to our school. She transferred and made friends. Whatever people said about her they whispered behind her back. Like the joke James cracked when the principal announced over the staticky intercom, "Lost and Found: there is a black, girl's watch in the office. A black, girl's watch. If this is your watch, please come and claim it."

"A black girl's watch?" said James. "Must be Christina's."

James whispered his wisecrack, but I so loved the idea of an inside joke that for weeks afterward, whenever James and I saw Christina in the hallways, I would say, "Hey, Christina, your watch is in the office" and Christina would smile, puzzled. I repeated the joke so many times that Christina started to greet me by saying, "Your watch is in the office" before I could say it to her. Classmates, certain there was a joke at Christina's expense, asked me to let them in on it, to explain what was so funny about a black girl and a watch. I enjoyed the attention.

Then—maybe because the humor of Christina's bewilderment wore thin, but more likely because I'd taken credit for a joke he made up—James turned the prank on me and told me he'd tipped off Christina. Knowing James, it's less likely he told Christina than pretended he had just to scare me and shame me. Or maybe that's just what I tell myself. If he wanted to shame me, it worked—I would like to say that my jokes stopped there, that the experience changed me right there on the spot, but mostly I learned to make quieter jokes. If Christina knew, she never let on. She still smiled when we passed in the hall, but I avoided her, afraid of a confrontation and deeply ashamed of myself. I can't remember ever speaking to her again.

I would rather not tell these stories, but it would be dangerous to misremember my own history. I made worse jokes, ones I'm ashamed to repeat here. I'd set out to mock the offhand racist comments made by the classmates I considered rednecks, but I'd ended up trafficking in racist humor myself. I think of the author Al Burian, apologizing for his own sexist jokes: "Let me offer that I am very susceptible to peer pressure, that the urge to please an audience is deeply ingrained in me. All humor is based in the suffering of others. There is a component of immorality to all laughter. It is the devil's voice coming out of us." I can't say I made racist jokes for shock value; nobody was shocked. Nobody challenged me at church, where we had an entirely white congregation and the deacons used the phrase "mongrelization of the races." It wasn't teachers who challenged my views—it was a classmate who first heard my jokes and had the guts to say, "That's not funny."

Twelve

EDUCATION IS THE APOLOGY

If my dad's country music shaped my class consciousness, and hip-hop made me have to think about what it means to be white, my education in social justice began with the handful of high school classmates who listened to punk rock. They were the ones who made me see the contradictions of listening to militant hip-hop while laughing at racist jokes. They had their own contradictions, of course. I had a rapport with the rednecks; I was kind enough to only make fun of them behind their backs, but the punk rock kids actively mocked them. They preached tolerance but mocked our school's morning prayer circle and the Fellowship of Christian Athletes. They were defiant and oppositional, from the way they dressed to the opinions they voiced, while I'd made it through high school pretending to agree with whatever group I happened to be sitting with at the time.

I went to church every Sunday because I'd always gone, because church told me that good people went to church. The punk rock kids were the first ones to ask me *why* I went. The first time I truly questioned my faith came the summer after I graduated from high school. I went to my first punk rock show at a dive club in Lexington, with my new friend who wore his hair in a bright red spiked Mohawk. We were accosted by old Pentecostal women in dresses and bonnets protesting out front, waving signs that proclaimed Club Wrocklage was the devil's den. My friend snickered, but I felt my heart pounding with the weight of betrayal—I was on the threshold of a major decision. Of the kids standing and snickering out front of the club, I suppose I looked the least punk—the least threatening or most rattled or easiest to save from a life of sin—so one of the women grabbed my arm and pleaded, "Don't go in that place."

I went in. I watched the band Fudge Tunnel play and I never looked back. I went to see show after show after show. I braved a blizzard to see Nirvana. I went to watch Willie Nelson play at the Kentucky State Fair. I saw De La Soul, A Tribe Called Quest, Souls of Mischief, the Beastie Boys. I read the first few books published on hip-hop: S. H. Fernando's *The New Beats*, Houston Baker's *Black Studies, Rap, and the Academy*, Tricia Rose's *Black Noise: Rap Music and Black Culture*. I didn't go back to church but I went to college. As I packed for college, neighbors gave me winks that said *We both know you're not going to learn anything worth knowing*. Neighbors presented college to me as jumping through hoops, a way to delay going to work as much as it was a path to a better-paying job. The people of Pulaski County, Kentucky, warned me that college would indoctrinate me to think I saw the world clearer than they did. I came to college determined not to be taught, so how did I learn? The way fiction might write it, I'd sink into my teenage, off-the-cuff, racist humor in high school but be assigned a black roommate in college. I'd hang up my Public Enemy poster and he'd eye me as suspiciously as I'd eye him when I'd find out he voted for Bush. In that tiny cement-block dorm room we'd soon come to see our differences melt away as soon as we truly talked and got to know each other. I'd take him to my Kentucky hometown on Fall Break and he'd return the favor and invite me to his mom's house in the Bronx for Thanksgiving. We'd become best friends, so close that we'd make whatever kinds of jokes we wanted with each other and no one would get offended. Racism would have all been a big misunderstanding.

In reality the story isn't nearly that heartwarming. My moment of transformation isn't that easy to pinpoint, but I know it took place in college. I look for a pivotal moment or conversation, but I see mainly missed learning opportunities that eventually coalesced and shifted my sensibilities. I went to college in the big city of Louisville and the professors looked at me—ME—as one of the uncultured rednecks I'd mocked in high school. The University of Louisville forced me to take a course called Campus Culture; the white professor forced us to attend a poetry reading by two middle-aged black women. This, my professor told me, is *diversity*. I didn't like how it felt to be looked down on. I resented my professor for making me look, for assuming I would never have looked on my own. (I wouldn't have, but I still didn't like his assumption.) My resentment of him made me reject the culture he insisted on showing me. I sneaked out while the poets performed Maya Angelou's "Phenomenal Women" and went to a record store to wait in line for the midnight release of Snoop Doggy Dogg's *Doggystyle*.

"When I saw the Snoop Doggy album with the pornographic, obscenity-laced cartoon inside, I couldn't believe it," anti-gangsta rap activist C. Delores Tucker told the *Chicago Tribune*, "I called up some record stores and found out that any child of any age could go into a record store and purchase that CD and see that graphic art . . . Everybody wants to look cool like the gangstas and carry guns to school. Even going to prison is cool. Young minds are being exploited to see only the worst in the African American community."[1] At eighteen, I could not for the life of me understand what she was talking about. *Snoop isn't showing me the worst in the African-American community*, I thought, shaking my head; *Snoop is showing me he's cool as hell.* The logic to her argument—that Snoop's lyrics were harming women and making black men look bad—was lost on me. I was a spectator, neither black nor a woman, and I'd never been pushed to think much about how it might feel to be either one.

Tucker's criticisms began to hit home for me, finally, in the course I took on the History of Country Music, which taught me that the American record industry was founded on segregation, splitting musicians who'd previously played together on front porches along the black/white color line as record labels divided artists into "race records" and "hillbilly" music. In defining the hillbilly, *Variety* wrote in 1926, "The great majority, probably 95 percent, can neither read nor write English. Theirs is a community all to themselves . . . illiterate and ignorant, with the intelligence of morons."[2] Country group the Skillet Lickers dressed in suits when they played the Grand Ole Opry, but their New York record label dressed them in straw hats and overalls for the press photos.[3] The bluesman Lead Belly posed barefoot, sitting on a bale of hay for the cover of *Negro Folk Songs as Sung by Lead Belly.* Alan Lomax, who toured Southern prisons in search of authentic black music, said of his star performer, "Leadbelly is a nigger to the core of his being."[4] "Leadbelly, Negro Minstrel," raved the *New York Herald Tribune,* "Sweet Singer of the Swamplands Here to do a few Tunes between Homicides."[5] "Bad Nigger Makes Good Minstrel," raved *Life* Magazine, above a close-up photo of Leadbelly's hands playing guitar, and the caption "These hands once killed a man."[6] These old notions carry forward, not only in music and marketing, but in the ways we look at each other in everyday life. White people, once thrilled to watch a black murderer play music on stage, will still today call the cops on a black child holding a toy gun. Police killed black children holding toy guns in Cleveland and Columbus—cities few Americans would call Southern—yet we still place racism at the feet of the illiterate and ignorant morons down south, who either don't know the words the white people on the coasts have agreed to use when referring to race, or else refuse to use them out of sheer Southern stubbornness.

I mention Lead Belly and the Skillet Lickers not to suggest that white and black Americans were equally harmed by the record industry's selling a stereotype, but to show the way such stereotypes divide the very Americans—poor and rural, in this case—who have the most in common. If we could get white Americans to see that when they feel the chips stacked against them they are feeling a hint of what black Americans feel, we might foster some solidarity rather than foment resentment. America's greatest scheme is to get poor white people to resent that their tax dollars support poor black people, when unfathomably huge corporations like AT&T don't pay a dime in taxes and the US uses taxpayer dollars to bail out the financial entities who went bust gambling with our mortgages.

But I'm guilty myself of being divisive. I criticize my neighbors for the racism inherent in their political views when I used to be so outwardly racist myself. It took me too long to learn, but I have no patience for the people who haven't learned yet. I hate a man at my university because he's plastered his office with posters from a reality TV show I've never watched. The show follows the lives of hunters who look and speak like the grown-up versions of children I went to school with in Kentucky. I've never watched it, but I know it offends me. One of the hunters spoke out against gay people, I remember, or women, maybe it was. The context escapes me. I've read the offensive tidbits shared by people either by way of taking offense or by way of taking vicarious pride in a man on TV who says what he wants without fear of reprisal.

The room is a shrine to the show. There are more posters than wall—men with and camouflage headbands and gray bushy beards dare professors and students to take offense as they enter the room to have their school IDs made or replaced. On a bookshelf in the corner, a small glass frame holds a medal from the Viet Nam war. This man went to Viet Nam, and I hate him because of a show he likes, or at least because he's so insistent I know he likes it. These are my people, his posters say; I am like them and not like you. He was sweating in a foreign jungle when he was eighteen, so he dares freshmen who've barely left Mama's house to walk in here thinking they know all the answers and seeking a reason to be offended, dares them to go back to their fancy dorm rooms and draw up a petition to take down the posters and limit a veteran's freedom of speech.

I didn't speak more than three words to him. A little handwritten sign on his desk says, "Tell me your name." When I say hello he huffs and points to the sign. He prints and laminates my replacement ID without even glancing at me to see if I match the face in the picture.

Is it okay for a man to say hateful things on TV, or for a university employee to hang posters of him in a room every student has to visit before they can park on campus or check out a library book? The right of a gay student not to be stared down by a hateful face trumps a war hero's right to hang up a poster.

Still filled with an anxious rage at the ID maker and the goddamned nerve of his posters, I sat down and prepared to complain. Should I email the student ID higher-ups or Multicultural Affairs? On the walls of my own little windowless office, I recognize a poster of Muhammad Ali—who went to jail for refusing to go to war—asks, "Why should they ask me to put on a uniform and go ten thousand miles from home and drop bombs and bullets on brown people in Vietnam while so-called Negro people in Louisville are treated like dogs?" Above my desk, framed albums and posters signed by my heroes, the rappers I write books about: a man who's said "fag" in his lyrics, a man who's said he loves money so much he'll even do business with the likes of the Jews. On my bookshelves, an author who broke his thumb beating his girlfriend, an author who shot his wife in the head. Two snooty authors who went on TV and called each other "crypto-Nazi" and "queer."[7]

The Norwegian Knut Hamsun, author of beautiful novels, shook Hitler's hand and gave Goebbels his Nobel Prize. Ezra Pound, the American poet who mentored everyone from Ernest Hemingway to Robert Frost, said he "never met anyone who seemed to GET my ideas" the way Mussolini did.[8] There's no way around it: our artists are assholes. So why did the rumors of some ignorant offhand comments make me hate a man who hung up a poster? The truth is I didn't write off that hunting show because I heard the man make controversial remarks. I wrote it off as soon as I saw his camouflage headband and bushy gray beard, and when he spoke hateful words I congratulated myself for having avoided him. Such a self-congratulatory approach to having figured out how to speak about race does nothing but reinforce the division between the white people who want to bring others around and the ones their message might reach. Instead, we need to bring them around to listen to black voices without resorting to the knee-jerk reaction of crying reverse racism when those voices prompt them to think about what it means to be white.

•

I apologize.

I apologize, like so many white people before me. "I lost my temper onstage," said the white comedian Michael Richards, best known for playing Kramer on *Seinfeld*. "I said some pretty nasty things to some Afro Americans . . . You know, I'm really busted up over this and I'm very, very sorry."[9] Richards, speaking in 2006, had assaulted a black heckler with a history lesson. "Fifty years ago," he screamed from the stage, "they'd have you hanging upside down with a fucking fork up your ass. Throw his ass out. He's a nigger! He's a nigger! He's a nigger! A nigger. Look, there's a nigger!"[10] Richards' rant was so shocking that Paul Mooney—who'd built a comedic career alongside Richard Pryor making the word funny—swore he'd never use the word onstage again: "I had a romance with the word. I worked with Richard Pryor using the word. It was so destructive—it was created by whites to hurt and destroy—and we were trying to defuse it, trying to desensitize people to it. We did it every chance we got, we would drive people crazy."[11] But hearing Richards, a fellow comedian he'd known for two decades, use the word to assault a black heckler made Mooney never want to say the word onstage again: "It was so ugly, so horrible. I hadn't heard (the n-word) like this—from someone I knew. Suddenly, I was directly connected. I was able to look at it not just through my eyes but through the eyes of the world. I had always thought it was endearing. It's NOT. It's not an equal opportunity word. I don't want everyone running around saying it."[12] Mooney's memoir *Black Is the New White* traces this impulse back to Mooney's childhood and his neighbor's parrot, Feathers: "Feathers screams out 'Nigger' all day long, every single day. It's the only fucking word he knows. Everyone in the neighborhood can hear it. Maybe it's only fitting. The first time I hear the word *nigger*, it's out of the mouth of a parrot. All my life, I hear that word parroted mindlessly, and I think of Feathers."[13]

Richards' apology was fumbling and tone-deaf. Jerry Seinfeld went on *The Late Show with David Letterman* to speak on his co-star's behalf, and Richards patched in to repent via satellite, from a safe distance. But at least his apology came only days after he'd invoked the history of lynching to respond to a black man who hadn't found his jokes funny. It took America 144 years after the Civil War to apologize for slavery, and 170—counting from the Trail of Tears—to apologize to Native Americans. Yet my wife and I, on the advice of TV's SuperNanny, expected our small daughter to apologize. We sentenced her to a time-out on the bottom step of the stairs, then staged a parole hearing to ask her to acknowledge her transgression and express remorse. At first she complied, with probably no understanding of what the words meant or how they connected to whatever crime got her sent to her room. She was not so much sorry for what she did as she was sorry she got in trouble, so we couldn't tell if we were teaching her to recognize her emotions or to lie about them.

Then she began refusing to say she was sorry. We sent her back to the bottom step for more time and she still refused. We came to a stand-off. I let her leave the step but things remained tense. My wife and I discussed it under our breath—*What kind of a kid won't apologize?* Let it go, we decided. No need to push. Then, days later she did apologize when we accidentally injured her. I caught the skin of her bare thigh in the car seat buckle and she screamed, tears in her eyes, "I'm *sorry!*" My wife texted me at work to say I should talk to her about jabbing the cat with a pencil. Five hours later I came home and asked my daughter if she had something to tell me, if she had an apology to give to the cat. She sighed. "That was a long time ago, Daddy."

It reminded me of an apology I'd studied when I was writing about a white rapper who hit some Vietnamese men in the face with a stick while screaming, "slant-eye" and "gook" and threw rocks at some black schoolkids while screaming, "nigger." Three years after his hate crimes, Marky Mark Wahlberg was on MTV rapping about how much he loves money, flanked by a crew called The Funky Bunch, assembled as if to say, *Look, these are blacks and Latinos who are willing to work with me*. While Americans were distracted by Vanilla Ice trying to tell us he'd grown up poorer than he actually did, Marky Mark quietly apologized for his hate crimes: "I harassed a group of school kids on a field trip. Many of them were African American . . . I assaulted two Vietnamese men over a case of beer. I used racist language during these encounters and people were seriously hurt by what I did. I am truly sorry. I was a teenager and intoxicated when I did these things. But that's no excuse . . ."[14] Twenty years later he was a wealthy and prominent film actor, worth about $200 million. He petitioned the Massachusetts governor for a pardon but he never tried to track down those black kids he'd terrorized and pay their college tuition.

He did ask to meet face-to-face with one of the Vietnamese men, Johnny Trinh, who'd made it known he forgave him for hitting him in the head. Until they met, the white rapper didn't know the man he'd attacked was a veteran who'd fought alongside the Americans in the Viet Nam War. The veteran had "no idea he was attacked by a celebrity."[15] I imagine they shook hands and looked at each other expectantly.

It just don't feel right, I imagine the rapper saying, me standing here with my 200 million and you with one eye.

Aw, don't beat yourself up, I imagine the veteran saying. You cracked me over the head all right, but I'd already lost that eye in the war.

Wahlberg's petition explained that he sought a pardon so that his hate crimes would not cost him a concessionaire's license for his chain of restaurants, Wahlburgers. As a sort of bonus, he suggested the pardon would also make him a shining example of the power of redemption. Look: a man who used to hit people with sticks is now a pardoned and famous multimillionaire, free to sell burgers across this great nation. Do you see? No matter how many rocks you throw at black children—you too might become a multimillionaire who gives a little of his money to charity (although none of it to the black children you terrorized, or to Vietnamese-American charities). "I have not engaged in philanthropic efforts in order to make people forget about my past," Wahlberg wrote in his pardon petition. "To the contrary, I want people to remember my past so that I can serve as an example of how lives can be turned around and how people can be redeemed."[16]

But pardons, by their very nature, are about forgiving and forgetting. Pardons cancel out crimes, wrote Judith Beals, the attorney who'd originally prosecuted Wahlberg: "While private acts of reconciliation and forgiveness can be an important part of our shared racial history, that history should never be erased."[17] Beals argued that Wahlberg had never addressed the racist nature of his attacks, but instead continued to blame them on being teenaged and drunk.[18] Blame it on the recklessness of youth that Kristyn Atwood, a forty-year-old woman, still has a scar from a rock Wahlberg threw at her when she was in fourth grade. "It was a hate crime," she told CBS News, "and that's exactly what should be on his record forever . . . I don't really care who he is. It doesn't make him any exception. If you're a racist, you're always going to be a racist."[19]

I am inclined to agree with her. I was and am a racist, despite wishing I could erase my own teenage transgressions. The difference between me and Wahlberg may be that he sees racism as something he's grown out of, while I see it as something that haunts my psychology. I was a racist then, stealing jokes from In Living Color, and I am a racist now, sending my daughter to the South Jersey schools that seem most isolated from Camden's black and Hispanic poverty. America has come to a moment where "racist" is one of the worst things a man called be called, when it might be more useful for those of us who've moved beyond past transgressions to admit the ways racist thinking continues to color our thinking. Recovering addicts have to admit they are powerless against their addiction. Christians must face their original sin. But if Wahlberg was once and forever a racist, why didn't we call for his firing the way we did Paula Deen and Hank Williams Jr. and Don Imus? Instead, we watched Wahlberg move from rapping to starring in major motion pictures, despite the hate crimes on his record. We'd set Wahlberg's hate crimes so firmly aside that we chose him as our emissary when the Pope visited Philadelphia in 2015. "Holy Father, please forgive me," said Wahlberg, not apologizing for his hate crimes but cracking a joke about his latest movie, which co-starred a foulmouthed teddy bear.[20]

I would deny Wahlberg his pardon, but I've pardoned entities bigger than Marky Mark—or at least I'm willing to give them my money. My employer sells its faculty a group health insurance plan through Aetna, a company that once sold slave-owners insurance on the lives of their slaves. "We express our deep regret over any participation at all in this deplorable practice,"[21] Aetna wrote, offering a heartfelt apology in lieu of reparations, but my university gets a good group rate, so I buy in, along with the other professors. Every month, my employer sends part of my money to Wall Street to do God knows what with; I sign the forms and hope those evil bankers make me a rich retiree.

America was founded on disparity between whites and blacks. Racism is woven into the fabric of our institutions, from schooling to policing to real estate to religion. I was raised a member of the Southern

Baptists, a denomination founded when it split, pre-Civil War, with the regular Baptists, who could no longer make the Bible's teachings jibe with owning slaves. It was not until 1995 that the Southern Baptists apologized: "Our relationship to African-Americans has been hindered from the beginning by the role that slavery played in the formation of the Southern Baptist Convention . . . In later years Southern Baptists failed, in many cases, to support, and in some cases opposed, legitimate initiatives to secure the civil rights of African-Americans."[22] 130 years after the end of the Civil War, Southern Baptists issued a Resolution on Racial Reconciliation to "unwaveringly denounce racism, in all its forms, as deplorable sin."[23] My mother had taken me to a Southern Baptist church since I was an infant, but I didn't learn until adulthood that its roots stood in slavery and racism.

"Education is the apology," wrote *Boston Globe* columnist Derrick Z. Jackson in 1997. "White folks need to study slavery to see that they are in the same trap as the 1800s" when "elite white industrialists raked in the profits [while] shafted white workers were left with the consolation that they were still better than black folks. Unwilling or unable to claw at the mansions, many white Americans commenced sixty years of lynching and segregation."[24] The trap in 1997, according to Jackson? "Millions of white Americans are genuine victims of the new economy, with widening gaps in wealth and far less job security. But instead of focusing on that or universal health care or runaway college tuitions, a huge chunk of energy has been diverted to welfare and crime, issues that several studies confirm has been given an unfair black face."[25] In a country founded on the division between white and black people, the conversation about race divides whites into camps convinced they're better than the other whites. Whether the split is between those whites who pride themselves on education versus common sense, or school versus church, or tradition versus progress, or rural vs. urban identity, the division breeds an anti-intellectualism which leads both groups of whites to believe they've already figured things out.

If education is the apology, how can I best help teach others what I've learned? It would be ridiculous to expect black people to be patient in the face of racism, as America has urged its black citizens to do for so many decades now. It's the white Americans who have a responsibility to educate themselves, and then others, in the painful history of race in this country. As a white person speaking to another white person, I may achieve more when I open not with a condemnation of their ignorance but by admitting my own ignorance and telling the story of how I continue to read and listen in order to overcome it. I am not urging civility toward white supremacist groups, but toward the whites who don't quite see what's so wrong with the white supremacist slogans, statues, and flags because they just haven't learned their history. We might borrow a strategy from the novelist Kurt Vonnegut, who described his approach to classroom teaching in terms of battlefield triage: some students he knew he couldn't help and some would do perfectly well without his help, but he was most concerned with the middle third—those students who he felt could immediately benefit from the lessons he had to offer.[26] White people speaking to other whites about racism might follow Vonnegut's triage approach and not give up on the lost causes and sure things so much as feel a real urgency to first reach that middle third whose minds we are most likely to change.

Of course we should also feel an urgency to act when white nationalist groups march onto our campuses and into our communities. Heather Heyer died standing up against white supremacists in Charlottesville, Virginia. She is the hero I'll never be with my lectures and lesson plans, but the activist and the educator each has our role. I admire the hell out of Heather Heyer, same as I look up to my wife for tying a black bandana over her face and marching for justice in Philly while I finish this book. I wish I had their courage, but I hope I can contribute by giving my students the education I never got. The poet and memoirist M. K. Asante says that observation equals obligation—recognizing a problem makes it your responsibility to try to fix it.[27] I see our educations failing us. It's easier to believe the police intend to protect and serve people of all colors when you don't know the history of lynchings and slave patrols. It's easier to write off a racist joke when you don't know the history of the minstrel show. I am not urging patience in the face of such ignorance—far from it. The journey shouldn't have taken me nearly as long as it did. If I heard my child make some of the jokes I did I would make her write me a report on the history of lynchings in America. Still think it's funny?

We have to call out ignorance, even as we must employ a teacher's patience—not to spare their feelings but to make sure our lessons are heard. We can't simply call out their racism and walk away, and we can't risk making them feel so attacked that they dig in their heels. The problem with urging patience in the face of racism is that the effort often stops there. It took me far too long to learn because there was so little effort to teach me and so little support for my efforts to learn. At the same time, there's a certain self-satisfaction that I want to avoid— the self-satisfaction that too often develops when someone takes on the role of the learned teacher or expert. White people take a particular pride in having figured out the right thing to say or do when it comes to race, but they often continue to speak in a way that talks down to whites who haven't had the same educational opportunities, and speak into a void that does not include black voices.

•

"Please do not comment on black music anymore," Kanye West asked every "white publication" in 2016. "I love love love white people but you don't understand what it means to be the great grandson of ex-slaves and make it this far."[28] White publications, in West's definition, included *Pitchfork, Rolling Stone,* and the *New York Times,* each of whom he called out by name. But almost defiantly, sooner than six months after West's statement, the *New York Times* ran an article that said hip-hop had entered an era in which white rappers could fare just fine without the approval of black stars. Jon Caramanica's "White Rappers: Clear of a Black Planet" claimed that a new wave of white rappers like G-Eazy, Mike Stud, and Lil Dicky were "finding paths to success that have little if anything to do with black acceptance."[29] The article—by a white writer—included not one black voice.

Caramanica's title played off Public Enemy's seminal 1990 album *Fear of a Black Planet,* which dealt head-on with white supremacy and institutional racism—topics barely mentioned in Caramanica's article, which twenty-six years later suggested that white rappers were finally free and clear of the reach of such issues. *Clear at last! White people can finally rap and write about hip-hop without the burden of this country's history of race relations!* That is, if you ignored what black rappers said. If you ignored Lord Jamar calling white rappers guests in the house of hip-hop. If you ignored J.Cole and Vince Staples commenting on white appropriation in their lyrics. If you ignored Kanye West telling the *New York Times* to stop writing about hip-hop, and if you ignored Caramanica's own dispute with Solange Knowles. Just six months before Caramanica declared white rappers "clear of a black planet," Knowles complained that he wrote about that which he did not know. Caramanica warned her not to bite the (white music journalist) hand that feeds her, and she responded, in part: "The music business was built brick by brick off the backs, shoulders, heartache and pain of black people, and everyone is just exhausted"[30] and "Don't you EVER tell a Black woman not to 'Bite the hand that feeds you' while speaking in reference to white people."[31] A white journalist said rap had moved beyond race, was now post-racial; it was an easy case to make, as long as you ignored the words of black people.

It wasn't that Caramanica was particularly impressed with the assimilation skills of G-Eazy and Lil Dicky. He'd been making some version of the same argument for years, anytime a white rapper made any kind of a splash. In 2014 he wrote, "Yung Lean is a reminder that the new hip-hop underground isn't geographically or racially specific in any way: A seventeen-year-old Swedish kid can rack up millions of YouTube views and SoundCloud plays without making so much as a ripple in the mainstream hip-hop world. It's a potent reminder that success as a rapper no longer requires traditional hip-hop gate-keepers."[32] In 2009, he wrote about Ke$ha as "part of the continuing deracination of the act of rapping, which used to be inscribed as a specifically black act, but which has been appropriated so frequently and with such ease that it's been, in some cases, re-racinated. The very existence of the casually rapping white girl reflects decreasingly stringent ideas about race and gender."[33] What Caramanica calls "re-racination" is nothing more than what black writers have called erasure—the process by which whites removed blacks from the histories of everything from the cotton scraper to rock music. Caramanica seemed to celebrate segregation, to see progress in the fact that white rappers are rapping to white fans in venues beyond the purview of black rappers. Publicists and journalists in the Nineties and Aughts celebrated the white rappers, like Vanilla Ice and Eminem, who claimed to have wandered into a black neighborhood and outshined the black musicians. But Caramanica seemed fixated on the white rappers who'd become stars without ever visiting a black neighborhood or seeking the mentorship of black rappers or using lyrics to talk about the ways they fit, or didn't fit, into the larger history of hip-hop as a part of black culture. What was so compelling about the idea that one day, if this new breed of white rapper continued to find an audience, it would no longer matter if a rapper were black or white?

It has long been suggested that if we'd just stop talking about our differences they'd dissolve, but we have to ask ourselves *who* exactly do we wish would stop talking? After all, white Americans talking self-critically about race is an incredibly recent development, so it's hard for me to join in applauding the young white YouTube rappers who've gone back to the old tradition of leaving the race talk to the minorities. It seems to me that progress happens when white Americans think *more* about race, not less. As correct as Kanye is that I don't know how it feels to be the great grandson of ex-slaves, I have learned a lot by studying the stories told by black rappers and the ways white fans and white critics and white rappers relate to those stories, and the best use I can make of what I've learned is to share it with others by writing about it and using that writing to point them to the ideas of black writers and rappers. But no matter how many books I publish, I have to remember I remain a guest in the house of hip-hop. Having studied hip-hop for nearly twenty years, I'd be a saint not to come to feel like I have some claim to the subject, but if all that studying taught me nothing else, it taught me that I have to catch myself and remind myself it's not mine.

I could end this book by walking away from hip-hop entirely. I could develop a new and more definitive sense of belonging. Or I could end up right back where I started, still doing it even as I question the very correctness of doing it. It would be a tidier ending if I were to quit teaching and writing about hip hop, but I don't trust myself to stay away. I don't want to write one of those retirement-threat efforts like Jay-Z's *Black Album* or Kurt Vonnegut's *Breakfast of Champions*, much as I love them both. As compelling a device as the swan song is, no real fan believed for a second that Jay would quit rapping or Kurt would quit writing. I can't promise to leave hip-hop alone. It's a part of me, whether or not I'm a part of it. But my long-term involvement doesn't mean I stop asking myself questions. When white rappers, professors, and writers stop having to think about being white, then we'll know black folks have truly lost hold of this thing they created called hip-hop.

•

Yet even knowing hip-hop was not mine, I felt like it was being stolen from me when my university hired a new president who declared he would shut down the American Studies program that houses my hip-hop class. (Our faculty union—the kind of organization presented to me in my youth as lazy and parasitic and anti-American—gave back two years of raises to keep the programs open and keep students from having to switch majors and professors from losing their jobs.) I felt a tinge of possessiveness when newer professors proposed their own courses on hip-hop. A white man (a music professor) and a black woman (an arts administration professor) proposed a new course on hip-hop and gender studies. I'd always told myself that I'd step aside if a black professor wanted to teach the course, but I hadn't considered how I'd feel if it were another white guy. I couldn't very well tell a black woman she couldn't teach the topic of women in hip-hop because I felt like I'd staked my claim first. Nor could I tell the music professor he couldn't then teach a new course on Dirty South hip-hop, or a fellow English professor (a white woman) that she couldn't teach a new course on Beyoncé. But the problem was not at all whether *my* territory was being encroached upon; it was that a decade after I first taught Hip-Hop and American Culture, my campus offers four classes in black music culture. White professors teach three of the four, and none is taught solely by a black professor.

How do I use my position to correct this imbalance? I can work to correct the cultural imbalance by educating my students—and my readers—to these facts, but the greater imbalance is economic. Professors have far less power with the university administrators who control the money than you might think—remember, I just gave back my last two raises so that I could keep doing my job. I could step aside and give up my job and hope to improve the numbers, but I have no faith that I'd be replaced by a black professor. In my first years on campus, I volunteered to serve on a diversity committee that never even successfully called a meeting. So I keep teaching, and I keep assigning the work of black rappers and scholars and inviting them to speak on campus. I joined forces with my colleagues at Rider to organize a Hip-Hop Conference and bring in black hip-hop scholars and rappers. Baruch professor Kyra Gaunt, author of *The Games Black Girls Play: Learning the Ropes from Double-Dutch to Hip-Hop*, spoke about teenage girls twerking for money on Youtube. Cornell professor Travis Gosa spoke about hip-hop and neoliberalism and the police surveillance of rappers. Traum Diggs presented the chapter he published on hip-hop as expressive therapy. Rah Digga joined a panel discussion in the afternoon and played a concert that night.

It was a triumphant semester. I felt a new sense of legitimacy when Rah Digga—who was setting up some hip-hop workshops in her hometown of Newark, NJ—emailed to ask for a peek at my syllabus. I felt proud when one of my old students recorded a verse for a song with Treach from the Grammy-winning group Naughty by Nature. I felt like I was helping a student make back some of her tuition money when I was able to help her land an internship with Eva Ries, who's spent the past twenty years booking the European tours of rappers ranging from Big Pun to Wu-Tang Clan. Another alumna interviewed Ol' Dirty Bastard's kids for a Father's Day piece in *Vibe* magazine. I felt like I was doing some good after all.

But is my bringing hip-hop into the classroom a misappropriation no matter how I frame it or how many black voices get heard? Hip-hop in the university can't be a one-way street. Education is the apology, but what can I do to extend educational opportunities to the artists involved in creating hip-hop, and to the communities where they grew up? Rappers are going back to college. Wordsworth, from EMC and Lyricist Lounge, recently completed a master's degree in education. Sadat X tweets about the math and education classes he's taking. Record contracts don't come with a college savings fund or a 401(k), and artists approaching middle age often find themselves tossed aside by the record industry and seeking a new career. Rappers I've brought in as guest speakers have children in college, and they're co-signing student loans while universities charge students to study the music they made. It's an honor for an artist to have his or her work studied, but that honor doesn't put anyone's kids through college. Rapper Boots Riley, when asked about the spate of college courses on hip-hop, replied, "I don't need to be validated by academia because that presupposes that academia is a pure endeavor and not guided by market forces, which is not the case."[34] Universities are making tuition dollars from hip-hop courses that assign their music as required listening, so we should look for ways to give back. Universities are making money, so they should give back money.

I challenge every university that teaches a hip-hop course to offer a competitive scholarship for rappers and the children of rappers. This small initiative would fit with other recent efforts on the part of universities to extend a hand to the black Americans they've exploited. In 2016, Georgetown University issued "an apology for the university's historical relationship with slavery,"[35] renamed buildings, hired more black professors, promised to found an Institute for the Study of Slavery and Its Legacies, and began to offer "admissions preference" to the descendants of the 272 slaves the university sold in 1838 in an effort to stay afloat.[36] Following suit in early 2017, Harvard, Yale, and Columbia each addressed their institution's investment in slavery, but these apologies and initiatives had a long way to go in correcting the imbalances of segregated high schools and unaffordable tuition and legacy admissions that had maintained white bloodlines in the student body by giving preference to applicants whose parents and grandparents were alumni. Critics of Georgetown's plan pointed out that it did little to correct nearly two centuries of practices that gave every advantage to whites at the expense of blacks. Samantha Master, writing at *The Root*, called Georgetown's plan "worthless white guilt repackaged as justice," and added "this is not a reparations package—not even close."[37] PhD students at the University of Chicago proposed a new model for university reparations, writing, "This cannot be a question of what the university will do for black communities. It must be a function of what black communities demand as payment to forgive an unforgivable debt. Black people do not need a seat at the university's reparations table. They need to own that table and have full control over how reparations are structured."[38]

University reparations, of course, are but a fraction of the national reparations black Americans will, and must, continue to demand. Ta-Nehisi Coates wrote in "The Case for Reparations":

> Something more than moral pressure calls America to reparations. We cannot escape our history. All of our solutions to the great problems of health care, education, housing, and economic inequality are troubled by what must go unspoken. "The reason black people are so far behind now is not because of now," Clyde Ross told me. "It's because of then."[39]

Ross had spent his life watching whites get ahead by knocking him down. As a child, he'd seen his family's property seized unlawfully by whites in Mississippi. As a young man he was denied a mortgage in Chicago, where banks would not offer mortgages to black citizens. Coates proposes that the U.S. model reparations upon West Germany's payments to Israel, which tripled Israel's GNP. On a much smaller scale, Georgetown should pay the descendants of the slaves it sold, not just offer them the same legacy consideration as a white highschooler whose dad went to Georgetown. Georgetown has not done enough, but its plan is a beginning. And the only thing wrong with beginning where it has is if people allow it to rest comfortably there, as if all debts have been repaid. As of March 2018, as I finish this book, a group of more than 200 people continues to push for Georgetown to pay restitution to the descendants of the slaves it sold.[40] I know the history of calls for reparations, so I don't believe for a second that Georgetown will agree to pay these descendants, but it's still encouraging to see this group pushing the school to do more than it's done.

It's encouraging to see the students who survived a shooting at Marjory Stoneman Douglas High School in Parkland, Florida, heed the criticism that Americans cheered on their activism in a way that they hadn't cheered on the Ferguson protestors or the Black Lives Matter movement. At a press event ahead of the March 24, 2018 March for Our Lives, Parkland student David Hogg said the media's biggest mistake was "Not giving black students a voice . . . My school is about 25 percent black, but the way we're covered doesn't reflect that."[41] Hogg's black classmates commended him for his words in support of them, but still argued he could take more action: "We're proud of him," said Mei-Ling Ho-Shing, "but he mentioned he was going to use his white privilege to be the voice for black communities, and we're kind of sitting there like, 'You know there are Stoneman Douglas students who could be that voice'"[42] On March 29, 2018, a group of black Stoneman Douglas students held their own press conference to say they don't want more police officers at their school because police make them feel threatened rather than protected. One student, Tyah-Amoy, insisted that any conversation about gun violence has to include police violence that killed blacks Americans like Stephon Clark and Alton Sterling. I found the drive of these kids inspiring, even though I went to college in the Nineties and remained as stuck in my era's apathetic political mindset as any hippie stuck pining for a good old Sixties sit-in. I grew up at the tail-end of Generation X, so I'd never bought into the romance of the picket sign. I'd so completely written off the power of collective action that I'd sat in my New Jersey office, a ninety-minute train ride away from the epicenter of the

2011 Occupy Wall Street protests, and never considered taking part, even as I boasted for weeks about having watched two guys at Home Depot stick it to the corporation by returning a snow-blower in April. But I felt hopeful watching the Concerned Student 1950 group secure the resignation of the University of Missouri's president and watching black activists from Dream Defenders and Black Lives Matter march along with the Parkland shooting survivors in the #NeverAgain movement in the March for Our Lives. So *this* was what those gray-headed hippies had pined for.

With plenty of gray in my own beard, I'm too old to be a student activist. I'm not skilled at organizing marches and giving speeches, but I will use my writing and teaching to arm my students with an education in what's worth fighting for, and to make every effort to extend opportunities for higher education to people who can't afford it. My proposal to fund scholarships for rappers and their kids, would be, at best, one tiny part of a much larger campaign, but it is one that extends the legacy of university exploitation of black Americans to the present-day investment in teaching a musical and cultural form invented and developed by black Americans who came from public schools and communities designed to keep them from the franchise of higher education. The larger campaign would expand from giving free tuition to the sons and daughters of rappers to community outreach that would connect professors and rappers to offer music education and college preparations work to public-school students who might live and breathe hip-hop but have little to direct them toward higher education. Look at the guest speakers who've come to my class: Rah Digga teaches hip-hop to seventeen to twenty-one-year-olds in her hometown of Newark, New Jersey, via The Newark Youth One Stop Career Training Center initiative. Reef the Lost Cauze teaches hip-hop to youth impacted by mass incarceration via Philly's Beyond the Bars program. I encourage universities to enhance these kinds of programs with resources to bridge community programs with university admissions. We've brought hip-hop to the university; now let's do everything we can to bring the university to the communities that created hip-hop, even as we recognize that this small step leaves a long way to go to repay our debt.

ACKNOWLEDGMENTS

To my friend Traum Diggs (aka David Shanks), thank you for the conversations that drove me to write this book, for your insight and humor, and for all those seitan wings we've shared at Dos Segundos in Philly. I thank Steve Sachs for our epic text threads as this book unfolded. I thank Reef the Lost Cauze for his music, for visiting my class and being so willing to answer follow-up questions on emails from students, and for my conversations with him during the long car rides to campus and back. I owe a debt of gratitude to my brothers in books—Sean Carswell, Todd Dills, and Joe Meno—with whom I've driven up and down the East and West Coasts and across the Midwest, our rental car trunk stuffed with our latest tomes. Thanks to my literary agent, Matt DiGangi at Bresnick Weil, for believing in this book and for his guidance and editorial insight. Thanks to Peter Richter, Shamika Mitchell, Robbie Clipper, and Denise Oswald for their feedback on early drafts of this book. Thanks to Mike Faloon for inviting me to read with you at Brickbat Books in Philly. Thanks to Ron Ventola his legal expertise and persistence—is this why you went to law school? Thanks to Chad Willenborg and Al Burian for their writing, friendship, and support. Thanks to Ricky Lorenzo for being Ricky Lorenzo. Thanks to my Rider University colleague Pearlie Peters for always having my back. Thanks to Luke Buckman, Kelly Buckman, Bronwyn Williams, and Dale Billingsley for holding things down at my alma mater, the University of Louisville. Thanks to Chad Patterson—the most literary surgeon I know—for letting me dub his Eazy-E and Sir Mixalot cassettes back in junior high. Thanks to Richard Prince for so graciously sharing his work with me. Thanks to the best interview subjects and guest speakers a professor could ask for: MF Grimm, Masta Ace, Reef the Lost Cauze, Rah Digga, Traum Diggs, Buddha Monk, Greg Nice, Da Beatminerz, Bahamadia, K-Blunt, Jus Rhyme, Prince Paul, and Count Bass D. And finally, thanks to my daughter, Coco Hess, who is growing up to be so kind and so insightful, and to her mom, Danielle Hess, who continues to be the perfect model of those attributes for our daughter and for me.

NOTES

INTRODUCTION: WHAT SHOULD A WHITE ALLY DO?

1. Glenn Kessler, "The Stale Statistic That One In Three Black Males 'Born Today' Will End Up In Jail," *Washington Post*, June 16, 2015, https://www.washingtonpost.com/news/fact-checker/wp/2015/06/16/the-stale-statistic-that-one-in-three-black-males-has-a-chance-of-ending-up-in-jail/?utm_term=.15502f803fc3.

2. "Felony Disenfranchisement in the Commonwealth of Kentucky: A Report of the League of Women Voters of Kentucky," February 2017, https://lwvky.files.wordpress.com/2017/02/kentucky-felony-disenfranchisement-report-feb-17-final-docx.pdf.

3. Derrick Z. Jackson, "Breaking Free from Slavery," *The Day*, December 9, 1997, A12, https://news.google.com/newspapers?nid=1915&dat=19971209&id=FSIiAAAAIBAJ&sjid=FXQFAAAAIBAJ&pg=4877,2327516&hl=en.

4. John B. Russworm and Samuel E. Cornish, *Freedom's Journal*, March 26, 1827.

5. Ibid.

6. Betsy Rader, "I was Born in Poverty in Appalachia. 'Hillbilly Elegy' Doesn't Speak for Me," *Washington Post*, September 1, 2017, https://www.washingtonpost.com/opinions/i-grew-up-in-poverty-in-appalachia-jd-vances-hillbilly-elegy-doesnt-speak-for-me/2017/08/30/734abb38-891d-11e7-961d-2f373b3977ee_story.html?utm_term=.3e86116fddb4.

7. Claudia Rankine, *Citizen: An American Lyric* (London: Penguin, 2015), 16.

8. Ibid, 10.

9. Ibid, 13.

10. Dr. Martin Luther King, Jr, "Letter from a Birmingham Jail," April 16,

1963, https://www.africa.upenn.edu/Articles_Gen/Letter_Birmingham.html.

11. "Martin Luther King, Jr.'s 'Where Do We Go from Here' Turns 50," June 20, 2017, http://www.beaconbroadside.com/broadside/2017/06/martin-luther-king-jrs-where-do-we-go-from-here-turns-50.html.

12. Ijeoma Oluo, "Bernie Sanders, Black Lives Matter and the Racial Divide in Seattle," *Seattle Globalist*, August 9, 2015, http://www.seattleglobalist.com/2015/08/09/bernie-sanders-black-lives-matter-race-divide-in-seattle/40394.

13. Lincoln Blades, "Bill Clinton's Black Lives Matter Comments were Revealingly Honest," *Rolling Stone*, April 8, 2016, https://www.rollingstone.com/politics/news/bill-clintons-black-lives-matter-comments-were-revealingly-honest-20160408.

ONE: DON'T PUSH IT TOO FAR

1. Shenequa Golding, "Kanye West Asks White Publications To 'Not Comment On Black Music Anymore,'" *Vibe*, February 15, 2016, https://www.vibe.com/2016/02/kanye-west-twitter-rant.

2. bell hooks, *Outlaw Culture: Resisting Representations* (New York: Routledge, 2015), 129.

3. Danielle Harling, "Lord Jamar Says White Rappers Are Guests in Hip-Hop," *Hip Hop DX*, September 23, 2013, https://hiphopdx.com/news/id.25530/title.lord-jamar-says-white-rappers-are-guests-in-hip-hop.

4. Alex Nichols, "You Should Be Terrified that People Who Like 'Hamilton' Run Our Country," *Current Affairs*, July 29, 2016. http://editor.currentaffairs.org/2016/07/you-should-be-terrified-that-people-who-like-hamilton-run-our-country.

TWO: WHY WHITE KIDS SHOULD LISTEN TO HIP-HOP

1. Dyson, Michael E., *Know What I Mean?: Reflections on Hip-Hop* (New York: Basic Civitas Books/Perseus Books Group, 2010), 11.

2. John Conlee, "Common Man," *Songs for the Working Man*, MCA, 1986.

3. City of Science Hill, "Our City History," http://www.cityofsciencehill.com/commissioners.html.

4. Rob Gallagher and Lori DeWinkler, "Kentucky Lynchings 1882–1921," http://genealogytrails.com/ken/ky_southernlynchings.html.

5. Jerry Heller, *Ruthless: A Memoir* (New York: Simon & Schuster, 2007), 4.

6. N.W.A. featuring Snoop Dogg, "Chin Check," *Next Friday*, Priority Records, 1999.

7. Jerry Heller, *Ruthless: A Memoir* (New York: Simon & Schuster, 2007), 4.

8.. Jon Pareles, "Public Enemy Rap Group Reorganizes After Anti-Semitic Comments," *New York Times*, August 11, 1989, http://www.nytimes.com/1989/08/11/arts/public-enemy-rap-group-reorganizes-after-anti-semitic-comments.html.

9. Mark Memmott, "Hank Williams Jr.: 'Sorry If It Offended Anyone,'" *The Two-Way: Breaking News from NPR*, October 5, 2011, https://www.npr.org/sections/thetwoway/2011/10/05/141072327/hank-williams-jr-sorry-if-it-offended-anyone.

THREE: "IT'S ABOUT CLASS, NOT RACE" (NO IT'S NOT)

1. "Bootstrap Story," *The Daily Show with Jon Stewart*, Comedy Central 28 July 2004, http://www.cc.com/video-clips/wdl392/the-daily-show-with-jon-stewart-bootstrap-story.

2. "A Very Slow Recovery: The Annual Report on the Economic Status of the Profession, 2011–12," https://www.aaup.org/reports-publications/2011-12salarysurvey.

3. Ken Parish Perkins, "Under Raps: Hot Pop Vocalist Vanilla Ice Shrugs off Conflicting Versions of his Background," *The Dallas Morning News*, November 18, 1990, 1A.

4. Ibid.

5. Naughty by Nature, "Everything's Gonna Be Alright (Ghetto Bastard)," *Naughty by Nature*, Tommy Boy, 1991.

6. Richard Prince, "Ken Perkins: 'I Just Can't Take the Lies,'" *Maynard Institute*, November 23, 2005, http://mije.org/richardprince/ken-perkins-i-just-cant-take-lies.

7. Tom Moon, "The Making of Vanilla Ice: His Rap Music Has His Female Fans Melting. He'll Be at the Tower Tomorrow. But How Real is His Sound? And Who is He, Really?" *Philadelphia Inquirer*, February 6, 1991, http://articles.philly.com/1991-02 06/news/25773507_1_robbie-van-winkle-rap-ice-ice-baby.

8. *The Arsenio Hall Show*, Vanilla Ice Interview, February 13, 1991. https://youtu.be/KAz-SF-329E.

9. Ibid.

10. Ibid.

11. Ibid.

12. Ibid.

13. Liam Stac,. "Debunking a Myth: The Irish Were Not Slaves, Too," *New York Times*, March 17, 2017, https://www.nytimes.com/2017/03/17/us/irish-slaves-myth.html?mtrref=www.google.com.

14. Harry Allen, "The Unbearable Whiteness of Emceeing: What the Eminence of Eminem says about Race," *The Source*, February 2003, 3. Available at http://harryallen.info/wp-content/uploads/2008/01/The-Unbearable-Whiteness-of-Emceeing.pdf.

15. Ibid, 3.

16. Eric Lacy, "Wanna Buy Eminem's Old 'Marshall Mathers LP' House in Detroit? Michigan Land Bank Accepts Bids," *MLive*, September 17, 2013, http://www.mlive.com/entertainment/detroit/index.ssf/2013/09/wanna_buy_eminems_old_mashall.html.

17. "Meet Ben Carson," June 24, 2015, http://www.p2016.org/ads/carsonv062415.html.

18. Scott Glover and Maeve Reston, "A Tale of Two Carsons." *CNN*, December 5, 2016. http://www.cnn.com/2015/11/05/politics/ben-carson-2016-childhood-violence.

19. Ibid.

20. Eric Levitz, "Ben Carson Might Be Next on Trump's Chopping Block," *Daily Intelligencer*, March 23, 2018, https://nymag.com/daily/intelligencer/2018/03/ben-carson-might-be-next-on-trumps-chopping-block.html.

21. Ben Carson and Cecil Murphey, *Gifted Hands: The Ben Carson Story* (Grand Rapids, MI: Zondervan, 2011), 56.

22. "Rapper Ice-T Takes A Quiz On Pantyhose," *NPR*, July 7, 2012, http://www.npr.org/2012/07/07/156251697/ice-t-takes-a-quiz-about-pantyhose.

FOUR: HIP-HOP COMES TO CAMPUS

1. Donald Bogle, *Toms, Coons, Mulattoes, Mammies, and Bucks: An Interpretive History of Blacks in American Films* (New York: Continuum, 1994), 82.

2. Jake Brown, *Ready to Die: The Story of Biggie Smalls* (Phoenix: Amber, 2004), 50.

3. Karam Tumulty, "Obama Says This Hope Stuff Only Goes So Far," *Time*, July 8, 2008. http://swampland.time.com/2008/07/08/obama_says_this_hope_stuff_onl/.

4. *The MC: Why We Do It*, directed by Peter Spirer (QD3, 2004).

5. Ewuare X. Osayande, *Misogyny and the Emcee* (Philadelphia: Machete, 2008), 14.

6. Grandmaster Flash with David Ritz, *Adventures of Grandmaster Flash: My Life, My Beats* (New York: Broadway, 2008), 157–59.

7. "Black Mayoral Candidates Respond to Racist graffiti on City Hall," WISTV.com, 2009, http://www.wistv.com/Global/story.asp?S=11746767.

8. "An Open Letter Calling for the Termination of Dr. Andrea Quenette for Racial Discrimination," *Medium*, November 17, 2015, https://medium.com/@schumaal/what-follows-is-a-letter-collectively-written-by-the-students-currently-enrolled-in-coms-930-at-the-8f4914d4bbd5.

9. Scott Jaschik, "Professor Cleared to Teach After Furor Over Race," *Inside Higher Ed*, March 21, 2016, https://www.insidehighered.com/news/2016/03/21/u-kansas-professor-cleared-teach-after-controversy-over-discussion-race.

10. Ibid.

11. Ibid.

12. "Email From The Intercultural Affairs Committee," *The Fire*, October 27, 2015, https://www.thefire.org/email-from-intercultural-affairs.

13. "Email From Erika Christakis: 'Dressing Yourselves,' email to Silliman College (Yale) Students on Halloween Costumes," *The Fire*, October 30, 2015, https://www.thefire.org/email-from-erika-christakis-dressing-yourselves-email-to-silliman-college-yale-students-on-halloween-costumes.

14. Conor Friedersdorf, "The Perils of Writing a Provocative Email at Yale," *The Atlantic*, May 26, 2016, https://www.theatlantic.com/politics/archive/2016/05/the-peril-of-writing-a-provocative-email-at-yale/484418.

15. Ibid.

16. Hunter Walker, "Paula Deen on Her Dream 'Southern Plantation Wedding,'" *Talking Points Memo*, June 19, 2013, https://talkingpointsmemo.com/dc/paula-deen-on-her-dream-southern-plantation-wedding.

17. Alan Scher Zagier, "Missouri Students Apologize for Cotton Ball Prank," *Diverse: Issues in Higher Education*, March 8, 2010, http://diverseeducation.com/article/13604.

18. "How Change Should—and Does—Come About," *St. Louis American*, November 12, 2015, http://www.stlamerican.com/news/editorials/how-change-should-and-does-come-about/article_5ce5c218-88eb-11e5-ac2f-3709307d21fa.html.

19. Ibid.

20. Eyder Peralta, "Two Personal Statements that Help Explain the

Situation At Mizzou," *The Two-Way: Breaking News from NPR*, November 8, 2015, https://www.npr.org/sections/thetwo-way/2015/11/08/455232301/read-two-personal-statements-that-help-explain-the-situation-at-mizzou.

21. Payton Head, "Sept 12 FB statement by Payton Head," https://www.facebook.com/PeoplesPowerAssemblies/posts/932921543409524.

22. Aviva Shen, "Police Arrest Suspect Who Threatened To Shoot Every Black Person At Mizzou," *Think Progress*, November 10, 2015, https://thinkprogress.org/police-arrest-suspect-who-threatened-to-shoot-every-black-person-at-mizzou-454d516029a3.

23. Clover Linh Tran, "CDS Appropriates Asian Dishes, Students Say," *Oberlin Review*, November 6, 2015, https://oberlinreview.org/9055/news/cds-appropriates-asian-dishes-students-say.

24. Conor Friedersdorf, "A Cook Explains Why 'Inauthentic' Menu Items Are Inevitable," *The Atlantic*, December 29, 2015, http://www.theatlantic.com/notes/2015/12/a-chef-explains-why-inauthentic-menu-items-are-inevitable/422106.

FIVE: POLITICAL CORRECTNESS AND WHITE IDENTITY

1. Kool Moe Dee ft. KRS-ONE and Chuck D, "Rise 'n' Shine," *Funke Funke Wisdom*, RCA, 1991.

2. "Racial Remark by 'Happy' Chandler Stirs Up Students," *Los Angeles Times*, April 7, 1988, http://articles.latimes.com/1988-04-07/sports/sp-1386_1_happy-chandler.

3. "'Happy' Chandler Apologizes for Remark," *Los Angeles Times*, April 8, 1988, http://articles.latimes.com/1988-04-08/sports/sp-1072_1_chandler.

4. Ibid.

5. Jo Ann Beard, *In Zanesville: a Novel* (New York: Little, Brown and Co, 2011), 3.

6. Tony Earley, "Somehow Form a Family," *Harper's*, March 1998, 59.

SIX: RACIAL ESSENTIALISM

1. J. Rawls ft. Sadat X and Wise Intelligent, "Face It," *The Hip-Hop Effect*, GSE 731, 2011.

2. Crispin Sartwell, *Act Like You Know: African American Autobiography and White Identity* (Chicago, IL: University of Chicago Press, 1998), 4.

3. J Cole, "Fire Squad," *2014 Forest Hills Drive*, Columbia, 2014.

4. Toni Morrison, "Comment," *New Yorker*, October 5, 1998, http://www.newyorker.com/magazine/1998/10/05/comment-6543.

5. Ibid.

6. Ta-Nehisi Coates, "It Was No Compliment to Call Bill Clinton 'The First Black President,'" *The Atlantic*, August 27, 2015, https://www.theatlantic.com/notes/2015/08/toni-morrison-wasnt-giving-bill-clinton-a-compliment/402517.

7. Toni Morrison, "Comment," *New Yorker*, October 5, 1998, http://www.newyorker.com/magazine/1998/10/05/comment-6543.

8. Ibid.

9. Ibid.

10. Ibid.

11. Ta-Nehisi Coates, "It Was No Compliment to Call Bill Clinton 'The First Black President,'" *The Atlantic*, August 27, 2015, https://www.theatlantic.com/notes/2015/08/toni-morrison-wasnt-giving-bill-clinton-a-compliment/402517.

12. Jonathan Capeheart, "Ben Carson and Cornel West Actually Agree: Obama's 'Not Black Enough,'" *Washington Post*, February 23, 2016, https://www.washingtonpost.com/blogs/post-partisan/wp/2016/02/23/ben-carson-and-cornel-west-actually-agree-obamas-not-black-enough.

13. Ibid.

14. Krissah Thompson and Scott Wilson, "Obama on Trayvon Martin: 'If I had a son, he'd look like Trayvon,'" *Washington Post*, March 23, 2012, https://www.washingtonpost.com/politics/obama-if-i-had-a-son-hed-look-like-trayvon/2012/03/23/gIQApKPpVS_story.html?utm_term=.8a908eca88ac.

15. Earl Sweatshirt, "Chum," *Doris*, Columbia, 2013.

16. Erik Wemple, "Fox News's Bill O'Reilly Blames Trayvon Martin's Death on Hoodie," *Washington Post*, September 16, 2013, https://www.washingtonpost.com/blogs/erik-wemple/wp/2013/09/16/fox-newss-bill-oreilly-blames-trayvon-martins-death-on-hoodie.

17. Ibid.

18. Biz Jones, "RZA Says Grab Your Suit and Tie, Says Dressing Better Could Lessen Police Brutality: 'I Tell My Sons, You Don't Have to Wear a Hoodie,'" *SOHH*, January 7, 2016, https://www.sohh.com/rza-says-grab-your-suit-tie-says-dressing-better-could-lessen-police-brutality-i-tell-my-sons-you-dont-have-to-wear-a-hoodie.

19. Richard Greelis, "Race and the Police: We Can't Avoid Talking about Behavior," *Star Tribune*, July 13, 2016, http://m.startribune.com/race-and-the-police-we-can-t-avoid-talking-about-behavior/386708571.

20. Open Mike Eagle, "Qualifiers," *Dark Comedy*, Mello Music Group, 2014.

21. Mellow Music Group, http://www.mellomusicgroup.com/products/open-mike-eagle-dark-comedy-cd.

22. CNN.com, http://www.cnn.com/TRANSCRIPTS/0612/03/sm.02. html.

23. Ibid.

24. Ibid.

25. Amanda Lee Myers, "Ariz. Cop had Black Men Rap Away Ticket," Associated Press, 2 Dec, 2006, http://www.foxnews.com/printer_friendly_ wires/2006Dec01/0,4675,PoliceTVShow,00.html.

26. Kelly Puente, "UC Irvine Hip-Hop Professor Seeks Poetic Justice," *Orange County Register*, December 28, 2015, http://www.ocregister.com/articles/ rap-697430-kubrin-says.html.

27. Charis Kubin, "The Threatening Nature of . . . Rap Music?," TedxOrangeCoast, https://www.youtube.com/watch?v=cjTIhRtFJbU.

28. Bakari Kitwana, *Why White Kids Love Hip-Hop: Wangstas, Wigger, Wannabes, and the New Reality of Race in America* (New York: Basic Civitas, 2006), 104.

29. Ibid, 105.

30. Phillip Mlynar, "Prince Paul and Son are 'Negroes on Ice,'" *MTV News*, January 11, 2012, http://www.mtv.com/news/2695248/ prince-paul-negroes-on-ice-interview.

31. Fran Ross, *Oreo* (New York: New Directions, 2015), 5.

32. Adam Krims, *Rap Music and the Poetics of Identity* (Cambridge: Cambridge University Press, 2000), 7.

33. Crispin Sartwell, *Act Like You Know: African American Autobiography and White Identity* (Chicago, IL: University of Chicago Press, 1998), 7, emphasis in the original.

34. Selwyn Seyfu Hinds, *Gunshots in My Cook-Up: Bits and Bites from a Hip-Hop Caribbean Life* (New York: Simon & Schuster, 2004), 53.

35. Ibid.

36. Ibid.

37. Ibid., 54.

SEVEN: PROFESSORS AND RAPPERS

1. Mickey Hess, ed., *Hip-Hop in America: A Regional Guide*, Vol. 1 (Westport, CT: Greenwood, 2010), 110.

2. Ibid., 115.

3. Ibid., 114.

4. Scott Merwin, "From Kool Herc to 50 Cent, the Story of Rap, So Far (Bustin' Rhymes/First in a Three Part Series)," *Pittsburgh Post-Gazette*,

February 15, 2004, http://www.post-gazette.com/ae/20040215rap0215 aep1.asp. 13 Feb 2005.

5. Erik Nielsen, "High Stakes for Hip-Hop Studies," *Huffington Post,* April 29, 2013, http://www.huffingtonpost.com/erik-nielson/high-stakes-for-hip-hop-studies_b_3170794.

6. Ezra Pound, "A Retrospect," *Literary Essays of Ezra Pound* (New York: New Directions, 2007), 4.

7. Tamara Palmer, "Black Steel in the Hour of Chaos: The Misunderstood Adventures f the Bishop of Hip-Hop," *San Francisco Weekly*, March 29, 2006, http://www.sfweekly.com/sanfrancisco/black-steel-in-the-hour-of-chaos/Content?oid=2159486.

8. Ibid.

9. A Tribe Called Quest, "Jazz (We've Got)," *The Low End Theory*, Jive/Zomba, 1991.

10. Claudia Rankine, *Citizen: An American Lyric* (London: Penguin, 2015), 10.

11. Ibid., 10.

12. "Background Facts on Contingent Faculty," *AAUP*, www.aaup.org/issues/contingency/background-facts.

13. Katy Waldman, "The White Poet Who Used an Asian Pseudonym to Get Published is a Cheater, Not a Crusader," *Slate*, September 7, 2015, http://www.slate.com/blogs/lexicon_valley/2015/09/07/yi_fen_chou_is_michael_derrick_hudson_the_best_american_poetry_from_2015.html.

14. Tanner Colby, "Can a White Author Write Black Characters?," *Slate,* September 19, 2012, http://www.slate.com/articles/arts/culturebox/2012/09/michael_chabon_s_telegraph_avenue_can_a_white_guy_write_about_black_characters_.

15. Ibid.

16. Ibid.

17. "Ol Dirty Bastard's Mother Calls For Biography Boycott," *Hip Hop DX*, November 14, 2008, http://hiphopdx.com/news/id.8089/title.ol-dirty-bastards-mother-calls-for-biography-boycott.

18. Dante Ross, "Worst Book Ever: Jaime Lowe, You Owe ODB an Apology and Then Some," *DanteRoss.com*, June 1, 2009, http://www.danteross.com/blogs/dante/2009/06/01/worst-book-ever-jamie-lowe-you-owe-odb-an-apology-and-then-some.

19. Jaime Lowe, *Digging for Dirt: The Life and Death of ODB* (New York: Faber and Faber, 2008), 35.

EIGHT: "WHERE WE ARE IS WHO WE ARE"

1. Jerald Walker, "How to Make a Slave," *Best American Essays 2016* (New York: Houghton Mifflin Harcourt, 2016), 187.

2. Ibid., 188.

3. Ibid., 190.

4. Camille Dungy, "Conspiracy (to Breathe Together)," *American Poetry Review* 42, no. 2, http://aprweb.org/poems/conspiracy-to-breathe-together.

5. Carvell Wallace, "The Lonely Hurt of Beautiful Things," *MTV News*, April 20, 2016, http://www.mtv.com/news/2870528/the-lonely-hurt-of-beautiful-things.

6. Lincoln Blades, "Bill Clinton's Black Lives Matter Comments were Revealingly Honest," *Rolling Stone*, April 8, 2016, https://www.rollingstone.com/politics/news/bill-clintons-black-lives-matter-comments-were-revealingly-honest-20160408.

7. David Kocieniewski, "Success of Elite Police Unit Exacts a Toll on the Streets," *New York Times*, February 15, 1999, http://www.nytimes.com/1999/02/15/nyregion/success-of-elite-police-unit-exacts-a-toll-on-the-streets.html.

8. Peter Noel, *Why Blacks Fear "America's Mayor": Reporting Police Brutality and Black Activist Politics Under Rudy Giuliani* (New York: iUniverse, 2007), 163.

9. Toni Cade Bambara, *Gorilla, My Love* (New York: Random House, 1972), 93.

10. Ibid., 94.

11. Ibid., 96.

NINE: SIT DOWN—CENSORSHIP, GRANDSTANDING, AND SHUTTING YOUR MOUTH

1. "Young Black Men Killed by US Police," *The Guardian*, December 31, 2015, https://www.theguardian.com/us-news/2015/dec/31/the-counted-police-killings-2015-young-black-men.

2. Robert G. Parkinson, "Did a Fear of Slave Revolts Drive American Independence?," *New York Times*, July 4, 2016, http://www.nytimes.com/2016/07/04/opinion/did-a-fear-of-slave-revolts-drive-american-independence.html?_r=0.

3. Bill D. Moyers, "What a Real President Was Like," *Washington Post*, November 13, 1998, https://www.washingtonpost.com/archive/opinions/1988/11/13/what-a-real-president-was-like/d483c1be-d0da-43b7-bde6-04e10106ff6c.

4. Tom LoBianco, "Report: Aide says Nixon's War on Drugs Targeted Blacks, Hippies," *CNN*, March 23, 2016, http://www.cnn.com/2016/03/23/politics/john-ehrlichman-richard-nixon-drug-war-blacks-hippie.

5. Rick Perlstein, "Exclusive: Lee Atwater's Infamous 1981 Interview on the Southern Strategy," *The Nation*, November 13, 2012, https://www.thenation.com/article/exclusive-lee-atwaters-infamous-1981-interview-southern-strategy.

6. Kris Ex, "Macklemore's 'White Privilege II' is a Mess, but We Should Talk about It," *Pitchfork*, January 22, 2016, http://pitchfork.com/thepitch/1003-macklemores-white-privilege-ii-is-a-mess-but-we-should-talk-about-it.

7. Justin Charity, "Macklemore's 'White Privilege II' is an Amazing Case Study of White Guilt," *Complex*, January 23, 2016, http://www.complex.com/music/2016/01/macklemore-white-privilege-guilt.

8. Ibid.

9. Rembert Browne, "Macklemore, Hillary, and Why White Privilege Is Everyone's Burden," *Vulture*, February 8, 2016, http://www.vulture.com/2016/02/why-white-privilege-is-everyones-burden.html.

10. Ibid.

11. Gene Demby, "I Guess We Gotta Talk About Macklemore's 'White Privilege' Song," *Code Switch*, NPR, January 29, 2016, http://www.npr.org/sections/codeswitch/2016/01/29/464752853/i-guess-we-gotta-talk-about-macklemores-white-privilege-song.

12. Kris Ex, "Macklemore's 'White Privilege II' Is a Mess, but We Should Talk about It," *Pitchfork*, January 22, 2016.

13. Gene Demby, "I Guess We Gotta Talk About Macklemore's 'White Privilege' Song," *Code Switch*. NPR, January 29, 2016.

14. Kris Ex, "Macklemore's 'White Privilege II' is a Mess, but We Should Talk about It," *Pitchfork*, January 22, 2016.

15. Kelsey Kennedy, "'The Burden of the Brutalized Is not to Comfort the Bystander': Jesse Williams' Electrifying Speech on American Racism," *Quartz*, June 27, 216, https://qz.com/717761/the-burden-of-the-brutalized-is-not-to-comfort-the-bystander-jesse-williams-electrifying-speech-on-american-racism.

16. Eric Bradner, "Bill Clinton Spars with Black Lives Matter Protestors," *CNN*, April 8, 2016, http://www.cnn.com/2016/04/07/politics/bill-clinton-black-lives-matter-protesters.

17. "Remarks by the President at Commencement Address at Rutgers, the State University of New Jersey," White House Office of the Press Secretary,

May 16, 2015, https://www.whitehouse.gov/the-press-office/2016/05/15/remarks-president-commencement-address-rutgers-state-university-new.

18. John Kelley, "Antidepressants: Do they 'Work' or Don't They?," *Scientific American*, March 2, 2010, http://www.scientificamerican.com/article/antidepressants-do-they-work-or-dont-they.

19. "Nelly Wanted To 'Kick Somebody's Ass' Over Spelman's Protest Of 'Tip Drill,'" *Huffington Post*, November 12, 2013, http://www.huffingtonpost.com/2013/11/12/nelly-kick-somebody-ass-spelman-protest-tip-drill_n_4262503.html.

20. Ibid.

21. "Hip Hop vs. America (The World) Volume 10: Misogyny," *BET*, September 26, 2007, https://www.youtube.com/watch?v=UkQd0Tk7_mQ.

22. Ibid.

23. Ibid.

24. "Angry Black Women Take Aim at Rappers," April 23, 2004, https://www.today.com/popculture/angry-black-women-take-aim-rappers-wbna4816719.

25. "Hip Hop vs. America (The World) Volume 10: Misogyny." *BET*, September 26, 2007. https://www.youtube.com/watch?v=UkQd0Tk7_mQ.

26. Ibid.

27. Michael Eric Dyson, *Open Mike: Reflections on Philosophy, Race, Sex, Culture, and Religion* (New York: Basic Civitas, 2003), 7.

28. Ibid.

29. "Hip Hop vs. America (The World) Volume 10: Misogyny," *BET*, September 26, 2007.

30. "Governor Mike Huckabee: Ivy League Schooling," *Awaken Now*, LifetodayTV, https://www.youtube.com/watch?v=diRRq-keb1o.

31. Sophia Tesfaye, "6 Mike Huckabee Quotes on Women That'll Make You Cringe," *Bustle*, May 8 2015, http://www.bustle.com/articles/81798-6-mike-huckabee-quotes-on-womens-rights-thatll-make-you-cringe.

32. Kurtis Lee, "Mike Huckabee Jokes about Posing as Transgender to Shower with Girls," *Los Angeles Times*, June 2, 2015, http://www.latimes.com/nation/politics/politicsnow/la-pn-mike-huckabee-transgender-comments-20150602-story.html.

33. Lea Kahn, "Lawrence: Protestors Ready for Mike Huckabee," *CentralJersey.com*, April 1, 2009, http://www.centraljersey.com/archives/lawrence-protesters-ready-for-mike-huckabee/article_cd48e941-3c50-5ecf-9b27-6acc5f770b22.html.

34. Monica Fountain, "Crying Foul: Tucker Battles Against Lyrics Of Gangsta Rap," *Chicago Tribune*, November 10, 1996, http://articles.

chicagotribune.com/1996-11-10/features/9611100411_1_national-political-congress-lyrics-of-gangsta-rap-tucker-talks.

35. Chuck Phillips, "Anti-Rap Crusader Under Fire," *Los Angeles Times*, March 20, 1996, http://articles.latimes.com/1996-03-20/news/mn-49205_1_c-delores-tucker.

36. Luther Campbell, "'Stale White Bitches Tried to Take us Down': Luther Campbell on 2 Live Crew, Race, Hip-Hop and the Conservative, Southern '80s," *Salon*, August 29, 2015, https://www.salon.com/2015/08/29/stale_white_bitches_tried_to_take_us_down_luther_campbell_on_2_live_crew_race_hip_hop_and_the_conservative_southern_80s.

37. Ibid.

38. Ibid.

39. Kimberlé Crenshaw, "Beyond Racism and Misogyny: Black Feminism and 2 Live Crew." *Boston Review*. http://bostonreview.net/archives/BR16.6/crenshaw.html.

40. Shaheem Reid, "Snoop Says Rappers and Imus are 'Two Separate Things,'" *MTV News*, April 10, 2007, http://www.mtv.com/news/1556803/snoop-says-rappers-and-imus-are-two-separate-things-talks-new-comp.

41. T. Denean Sharpley-Whiting, *Pimps Up, Ho's Down: Hip Hop's Hold on Young Black Women* (New York: New York University Press, 2008) 62.

42. Krissah Thompson, "Obama Addresses Race and Louis Gates Incident," *Washington Post*, July 23, 2009, http://www.washingtonpost.com/wp-dyn/content/article/2009/07/22/AR2009072203800.html.

43. "Obama: Police Who Arrested Professor 'Acted Stupidly,'" *CNN*, July 23, 2009, http://www.cnn.com/2009/US/07/22/harvard.gates.interview.

TEN: WHO WILL TELL HIP-HOP'S STORY?

1. President William Jefferson Clinton, "Address Before a Joint Session of Congress on Administration Goals," February 17, 1993, http://www.presidency.ucsb.edu/ws/?pid=47232.

2. "Ol' Dirty Bastard Gets Paid," *MTV News*, March 30, 1995.

3. William Shaw, "Portrait of the Artist in Jail," *The Guardian*, March 21, 2002, https://www.theguardian.com/lifeandstyle/2002/mar/22/shopping.artsfeatures.

4. Richard Iton, *In Search of the Black Fantastic: Politics and Popular Culture in the Post-Civil Rights Era* (Oxford: Oxford University Press, 2010), 181.

5. Dream Hampton, "I Like it Raw," *Village Voice*, May 30, 1995, 63.

6. Buddha Monk and Mickey Hess, *The Dirty Version: On Stage, in*

the Studio, and in the Streets with Ol' Dirty Bastard (New York: Dey Street/ HarperCollins, 2014), 3.

7. Ibid, 84.

8. Gay Talese, "Frank Sinatra Has a Cold," *Esquire*, April 1966, http:// www.esquire.com/news-politics/a638/frank-sinatra-has-a-cold-gay-talese.

9. John Jeremiah Sullivan, "The Last Wailer," *GQ*, February 9, 2011, https://www.gq.com/story/bunny-wailer-john-jeremiah-sullivan.

10. Ta-Nehisi Coates, "The Mask of Doom: A Nonconformist Rapper's Second Act," *New Yorker*, September 21, 2009, https://www.newyorker.com/ magazine/2009/09/21/the-mask-of-doom.

11. Monk and Hess, *The Dirty Version*, 11.

12. Sacha Jenkins, "Looking for Jesus," *Vibe*, December 1999/January 2000, 172.

13. Monk and Hess, *The Dirty Version*, 2.

14. "Ol' Dirty Bastard Estate Halts ODB Documentary Screening," *Vibe*, November 18, 2013, https://www.vibe.com/2013/11/ol-dirty-bastard-estate-halts-odb-documentary-screening.

15. Andres Tardio, "Ol' Dirty Bastard's Digital Performance at Rock The Bells Will Be 'Beautiful,' Says U-God," *Hip Hop DX*, May 19, 2013, https:// hiphopdx.com/news/id.24012/title.ol-dirty-bastards-digital-performance-at-rock-the-bells-will-be-beautiful-says-u-god.

16. Brian Koerber, "Some 'Dope Stuff' Happened to this Guy, So He's Handing out $100 bills to Strangers," *Mashable*, December 11, 2016, https://mashable.com/2015/12/11/shea-serrano-giving-out-money/ #zqSxV0EZDSqs.

17. "Ol' Cheeky Bastard," *NME*, Nov 22, 2000, http://www.nme.com/ news/music/ol-dirty-bastard-18-1395255.

18. Monk and Hess, *The Dirty Version*, 46.

19. Ibid., 134.

ELEVEN: REVISIONIST HISTORY

1. Ezra Klein, "AIG CEO: Anger Over AIG Bonuses 'Just as Bad' as Lynchings," *Washington Post*, Sept 24, 2013, https://www.washingtonpost. com/news/wonk/wp/2013/09/24/aig-ceo-anger-over-aig-bonuses-just-as-bad-as-lynchings/?utm_term=.605ce3b04c9f.

2. Jeremy Pelofsky, "AIG Home Loan Units Deny But Settle Bias Complaints," *Insurance Journal*, March 5, 2010, https://www.insurancejour-nal.com/news/national/2010/03/05/107903.htm.

3. "Racial Pranks at Fraternity Bring Rebuke From College," *New York*

Times, January 23, 1993, http://www.nytimes.com/1993/01/23/nyregion/racial-pranks-at-fraternity-bring-rebuke-from-college.html.

4. M.K. Asante, "Racism Is Part of Our Country's Past and Present History, and We Should Never 'Forget' It," *New York Times*, April 9, 2014, https://www.nytimes.com/roomfordebate/2013/04/10/accidental-racist-and-lyrical-provocation/racism-is-part-of-our-countrys-past-and-present-history-and-we-should-never-forget-it.

5. Alan Light, "Ice-T," *Rolling Stone*, August 20, 1992, 31.

6. Brian Smith, "Same as the Old Boss," *Detroit Metro Times*, https://www.metrotimes.com/detroit/same-as-the-old-boss/Content?oid=2178805.

7. King Fantastic, "Why? What? Where?" *Finger Snaps and Gun Claps* (Jacknife Records, 2010).

8. Twitter post since taken down, previous accessed at https://twitter.com/kingfantastic/status/235805361557364737.

9. "Art or Evidence? After Appeal, Court Rules Violent Rap Lyrics Not a Confession," *PBS News Hour*, Aug 9, 2014, https://www.pbs.org/newshour/show/art-evidence-appeal-court-rules-violent-rap-lyrics-confession.

10. Frank Owen, "Paid in Full," *Spin*, October 1989, 36

11. Alan Light, ed., *Vibe History of Hip-Hop* (New York: Vibe, 1999), 124.

12. Emanuella Grinberg, "Perm or Weave? Rachel Dolezal Puts Hair Questions to Rest," *CNN*, June 16, 2015, https://www.cnn.com/2015/06/16/living/rachel-dolezal-perm-weave-feat/index.html.

13. Belva Davis and Vicki Haddock, *Never in My Wildest Dreams: A Black Woman's Life in Journalism* (San Francisco: Berrett-Koehler, 2012), 66.

14. Ibid.

15. Ibid.

16. Ibid.

17. Michael Marriot, "Rap's Embrace of 'Nigger' Fires Bitter Debate," *New York Times*, January 24, 1993, http://www.nytimes.com/1993/01/24/nyregion/rap-s-embrace-of-nigger-fires-bitter-debate.html?pagewanted=all.

18. Bill Chappell, "'We Are Not Cured': Obama Discusses Racism in America with Marc Maron," *The Two-Way: Breaking News from NPR*, June 22, 2015, https://www.npr.org/sections/thetwo-way/2015/06/22/416476377/we-are-not-cured-obama-discusses-racism-in-america-with-marc-maron.

19. Ansel Herz, "'Go Read *N*gger*,' Seattle University Humanities Dean Told Black Student Who Complained About Curriculum," *The Stranger*, May 13, 2016, https://www.thestranger.com/slog/2016/05/13/24081531/go-read-ngger-seattle-university-humanities-dean-told-black-student-who-complained-about-curriculum.

20. Rosie Gray, "Trump Defends White-Nationalist Protesters: 'Some Very

Fine People on Both Sides,'" *The Atlantic*, August 15, 2017, https://www.the-atlantic.com/politics/archive/2017/08/trump-defends-white-nationalist-protesters-some-very-fine-people-on-both-sides/537012.

21. NAACP Press Release, "The 'N' Word Is Laid to Rest by the NAACP," July 9, 2007, http://www.naacp.org/latest/the-n-word-is-laid-to-rest-by-the-naacp.

22. Ben Westhoff, "Not Your Father's N-Word," *Houston Press*, April 2, 2008, http://www.houstonpress.com/music/not-your-fathers-n-word-6542193.

23. "Lynching in America: Confronting the Legacy of Racial Terror," Equal Justice Initiative, accessed August 28, 2018, https://lynchinginamerica.eji.org/.

24. Dennis Abrams, *Beastie Boys* (New York: Chelsea House, 2007), 47.

25. Michael Odell, "The Greatest Songs Ever! Fight for Your Right," *Blender*, February 15, 2004, http://www.blender.com/guide/67366/greatest-songs-ever-fight-for-your-right.html.

26. Craig Marks and Rob Tannenbaum, *I Want My MTV: The Uncensored Story of the Music Video Revolution* (New York: Dutton, 2011), 248.

TWELVE: EDUCATION IS THE APOLOGY

1. Brenda Herrmann, "Radio Tuning Out Gangsta Rap," *The Chicago Tribune*, January 18, 1994, http://articles.chicagotribune.com/1994-01-18/features/9401180012_1_delores-tucker-rap-black-women.

2. Richard A. Peterson, *Creating Country Music: Fabricating Authenticity* (Chicago: University of Chicago Press, 1999), 68.

3. Ibid., 125.

4. Patrick B. Mullen, *The Man Who Adores the Negro: Race and American Folklore* (Urbana: University of Illinois Press, 2008), 85.

5. Jennifer L. Stoever, *The Sonic Color Line: Race and the Cultural Politics of Listening* (New York: New York University Press, 2016), 201.

6. "Lead Belly: Bad Nigger Makes Good Minstrel," *Life Magazine*, Single Issue magazine, April 19, 1937.

7. Hendrik Hertzberg, "Buckley, Vidal, and the 'Queer' Question," *New Yorker*, July 31, 2015, https://www.newyorker.com/news/daily-comment/buckley-vidal-and-the-queer-question.

8. "Pound, Politics, Poetry," *Today in Literature*, January 28, 2018, http://www.todayinliterature.com/print-today.asp?Event_Date=1/30/1933.

9. Paul Farhi, "*Seinfeld* Comic Richards Apologizes for Racial Rant," *Washington Post*, November 21, 2006, http://www.washingtonpost.com/wp-dyn/content/article/2006/11/21/AR2006112100242.html.

10. Dan Glaister, "*Seinfeld* Actor Lets Fly with Racist Tirade," *The Guardian*, November 22, 2006, https://www.theguardian.com/world/2006/nov/22/usa.danglaister.

11. Erin Texeira, "Kramer Aftermath: Paul Mooney Renounces N-word after Michael Richards Rant," *Times Herald-Record*, November 29, 2006, http://www.recordonline.com/article/20061129/entertain/61129019.

12. Ibid.

13. Paul Mooney, *Black Is the New White: A Memoir* (New York: Gallery Books, 2010), 43–44.

14. Katy Kelly, "Marky Regrets Remarks," *USA Today*, February 19, 1993, 2D.

15. Paul Thompson, "Wahlberg Gets His Pardon from the Only Person Who Matters: the Victim," *Daily Mail*, December 11, 2014, http://www.dailymail.co.uk/news/article-2868589/Mark-Wahlberg-s-blinding-race-attack-victim-Johnny-Trinh-backs-bid-pardon-saying-course-forgive-didn-t-blind-Communist-Vietnamese-did-that.html.

16. William J. Kole, "Mark Wahlberg Seeks Pardon for 1988 Assaults," *AP News*, December 5, 2014.

17. Judith Beals, "Don't Pardon Mark Wahlberg," *Boston Globe*, January 12, 2015, https://www.bostonglobe.com/opinion/2015/01/12/don-pardon-mark-wahlberg/2zCWxyVay7QLD4MDGjGbAN/story.html.

18. Ibid.

19. "Mark Wahlberg Victim Says He Shouldn't Be Pardoned," *CBS News*, January 20, 2015, http://www.cbsnews.com/news/mark-wahlberg-victim-says-he-shouldnt-be-pardoned.

20. B. G. Henne, "Mark Wahlberg Asked Pope Francis to Forgive Him for His Talking Bear Sins," *AV Club*, September 28 2015, https://news.avclub.com/mark-wahlberg-asked-pope-francis-to-forgive-him-for-his-1798284772.

21. "Aetna Apologizes for Slave Insurance," March 11, 2000, http://articles.latimes.com/2000/mar/11/business/fi-7637.

22. Southern Baptist Convention, "Resolution on Racial Reconciliation on the 150th Anniversary of the Southern Baptist Convention," 1995. http://www.sbc.net/resolutions/899/resolution-on-racial-reconciliation-on-the-150th-anniversary-of-the-southern-baptist-convention.

23. Ibid.

24. Derrick Z. Jackson, "Breaking Free from Slavery," *The Day*, December 9, 1997, A12.

25. Ibid.

26. Kurt Vonnegut, "Triage," *Fates Worse Than Death: An Autobiographical*

Collage (New York: Berkley Books, 2007), 76.

27. M. K. Asante, Jr, *It's Bigger Than Hip-Hop: The Rise of the Post-Hip-Hop Generation* (New York: St. Martin's Griffin, 2009), xi.

28. Shenequa Golding, "Kanye West Asks White Publications To 'Not Comment On Black Music Anymore,'" *Vibe*, February 15, 2016, https://www.vibe.com/2016/02/kanye-west-twitter-rant.

29. Jon Caramanica, "White Rappers: Clear of a Black Planet," *New York Times*, August 18, 2016, https://www.nytimes.com/2016/08/21/arts/music/white-rappers-geazy-mike-stud.html.

30. Naima Moore-Turner, "Here's Why Solange Drags *NY Times* Pop Critic," *BET*, February 4, 2016, https://www.bet.com/news/music/2016/02/04/solange-drags-ny-times-pop-critic.html.

31. Ibid.

32. Jon Caramanica, "Yung Lean Evolves into a Full-Fledged Practitioner," *New York Times*, July 10, 2014, https://www.nytimes.com/2014/07/11/arts/music/yung-lean-in-new-york-a-rapper-evolves.html.

33. Jon Caramanica, "Changing the Face (and Sound) of Rap," *New York Times*, Dec 23, 2009, http://www.nytimes.com/2009/12/27/arts/music/27rappers.html.

34. Reyhan Harmanci, "Academic Hip-Hop? Yes, Yes, Y'all," *SF Gate*, March 5, 2007, https://www.sfgate.com/entertainment/article/ACADEMIC-HIP-HOP-YES-YES-Y-ALL-2613595.php.

35. "Georgetown Shares Slavery, Memory, and Reconciliation Report, Racial Justice Steps," Georgetown University, Sept. 1, 2016, https://www.georgetown.edu/slavery-memory-reconciliation-working-group-sept-2016.

36. Haley Samsel, "Their Ancestors Were Slaves Sold by Georgetown. Now They're Going to School There," *USA Today College*, June 9, 2017, http://college.usatoday.com/2017/06/09/their-ancestors-were-slaves-sold-by-georgetown-now-theyre-going-to-school-there.

37. Samantha Master, "Georgetown University's 'Reparations' Plan Is Worthless White Guilt Repackaged as Justice," *The Root*, September 5, 2016, https://www.theroot.com/georgetown-university-s-reparations-plan-is-worthless-1790856615.

38. Caine Jordan, Guy Emerson Mount, and Kai Parker, "A Case for Reparations at the University of Chicago," *Black Perspectives*, May 22, 2017, https://www.aaihs.org/a-case-for-reparations-at-the-university-of-chicago.

39. Ta-Nehisi Coates, "The Case for Reparations," *The Atlantic Monthly*, June 2014. https://www.theatlantic.com/magazine/archive/2014/06/the-case-for-reparations/361631/.

40. Susan Svrluga, "'Make It Right': Descendants of Slaves Demand Restitution from Georgetown," *Washington Post*, January 17, 2018, https://www.washingtonpost.com/news/grade-point/wp/2018/01/16/__trashed-2/?utm_term=.447b9f43d93f.

41. Tim Marcin, "Parkland Student David Hogg Says Black Classmates Weren't Given a Voice by Media," *Newsweek*, March 23, 2018, http://www.newsweek.com/parkland-student-david-hogg-says-black-students-werent-given-voice-media-858606.

42. Sarah Ruiz-Grossman, "Black Parkland Students Want Peers to 'Share The Mic,'" *Huffington Post*, April 5, 2018, https://www.huffingtonpost.com/entry/black-students-marjory-stoneman-march-for-our-lives-gun-violence-movement_us_5ac5548ce4b056a8f59810f9?ncid=tweetlnkushpmg00000051.